UTOPIA IN PERFORMANCE

Utopia in Performance

Finding Hope at the Theater

Jill Dolan

The University of Michigan Press
Ann Arbor

2008   2007   2006   2005   4   3   2   1

A CIP catalog record for this book is available from the British Library.

Library of Congress Cataloging-in-Publication Data

Dolan, Jill, 1957–
    Utopia in performance : finding hope at the theater / Jill Dolan.
        p.   cm.
    Includes bibliographical references and index.
    ISBN-13: 978-0-472-09907-8 (cloth : alk. paper)
    ISBN-10: 0-472-09907-8 (cloth : alk. paper)
    ISBN-13: 978-0-472-06907-1 (pbk. : alk. paper)
    ISBN-10: 0-472-06907-1 (pbk. : alk. paper)
    1. One-person shows (Performing arts)   2. Monodrama—
History and criticism.   3. Theater—Psychological aspects.
I. Title.
PN1936.D65   2005
791—dc22   2005009149

For Stacy, always,

and for our nieces, nephew, and godchildren,
Allison and Benjamin Furfine,
Rachael and Morgann Green,
Noémi Wolf and Liliana Schlossberg-Cohen Wolf,
Flora Berklein and Hannah Zoe Diamond Lowe,
and Max and Milo Darlington,
and all the people we love,
young and old,
who give us hope

Acknowledgments

The process of writing *Utopia in Performance* has, happily, been its own utopian performative. A number of people have commented on these words and ideas, engaging with me in critically generous and generative ways.

Susan Bennett, Harry Elam, Ann Pellegrini, and David Román offered detailed comments on an earlier version of chapter 2; David's invitation to keynote a graduate student conference at University of Southern California in February 2001 provided the occasion for me to begin writing this book.

Janelle Reinelt, Elin Diamond, and Linda Kintz responded helpfully to an early draft of chapter 3 at the Association for Theatre in Higher Education conference in San Diego in 2002. Elin also offered very helpful responses to the keynote I presented at the International Federation for Theatre Research conference in Washington, D.C., in June 2005, which was based on this work.

Michal Kobialka, Sonja Kuftinec, Lauren Love, and John Fleming were acute interlocutors during the Nolte Lectures I gave, all based on this book, at the University of Minnesota in April 2003. Jim Peck, Beth Schachter, and the students at Muhlenberg University, where I presented earlier versions of chapters 4 and 5, in 2003, also offered smart and helpful feedback.

Katie Stewart and the generous friends and colleagues who attended my talk at the Cultural Studies Colloquium at the University of Texas in November 2004 provided generous comments on the introduction as I was in the throes of finishing the manuscript.

Working with Ric Knowles on an earlier version of chapter 3 was a pleasure, as was our working relationship on the special issue of *Modern Drama* on utopian performatives he invited me to edit. The authors in that issue—Maurya Wickstrom, Erin Hurley, Ehren Fordyce, Shannon Baley, Anita Gonzalez, Ramón Rivera-Servera, Judith Hamera, and Stacy Wolf—convinced me that other people could use the utopian performative productively.

Gayle Wald and Maurya Wickstrom suggested resources that proved key to my writing.

A number of friends and colleagues inspired me through their own thinking and commitments to theater and performance. I'd like to thank especially Herb Blau, Charlotte Canning, the late Dwight Conquergood (whose foundational work on performance ethics and "copresence" will always move me), Ann Cvetkovich, Ann Daly, Sharon Grady, Richard Isackes, Joni Jones, Lynn Miller, Deborah Paredez, Vicki Patraka, the faculty, staff, and students of the Department of Theatre and Dance at the University of Texas at Austin, and the graduate students in our M.A./Ph.D. program's Performance as Public Practice emphasis. Our determination to make theater matter, and to use our talents to explain how and why it should, continually convinces me of the necessity of this work.

I wouldn't have experienced utopian performatives without the always moving and provoking work of artists Sharon Bridgforth, Ann Carlson, Ann Ciccolella, Terry Galloway, Marga Gomez, Holly Hughes, Deb Margolin, Tim Miller, Jason Neulander, Marty Pottenger, Peggy Shaw, Dave Steakley, Carmelita Tropicana (Alina Troyano), Paula Vogel, Lois Weaver, and the remarkable Rude Mechs—Madge Darlington, Lana Lesley, Kirk Lynn, Sarah Richardson, and Shawn Sides—who make so many things in my artistic and intellectual life in Austin possible.

My research assistants, Paul Bonin-Rodriguez, Susanne Shawyer, and Amy Steiger, helped me in numerous ways, always with a warm "can-do" spirit that made everything seem easy and often even fun.

My family—Cyma and Jerry Dolan, Randee and David Green, and Ann Dolan, and Saralee Wolf, Ellis Fribush, Larry and Alice Wolf, Allie and Jay Schlossberg-Cohen Wolf, and Josh and Vanina Wolf—loved me and cared for me in increasingly valuable ways over the years I was writing this book.

Lisa Moore heard me talk about the book's introduction at the University of Texas colloquium and persuaded me that I was writing a "spiritual autobiography." Her emotional and intellectual support, as a colleague and as part of my Austin family, means more than I can say.

Jaclyn Pryor, in addition to her extraordinary research assistance, read every word of the book and wrote detailed, generous, generative responses that carried me through the final stages of writing and helped me to continue believing in this work.

David Román remains an exemplary colleague and friend. His comments on an early draft shaped and refined the project because he understood it, felt it, and gave me permission to write about how performance makes me feel.

LeAnn Fields, my editor at Michigan, as well as my friend and my colleague, has been an inspiration throughout my career. Her unwavering support for publishing about performance motivates us all. I'd also like to thank Marcia LaBrenz and the wonderful copyediting team at the press.

Stacy Wolf, my exacting in-house editor and always willing cospectator, saw most of the performances I describe here with me. Our discussions afterward provided the foundation for much of my analysis. Stacy continually helps me find the balance between feeling and excess, between florid and finessed, between theory and practice, between work and rest. With her, I find my humanity, and my hope.

An earlier version of chapter 2 was published as "Performance, Utopia, and the 'Utopian Performative,'" *Theatre Journal* 53 (October 2001): 455–79. An earlier version of chapter 3 was published as "Finding Our Feet in the Shoes of One (An)Other: Multiple Character Solo Performers and Utopian Performatives," *Modern Drama* 45 (winter 2003): 495–518. I'd like to thank Johns Hopkins University Press and the University of Toronto Press, respectively, for permission to use this work.

Contents

"There are these rare moments when musicians [or performers] together touch something sweeter than they've ever found before in rehearsals or performance, beyond the merely collaborative or technically proficient, when their expression becomes as easy and graceful as friendship or love. This is when they give us a glimpse of what we might be, of our best selves, and of an impossible world in which you give everything you have to others, but lose nothing of yourself. Out in the real world there exist detailed plans, visionary projects for peaceable realms, all conflicts resolved, happiness for everyone, for ever—mirages for which people are prepared to die and kill. Christ's kingdom on earth, the workers' paradise, the ideal Islamic state. But only in music [or theater], and only on rare occasions, does the curtain actually lift on this dream of community, and it's tantalizingly conjured, before fading away with the last notes."

—Ian McEwan, *Saturday*

chapter one

Introduction

Feeling the Potential of Elsewhere

Since the early nineteenth century, "utopia" has become
a polemical political concept that everyone uses against
everyone else.
—Jürgen Habermas, *Jürgen Habermas on Society and Politics*

The consideration of the power inherent in performance to
transform social structures opens the way to a range of additional considerations concerning the role of the performer in
society. Perhaps there is a key here to the persistently docu-
mented tendency for performers to be both admired and
feared—admired for their artistic skill and power and for the
enhancement of experience they provide, feared because of
the potential they represent for subverting and transforming
the status quo. Here too may lie a reason for the equally persistent association between performers and marginality or
deviance, for in the special emergent quality of performance
the capacity for change may be highlighted and made manifest to the community.
—Richard Bauman, *Verbal Arts on Performance*

Artaud believed that the function of theatre was to teach us
that "the sky can still fall on our heads." We've known for
some time that this vision of theatre is impossible, Utopian,
possibly even hysterical (Artaud as Chicken Little). But the
Slapstick Tragedy that opened on September 11th was also a
Theatre of Cruelty and might warrant some utopian explorations. The sky has fallen on our heads, and what we are seeing . . . threatens to blind us. At a time when every cultural
practice is reassessing itself and its role, perhaps we will re-
entertain Artaud's mad vision of theatre as a place to

encounter the unknown and the unimaginable, a place that
teaches the necessary humility of not knowing.
—UNA CHAUDHURI, "A Forum on Theatre and Tragedy in the
Wake of September 11th, 2001"

All true feeling is in reality untranslatable. To express it is to
betray it. . . . This is why true beauty never strikes us directly.
The setting sun is beautiful because of all it makes us lose.
—ANTONIN ARTAUD, *The Theatre and Its Double*

Utopia in Performance argues that live performance provides a place where
people come together, embodied and passionate, to share experiences of
meaning making and imagination that can describe or capture fleeting intimations of a better world. *Utopia in Performance* tries to find, at the theater,
a way to reinvest our energies in a different future, one full of hope and reanimated by a new, more radical humanism. This book investigates the potential of different kinds of performance to inspire moments in which audiences feel themselves allied with each other, and with a broader, more
capacious sense of a public, in which social discourse articulates the possible,
rather than the insurmountable obstacles to human potential.

I take my performance examples from a variety of contemporary performance genres and locations: feminist autobiographical solo performance by Holly Hughes, Peggy Shaw, and Deb Margolin; "monopolylogues" by Lily Tomlin, Danny Hoch, and Anna Deavere Smith, in which
a single performer enacts a number of different characters, knit together in
various narratives of experience; *Russell Simmons Def Poetry Jam on Broadway* and *The Laramie Project*, which address audiences as citizens of the
world and model political critique and engagement; and choreographer
Ann Carlson's solo performance *Blanket*, Mary Zimmerman's *Metamorphoses*, and Deborah Warner and Fiona Shaw's *Medea*, the dark beauty
and poignancy of which lead to what I see as moments of utopia in performance. The aesthetics of these performances lead to both affective and
effective feelings and expressions of hope and love not just for a partner, as
the domestic scripts of realism so often emphasize, but for other people,
for a more abstracted notion of "community," or for an even more intangible idea of "humankind." From the particular slant offered by theater
and performance as practices of social life, this book addresses the cynicism of progressive commentators who believe the Left, especially, has
given up on the possibility of a politics of transformation. Leftist academic
pundit Russell Jacoby, for example, suggests, "Today, socialists and leftists

do not dream of a future qualitatively different from the present. To put it differently, radicalism no longer believes in itself."[1] *Utopia in Performance* answers this claim with my own set of beliefs in the possibility of a better future, one that can be captured and claimed in performance.

Utopia in Performance, of course, is written in what has become the long moment after September 11, one in which progressive citizens of the United States have plenty about which to be cynical. The attacks on the World Trade Center and the Pentagon and the crash of the third plane-turned-missile in a Pennsylvania field left the country frightened, insecure about our ability to protect ourselves, too scared, some might suggest, to dream of brighter futures. Worse, the attacks that day prompted an already conservative administration to use its power to curtail civil liberties, tacitly condoning racial profiling, wiretaps, and warrantless searches and seizures to weed out potential terrorists who tragically escaped federal notice before September 11. And as Michael Moore suggests in his trenchant documentary, *Fahrenheit 9/11,* the Bush administration uses the calculated politics of fear to keep the citizenry passive, raising and lowering at random the Office of Homeland Security's threat level based on vague "chatter" on already unreliable spy networks.[2] In this climate, and under the dictates of the so-called U.S. Patriot Act, new definitions of citizenship insist on an uncritical acceptance of diminished privacy and nationalist racism; on blind flag-waving that supports fascist acts that supposedly secure the homeland; and a virulent, war-mongering enforcement of xenophobic definitions of "America." How can we hope for a better future in such an environment? What can hope mean, in a world of terror? What can performance *do,* politically, against these overwhelming odds?

For me, performance and politics have always been intertwined. At the theater, I first learned to articulate and sometimes to see realized my own hopes for some otherwise intangible future. I grew up on the tail end of the baby boom in a middle-class neighborhood in Pittsburgh, Pennsylvania, in which our community's hopes were focused on upward mobility of a social, pecuniary sort. The Jewish traditions into which I was inculcated were conservative from a religious perspective, but culturally liberal, expressing a more inclusive commitment to caring for "all humankind." Endowed with a post-Holocaust caution about the status of American Jewry, we nonetheless believed in a world of potential, if not for a brighter future, at least for one in which the traumas of the past wouldn't repeat. Somehow, as I grew up, I incorporated the rhetoric of 1960s social radicalism into my own cosmology, devising a critique of the racism that surrounded me and soon developing an awareness of gender and sexuality that was later articulated by feminist and queer theory and practice.

As Jews, my family suffered implicit discrimination in late 1950s and 1960s America, but we insulated ourselves from its excess by living in predominantly Jewish neighborhoods, belonging to the local temple and the Jewish Community Center, and otherwise trading in mostly Jewish businesses and culture. Because of these choices, the discrimination I saw was against the few Christians among us at school, or against the still fewer people of color in our neighborhood, until I started high school and the majorities and minorities reshuffled. Early on, though, my sense of compassion and indignity was aroused on behalf of those *we* considered the others, the marginal—never for ourselves.

In high school, my friends and I were integrated into a much more diverse world, one in which I found my own generous politics tried by my own sense of exclusion. My commitment to theater began at the same time, which is perhaps why I've always connected performance and the possibility for something better in the world. Leaving the ghetto of my erstwhile Jewish world, I traveled downtown to perform at the Pittsburgh Playhouse, taking acting lessons and mounting productions with people who never mixed with Jews. As a "Dolan," I passed as a non-Jew in those circumstances; I was young, thirteen years old when I started acting, but I could sense right away that suddenly, my identity made me vulnerable, rather than protecting me. My Jewishness remained invisible as I learned, turning my cheek to casual anti-Semitism, watching how this larger world worked, and losing myself in the fictions and fantasies and the displaced tragedies of drama. In theater, I learned to both disguise myself and revel in my visibility under the mask of character, performing ebullient turns of phrase and dress as Mrs. Malaprop in Sheridan's *The Rivals* and fierce, sex-denying poses for *Lysistrata,* before I really even understood what a sex strike might entail, knowing that the play's antiwar message was its most important point. In theater, I found ways to both free and constrain myself, to say who I was and to hide myself carefully. I watched, falling in love with my fellow women performers and surrendering to the seductions of performance. Whatever I would become in my life, I knew I would always be anchored here, in the ephemeral maybes of this magic place.

Although I've long since stopped performing, and more recently stopped directing theater productions, I've never given up my stance as a passionate spectator of performance. Performance continues to entice me with magic, to give me hope for our collective future. The performances I discuss in *Utopia in Performance* are ones that moved or captivated me, that I've seen performed live in all kinds of venues across the country, since I hope that utopia can be grasped in performance in any location. My intent is not to provide a recipe or even a road map; creating or finding utopia in performance is of necessity idiosyncratic, spontaneous, and unpredictable. I know there are playwrights and performers whose work I'll travel long distances to see, but even so, I can't assure myself that any given experience at the theater will bring me one of those exquisite moments in which I feel charged, challenged, and reassured. My spectatorial anticipation often comes up empty, my horizon of expectations frequently disappointed. But every ticket I buy contains a certain promise. I agree with Marvin Carlson, a preeminent theater historian, who writes about his own theatergoing in a lovely, autobiographical moment of scholarship:

> I also have now and then experienced moments of such intensity that they might be called epiphanies. It seems to me that theatre is perhaps particularly well suited as an art to generate such moments because it constantly oscillates between the fleeting present and the stillness of infinity. . . . Such moments of apotheosis are not everyday occurrences, of course. . . . Such moments will be different for every theatergoer, but I feel certain that we all have them, and treasure them. In an art that lives by, and survives largely in, the memory, such experiences have served me as touchstones, as permanent reminders of what I have been seeking in a lifetime of theatergoing.[3]

Such moments return me, too, to performance, lured by the possibility that in its insistent presence (and *present*), my fellow spectators and I might connect more fully with the complexities of our past and the possibility of a better future.[4]

Utopia in Performance defines and charts what I call *utopian performatives*.[5] Utopian performatives describe small but profound moments in which performance calls the attention of the audience in a way that lifts everyone slightly above the present, into a hopeful feeling of what the world might be like if every moment of our lives were as emotionally voluminous, generous, aesthetically striking, and intersubjectively intense. As a performative, performance itself becomes a "doing" in linguistic philosopher J. L. Austin's sense of the term, something that in its enunciation *acts*—that is, performs an action as tangible and effective as saying "I do" in a wedding ceremony.[6] Utopian performatives, in their doings, make palpable an affective vision of how the world might be better. As feminist performance theorist Elin Diamond so evocatively suggests,

> [A]s soon as performativity comes to rest on *a* performance, questions of embodiment, of social relations, of ideological interpellations, of emotional and political effects, all become discussable. . . . When performativity materializes as performance in that risky and dangerous negotiation between a doing (a reiteration of norms) and a thing done (discursive conventions that frame our interpretations), between someone's body and the conventions of embodiment, we have access to cultural meanings and critique.[7]

Theater and performance offer a place to scrutinize public meanings, but also to embody and, even if through fantasy, enact the affective possibilities of "doings" that gesture toward a much better world or, as director Joseph Chaikin, the famous founder of the Open Theater, once said, "a dynamic expression of the intense life."[8] By offering such concentrated, interpersonal, and "wish"-oriented moments, theater

> becomes a privileged, intimate area of human experience within which one can demand that the promise of another dimension of existence be revealed, and that the impossible be achieved/experienced here and now, in the presence of other living human beings—*the impossible,* namely a sense of unity between what is usually divided in our daily life: the material and immaterial, the human body and spirit, our mortality and our propensity for perfection, for infinity, for the absolute.[9]

The performatives under consideration in this book allow fleeting contact with a utopia not stabilized by its own finished perfection, not coercive in its contained, self-reliant, self-determined system, but a utopia always in process, always only partially grasped, as it disappears before us around the corners of narrative and social experience. As feminist theorist Angelika Bammer suggests, we "need to reconceptualize the utopian in historical, *this*-worldly terms, as a process that involves human agency."[10] She continues, "[I]t is often the partial vision, rather than the supposedly comprehensive one, that is most able to see clearly. In the sense that the gaze that encompasses less is often able to grasp more, the partial vision is the more utopian."[11] "My goal," she says, is to replace the idea of "a utopia" as something fixed, a form to be fleshed out, with the idea of "the utopian" as an *approach toward,* a movement beyond set limits into the realm of the not-yet-set. At the same time, I want to counter the notion of the utopian as unreal with the proposition that the utopian is powerfully real in the sense that hope and desire (and even fantasies) are real, never "merely" fantasy. It is a force that moves and shapes history.[12]

This sense of partiality and process informs the utopian performative, in which the various embodied, visual, and affective languages of the stage "approach toward" that which, as Bammer suggests, is "not-yet-set" but can be felt as desire, or as concrete fantasy, in the space of performance. Engaging the spectator in "a critical consideration of utopian enterprise, rather than simply aiming to secure his or her passive assent" makes the utopian performative nearly Brechtian in its gestic insistence.[13] In other words, utopian performatives are relatives of the famed German director and theorist Bertolt Brecht's notion of *gestus,* actions in performance that crystallize social relations and offer them to spectators for critical contemplation. In some ways, utopian performatives are the received moment of gestus, when those well-delineated, moving pictures of social relations become not only intellectually clear but felt and lived by spectators as well as actors.[14] Utopian performatives persuade us that beyond this "now" of material oppression and unequal power relations lives a future that might be different, one whose potential we can feel as we're seared by the promise of a present that gestures toward a better later. The affective and ideological "doings" we see and feel demonstrated in utopian performatives also critically rehearse civic engagement that could be effective in the wider public and political realm. These moments, then, are cousins to the ideas of Brazilian radical performance theorist Augusto Boal as well as to Brecht, in that they provoke affective rehearsals for revolution.[15]

My investigation into utopia in performance, then, resists the effort to find representations of a better world; the word *utopia* means, literally, "no place," and this book respects the letter of its sense by refusing to pin it down to prescription. I agree with Marxist philosophers Ernst Bloch and Herbert Marcuse, both of whom I reference in these pages, who "see art as an arena in which an alternative world can be expressed—not in a didactic, descriptive way as in traditional 'utopian' literature, but through the communication of an alternative experience."[16] Any fixed, static image or structure would be much too finite and exclusionary for the soaring sense of hope, possibility, and desire that imbues utopian performatives.[17] Utopian performatives exceed the content of a play or performance; spectators might draw a utopian performative from even the most dystopian theatrical universe.[18] Utopian performatives spring from a complex alchemy of form and content, context and location, which take shape in moments of utopia as doings, as process, as never finished gestures toward a potentially better future.

Arts critic John Rockwell, writing about Anne Bogart's production *bobrauschenbergamerica*, says, "Mesmerizing moments are what those of us addicted to performance live for. Suddenly and unexpectedly we are lifted from our normal detached contemplation into another place, where time stops and our breath catches and we can hardly believe that those responsible for this pleasure can sustain it another second."[19] He describes an experience of utopian performativity. Such moments make spectators ache with desire to capture, somehow, the stunning, nearly prearticulate insights they illuminate, if only to let them fill us for a second longer with a flash of something tinged with sadness but akin to joy. Bloch calls them instances of "anticipatory illumination," which "evade our efforts to apprehend them directly."[20] That evasion prompts the sadness in our joy. At the base of the utopian performative's constitution is the inevitability of its disappearance; its efficacy is premised on its evanescence. Performance's poignant ephemerality grounds all our experiences at the theater.[21] The utopian performative's fleetingness leaves us melancholy yet cheered, because for however brief a moment, we felt something of what redemption might be like, of what humanism could really mean, of how powerful might be a world in which our commonalities would hail us over our differences.

Spectatorship and Criticism

Given theater's ontological status, or its way of being, poised as it is between appearance and disappearance, and given the utopian performative's inherent ephemerality, this book poses several questions to the experience of writing about live performance. For example, how do we write about our own spectatorship in nuanced ways that capture the complicated emotions that the best theater experiences solicit? How do we place our own corporeal bodies in the service of those ineffable moments of insight, understanding, and love that utopian performatives usher into our hearts and minds? How do we theorize such moments, subjecting them to the rigor of our sharpest analysis while preserving the pleasure, the affective gifts that these moments share? Performance theorist and critic Ann Daly, writing on dance, says,

> Unlocking the dance is tantamount to unlocking myself. . . . Can I fine-tune myself to a new expressive frequency? Can I bring to this dance what it needs in order to be seen? . . . Criticism . . . is about sorting out the morass of perception into something orderly and interesting. It's about discerning relationships and making meaning. . . . [C]riticism takes a deferential position. . . . Criticism is the practice of appearing to disappear.[22]

Scholars, historians, and other thoughtful cultural critics face the continuing problem of how to capture and archive spectators' responses to performance. We rely on reviewers and their idiosyncratic reports of what they see not only to reconstruct the content and form of a given performance, but also to gain at least a glimmer of how it might have made the audience (and the performers, by virtue of their motivating presence) *feel*.[23] We write best about those performances we've been privileged to see. But part of the challenge of writing about performance as a public practice, one that circulates extensively and has some social impact, is to make it live well beyond itself, to hold it visually in memory, to evoke it with words, and to share it widely, so that its effects and potential might be known. Daly says, "Criticism is a gesture that carries the dance beyond its curtain time, extending it to readers near and far, present and future. Criticism transfigures dance into a much larger, discursive existence."[24] How can we capture, in our discourse, not just the outlines of a performance's structure and form, its content and the contours of its narrative, but the ineffable emotion it provokes in its moment of presence? How can we evoke, in writing, how its presence grounds us in a present, a moment of life at the theater, that seems somehow imbued with our past and our future, at once? How can I summon for you here my own experience of the simultaneity of time that infuses my argument, and that I feel during my richest, most memorable visits to the theater, many of which I want to conjure for you in these pages?[25]

During his tenure as the editor of *Theatre Journal,* the preeminent academic journal in theater and performance studies, David Román inaugurated a column in which various scholars write about their spectating experiences.[26] This recurring essay encourages theater and performance scholars to think about how we consume and experience performance and to inscribe the specific, material details of our theatergoing—with whom we went, how it made us feel, and what a performance made us think—into our memorializing analysis. These notations will leave behind a consciously marked trail of how performances felt in very local, historicized moments in time. *Utopia in Performance* is my own archive of spectatorship, documenting my own pleasures and desires, my hope and yearning, my experiences of intersubjectivity in rich exchange with flickering moments of theatrical performance.

Audiences as Participatory Publics

Documenting audience affect at performance requires a shift in focus, away from the notion of the singular spectator interpolated by representation, a trope my own work in *The Feminist Spectator as Critic* and in *Presence and Desire* has engaged repeatedly.[27] *Utopia in Performance* instead examines the audience as a group of people who have elected to spend an evening or an afternoon not only with a set of performers enacting a certain narrative arc or aesthetic trajectory, but with a group of other people, sometimes familiar, sometimes strange. I see, in this social choice, potential for intersubjectivity not only between performer and spectators but among the audience, as well.

Audiences form temporary communities, sites of public discourse that, along with the intense experiences of utopian performatives, can model new investments in and interactions with variously constituted public spheres. Feminist political theorist Nancy Fraser notes that according to the influential German philosopher Jürgen Habermas, "the idea of a public sphere is that of a body of 'private persons' assembled to discuss matters of 'public concern' or 'common interest.'"[28] Fraser goes on to suggest that public spheres are best considered multiple, since like community, or utopia, or other concepts at risk of totalitarian idealism, there can't be "one" public sphere in which all are included. Additional publics, then, aren't a distraction or fragmentation, but are a healthy sign of access and honesty. "Arrangements that accommodate contestation among a plurality of competing publics," Fraser argues, "better promote the ideal of participatory parity than does a single, comprehensive, overarching public."[29] "[T]o interact discursively as a member of a public, subaltern [meaning marginal or disempowered] or otherwise," she continues, "is to aspire to disseminate one's discourse to ever widening arenas."[30]

Considering theater audiences as such participatory publics might also expand how the *communitas* they experience through utopian performatives might become a model for other social interactions. Communitas, a term popularized in performance studies scholarship by anthropologist Victor Turner, describes the moments in a theater event or a ritual in which audiences or participants feel themselves become part of the whole in an organic, nearly spiritual way; spectators' individuality becomes finely attuned to those around them, and a cohesive if fleeting feeling of belonging to the group bathes the audience.[31] Attending performance, disparate people constitute these temporary publics; such spectatorship might encourage them to be active in other public spheres, to participate in civic conversations that performance perhaps begins. If, as Fraser theorizes, "public spheres are not only arenas for the formation of discursive opinion [but are also] arenas for the formation and enactment of social identities," then audiences at performance can be seen to be actively forming themselves as participating citizens of a perhaps more radical democracy.[32]

I saw a production at the Pittsburgh Public Theater that offers an example of how theater spectatorship can actively promote a sense of civic participation and emotional belonging. *The Chief* is a one-man show focused on Art Rooney, who owned the Steelers football team and stuck with them and the city that loved them through the team's derision and adulation for more than forty years and, in the process, became himself a much beloved fixture in the city.[33] The short production chose a folksy conceit to allow Tom Atkins, the virtuosic actor who played Rooney, to indulge in stories, and to reminisce directly with the audience: Rooney is due at a Knights of Columbus dinner, at which he's getting an award; his wife calls him to say he has some time before they need to leave. Rooney takes the occasion to "talk to some folks here"; he moves quickly into direct address and begins telling the audience stories about growing up in Pittsburgh; about boxing and gambling (for which Rooney was notorious); and mostly, about the historical exploits of the Steelers, which he relates in detail with a benign, patriarchal warmth and pride.

My family, with whom I attended *The Chief,* boasts a tradition of Steelers fandom nearly as long as Rooney's. My great-uncle Joe Tucker was an announcer for the team, and my grandfather, parents, aunts, and uncles are longtime season ticket holders.[34] Although I'm the only one in my family who's never been to a Steelers game, even I was caught up in the manufacture of communitas that the actor's impersonation of Rooney's stories produced. Clearly, the audience understood the play's references, not only to growing up in Pittsburgh, and to local neighborhoods, stores, and events, but to the "immaculate reception" and other highlights of the Steelers' years on the field, all of which were absolutely opaque to me. Clearly, from their attentiveness, their laughter of recognition, and the energy of their presence, they were persuaded by Atkins's full and affectionate portrait of Rooney and moved by the telling of a history in which many of them, as Steelers fans, played however small a part. By the time the show ended, the audience was on its feet, applauding, teary-eyed, and honoring the memories that had been so fully and lovingly wrought before them. After the curtain call, spectators approached the small thrust stage like anthropologists shopping for museum artifacts, looking closely at the detailed memorabilia decorating the set, touching (until hurried away by ushers) the photographs and objects that called up such nostalgia, such team spirit, such civic pride.

That evening was the first time I understood, affectively and intellectually, what it meant to root for the team. After a lifetime of perplexity (and sometimes, horror) at the vehemence of my family's fandom, I finally understood, because the expression of that powerful, moving commitment took place in a theater instead of a stadium. The production translated into terms through which I could relate that heightened sense of community, of belonging, of desire, of utopia that communitas at a football game or at the theater summons. In those ninety minutes in the O'Reilly Theater, the present housed a precious, explicitly local past, and beckoned toward a future full of hope for the athletic performance of a team and for a community that wants so much to rally around the players who somehow represent them all.

The play was a valentine for the team and the city, a powerful statement of pride in collective memory and wistful longing for a time in the team's history that seemed more local, less corporate, and more "real." *The Chief* made the theater audience a microcosm of the civic audience, relaying the conventions of communitas from the football field to performance and in the process creating a moving night at the theater that borrowed the emotional rituals of football. In other words, people cheered for the play as they do for the team; they "got it" by productively crossing modes of spectatorship. Suddenly, the theater *was* the city. The play hailed spectator-citizens and affirmed their belief in their team, their city, and their history. The present evoked the past and made the audience hopeful for the future.

Time and Utopia

The simultaneity of time brings force and effect to utopian performatives. Artist Ann Carlson, whose solo performance *Blanket* I discuss in chapter 6, as a motto for her work quotes Einstein's theory that all time exists in the present. This sense of monumentalism allows Carlson to capture, often on her own body, the flow of the past through the present into the future. By layering a representatively elderly body over a soundscape of much younger experience, and plotting a movement trajectory that appears rather elliptically to lead toward death, Carlson's performance in *Blanket* inspires utopian performatives that reassure us of the profundity of a confusion of temporal domains.[35] Such simultaneity characterizes more progressive arguments for utopia; the Marxist theorist Frederic Jameson, for example, suggests that utopian discourse can best be grasped as a "neutralization" of that which is, now.[36] Jameson believes that "[t]he force of the utopian text . . . is not to bring into focus the future that is coming to be, but rather to make us conscious precisely of the horizons or outer limits of what can be thought and imagined in our present."[37]

Thinking of utopia as processual, as an index to the possible, to the "what if," rather than a more restrictive, finite image of the "what should be," allows performance a hopeful cast, one that can experiment with the possibilities of the future in ways that shine back usefully on a present that's always, itself, in process. Such a view of utopia prevents it from settling into proscription, into the kind of fascism that inevitably attends a fully drawn idea of a better world. Angelika Bammer says that the difficulty faced by movements that work toward social change is "sustaining the very principle on which [they are] predicated, namely the idea of the future *as possibility* rather than as preset goal. The difficulty, in other words, is to sustain the concept of utopia as process."[38]

Performance's simultaneity, its present-tenseness, uniquely suits it to probing the possibilities of utopia as a hopeful process that continually writes a different, better future. While many commentators typically conceive of utopia as a space (and, as feminist philosopher Elizabeth Grosz writes, "usually an enclosed and commonly isolated space"),[39] performance allows us to see utopia as a process of spending time. Performance's temporality excites audiences with a slight disorientation; its spatiality often anchors it to an imagined place, a "what if" of matter and expression. But performance always exceeds its space and its image, since it lives only in its doing, which is imagining, in the good no-place that is theater. The utopic, Grosz writes, is "out of time";[40] performance, too, rests lightly in its own moment, referring to all of time in the images of its spectacle, in the projection of its presence, in its gesture of hope toward the wishes, predictions, and resolutions of its future.

Writing about performance while I'm watching, I try to capture time, to write it as it flees, with my pen in hand, scribbling on my program in the half-dark. But utopian performatives force me to stop transcribing my experience of the present to some sort of imagined future; in those moments, I sit bolt upright, caught in the density of a communal epiphany that I need to experience now, that gathers its power through the impossibility of doing it justice in any subsequent moment. These moments of communitas complement the processual nature of utopia in performance. Victor Turner suggests that any "social world is a world in becoming, not a world in being"; social worlds, like utopia, are too often, according to Turner, thought of as "static concepts."[41] On the contrary, Turner theorizes communitas as "anti-structural," as "most evident in 'liminality,' [which refers] to any condition outside or on the peripheries of everyday life," which includes, of course, performance.[42] Communitas doesn't conform to rules of law, to regulations or prior social agreements. The very existence of communitas "puts all social structural rules in question and suggests new possibilities. Communitas strains toward universalism and openness."[43] Although "social and cultural structures are not abolished by communitas," Turner argues, "the sting of their divisiveness is removed so that the fine articulation of their parts in a complex heterogeneous unity can be better appreciated."[44]

Turner's theory usefully describes the social potential of utopian performatives. That is, rather than resting on an old humanist legacy of universality and transcendence, utopian performatives let audiences experience a processual, momentary feeling of affinity, in which spectators experience themselves as part of a congenial public constituted by the performance's address. Hailed by these performatives, these moments of what Marvin Carlson calls "apotheosis" or "epiphany," spectators can be rallied to hope for the possibility of realizing improved social relations. They can imagine, together, the affective potential of a future in which this rich feeling of warmth, even of love, could be experienced regularly and effectively outside the theater.

I write about my experiences at performances as ones of both intellect and affect; at a performance, I watch performers and audiences think and feel, and do the same along with them. Part of my project is to describe the performance's effect on the audience as a temporary community, perhaps inspired by communitas to feel themselves citizens of a no-place that's a better place, citizens who might then take that feeling into other sites of public discourse. I write about performance to try to document, from a necessarily, productively partial perspective, its emotional efficacy as a way to think about its social potential. Feminist and Marxist theater scholar Janelle Reinelt, in her *Theatre Journal* record of her experiences as a spectator, writes, "The embodiedness of actors and spectators still trumps the mere page, but the belief, indeed the faith, that [theater] can entail intellectual rigor and ethico-political argument sustains me."[45] She captures the twofold project of experiencing performance, saying, "I still have experiences in theatre that cause me to question and cry, laugh and think, feel and reason, dream and critique. Sometimes other people do it with me."[46] Writing about the pull of those binaries, as part of our socially committed, aesthetically stirred spectatorship, lets performance critics like me and my colleagues document a complicated process of engagement with a live event whose presence I can only trace as I remember it in the future. I am left with words to describe what happens when, as Reinelt says, "I sometimes find my breath taken away by performances."[47]

Using Theater

I see and write about performance with hope for what it can mean politically, but also affectively, through my faith that emotions might move us to social action. That is, I believe that being passionately and profoundly stirred in performance can be a transformative experience useful in other realms of social life. Being moved at the theater allows us to realize that such feeling is possible, even desirable, elsewhere. People use their audience experiences at the theater in myriad ways; everyone relates differently to what it means to be a spectator. I am a voracious, indiscriminate spectator. I go to live performance regularly at home in Austin, Texas, running the gamut from university theater productions that my position as a professor requires I attend to new plays, musicals, and classics at the Equity-contracted, professional Zach Scott Theatre. I see experimental performance and new plays in converted warehouses in marginal Austin neighborhoods, squinting at addresses and studying rickety aluminum structures for signs of theatrical life. I attend touring Broadway productions of shows like *Mamma Mia, Phantom of the Opera,* and *Jesus Christ*

Superstar at the gigantic, twenty-eight-hundred-seat Bass Concert Hall on the University of Texas campus, and touring comedians and performance artists at the restored, vaguely baroque Paramount Theatre downtown. I see community-based performances in schools and senior centers, autobiographical work produced by teenage girls and people with disabilities. My eclectic tastes lead me to unforeseeable experiences, like feeling unexpectedly moved by a large-cast production of *Guys and Dolls* at a high school, or by seeing memoir-inspired solo performances by the graduating MFA acting class at the University of Texas.

I travel around the country and the world to see performance. In New York, I see cutting edge avant-garde work at P.S. 122 or LaMama on the Lower East Side; new plays off-Broadway at the Public Theater, New York Theatre Workshop, the Vineyard, Playwrights Horizons, Manhattan Theatre Club, and the Signature Theatre; chamber productions of rediscovered old musicals at City Center in midtown; and musicals and star-driven productions of straight plays on Broadway. I see regional theater productions, in Providence, San Diego, Chicago, Baltimore, Pittsburgh, San Francisco, Madison, Santa Fe, and other cities with professional theaters. I'm game to see anything, because I love the potential I feel sitting in a theater, the palpable sense that anything might happen once the lights go down.

For someone who only sees performance at home (wherever home might be), the experience of showing up at the theater might be completely different than for a spectator who seeks out performance around the world. Likewise, for the inveterate, itinerant spectator, seeing performance in many different places changes the experience each time, resituating our relation to the inside and outside markers of community, of the peculiarly "insider" knowledge that influences reception, and to local, as well as translocal social practices of spectatorship. For some people, the community that supports the theater is more important than the play; for others, the performance provides an excuse for social congress, to be seen at or to participate in an event.[48] For others, the place slips from prominence as soon as the light floods the stage, and the only reality that matters is the usable fiction crafted by the actors. Some people read their program notes and stay for talkbacks, to extend the moment of intimacy with strangers; some people push up the aisle at the curtain call, more concerned with postshow traffic than with demonstrating their appreciation or respect for the play.

Theater sustains some of us as a daily practice that helps us order and define an existence that becomes more incoherent with each new global political maneuver. Other people see theater as a novelty, whether boasting expensive tickets to a much-publicized Broadway production like *The Lion King* or *The Producers,* or gamely attending a local university performance by students in an Introduction to Acting class, or dutifully showing up for a high school production of a musical with a one-hundred-student cast and an awkward, tittering sold-out crowd. In *Utopia in Performance,* I'm interested in all these modes of spectatorship and audience practices. I consider what it means for people to collect the cultural capital (that is, the social "points" that sometimes derive from and can be flaunted about our spectating experiences) of seeing *Metamorphoses* on Broadway or seeing *Def Poetry Jam* live, rather than on HBO, as well as what it means for people to commit their time to attending a small city's local festival of performance that constitutes its own public audience from within a larger local community of spectators. I won't parse distinctions between "mainstream" and "alternative" or "community-based" and "popular" performance. I'm interested in how utopian performatives appear in many ways within, across, and among constantly morphing spectating communities, publics that reconstitute themselves anew for each performance.

The very present-tenseness of performance lets audiences imagine utopia not as some idea of future perfection that might never arrive, but as brief enactments of the possibilities of a process that starts now, in this moment at the theater. Many of us who've performed on stage ourselves, or who have participated in performance as collaborators, as well as spectators, know the magic, utopic moments that happen after weeks of rehearsals, of experimenting with people across a range of "what ifs" until we settle on the best choices. Those experiences resemble what musicologist MacKenzie Cadenhead calls the "phantom note" in choral singing. Cadenhead says, "In choral music there is a phenomenon called the phantom note. It exists octaves above the rest and is not sung by a human voice. It is magically heard when all vocal parts of a choir join together, the literal result of perfect harmony. In theater, this metaphorical phantom note is created by the component harmonies of all ensemble members."[49] In my own experiences participating in performance, I remember distinctly those moments of hearing the phantom note: performing, for instance, as the narrator in a bootleg production of Holly Hughes's underground lesbian classic *The Well of Horniness,* directed by a graduate student at the University of Wisconsin, where I taught in the late 1980s. Cast with nonprofessional actors holding their scripts, we performed in a basement bar with a large gay and lesbian clientele. The harmony of the performance came from the insane, hysterical glee with which the performers inhabited Hughes's campy characters, and the uproarious laughter with which the audience responded. The whole place swooned with inebriation, creating a bacchanalian atmosphere of communal transgression and delight. Performers and directors live to hear the phantom note and to make it audible for spectators.

But how can the profoundly moving experience of utopian performatives in performance (which might be considered phantom notes with community resonance and social implications) be conveyed or carried into the world outside the theater? Is the breathtaking moment of potential connection and emotion severed as soon as the house lights go up, and the audience returns to its more prosaic, individual arrangements of singles, couples, or trios to wade through the crowd to the exit doors? As theater theorist Bert States says, "The return from the play world is like the awakening from the dream: it is always an abrupt fall into the mundane, fraught with the nostalgia of exile."[50] Performers, too, often share such melancholic dislocation; singer Nina Simone once said that "the saddest part of performing" was that "it didn't mean anything once you were off-stage."[51] How can we sustain the wonder and intimacy and potential prompted by seeing, for instance, *Metamorphoses,* when the street outside the theater looks too bright, too blurry, too dirty, too fast-moving, when it clamors for our immediate attention, insisting that our pleasurable memory of the images created by the actors playing in water too quickly fade, leaving us only the residue of its loss?

Geography, though, changes the texture of these moments of departure. When I leave a theater in Austin, for example, the street isn't quite as loud or as bright as it is in New York. The soft air and thick trees cushion the shock of reentry and usually, the traffic has long since quieted down. Moving into the street with my companions, I can often hear other spectators murmuring about the performance, and sometimes I stop to talk to strangers about what we all just saw and felt. At a recent Laurie Anderson performance at the Paramount, for instance, I struck up a conversation with a stranger about Anderson's previous visits to Austin, about how this one seemed more intimate, slower, evidence perhaps of her own aging (and ours). I thanked him for his thoughts as we headed in separate directions, reminded of how spectators can take time together when we're not rushing to find taxis or steeling ourselves for the tumult of real life.

At a performance of *Jesus Christ Superstar* in the cavernous Bass Concert Hall, one of the four gay men seated in front of me and my partner turned around at intermission to confess that the musical was the first show he ever saw on Broadway, back when he was "seven," he joked. For no apparent reason, he wanted to talk, to reminisce, and when he turned, he found us receptive listeners (since I, too, was overrun with nostalgia for my own experience of seeing the show as a teenager, and my own amazement that these many years later, I still remembered every word of every song). Austin audiences have a reputation for standing ovations, indiscriminately rising to their feet at the end of most performances. Seasoned spectators tend to scoff and roll their eyes when this happens, before we, too, grudgingly get to our feet. But I'm moved by the respect and generosity of this gesture, this attempt to let the performers see us honoring their labor, each time. Perhaps these moments of public feeling that end our time together in the theater make us comfortable talking to each other as we move up the aisles and out onto the street. Perhaps the warm nights, and the proximity of our cars, and the generally relaxed and forgiving Austin atmosphere prompts us to be generous with each other and ourselves, allowing the moment of performance to linger longer.

In *Utopia in Performance,* I examine those moments, which performance theorist and practitioner Richard Schechner calls "cool down," so reminiscent of when the lights come up after last call in a bar to reveal the tired, too human, sweaty flesh of ordinary people who'd been transformed only a moment ago by flashing lights and a persistent, irresistible beat.[52] The moments before that letdown are what I like to call "disco ball moments," which are, in fact, utopian performatives.[53] How can we—or *should* we—bring the clarity of utopian performatives to the rest of our lives? Should utopian performatives work outside the frame of theatrical performance? Do they fail if they don't translate to more quotidian life? Many commentators measure political theater only by its effectiveness in the "real world." In *Utopia in Performance,* I try to resist such stark binaries between performance and reality, and suggest that the experience of performance, the pleasure of a utopian performative, even if it doesn't change the world, certainly changes the people who feel it.

Perhaps instead of measuring the utopian performative's "success" against some real notion of effectiveness, we need to let it live where it does its work best—at the theater or in moments of consciously constructed performance wherever they take place. The utopian performative, by its very nature, can't translate into a program for social action, because it's most effective as a *feeling.* Perhaps that feeling of hope, or that feeling of desire, embodied by that suddenly hollow space in the pit of my stomach that drops me into an erotics of connection and commonality—perhaps such intensity of *feeling* is politics enough for utopian performatives. Perhaps burdening such moments with the necessity that they demonstrate their effectiveness after the performance ends can only collapse the fragile, beautiful potential of what we can hold in our hearts for just a moment. The desire to feel, to be touched, to feel my longing addressed, to share the complexity of hope in the presence of absence and know that those around me, too, are moved, keeps me returning to the theater, keeps me willing to practice a utopian vision for which in some tangible way, no direct real-life analogy exists. The politics lie in the desire to feel the potential of elsewhere. The politics lie in our willingness to attend or to create performance at all, to come together in real places—whether theaters or dance clubs—to explore in imaginary spaces the potential of the "not yet" and the "not here."[54]

I won't claim that seeing *Def Poetry Jam* on Broadway or *Blanket* at a university theater changes the world. As philosopher Herbert Marcuse, whose writing about art and Eros profoundly influenced a generation of artists and activists in the 1960s, said, "Art cannot change the world, but it can contribute to changing the consciousness and drives of the men and women who could change the world."[55] He also says that art can invoke "an image of the end of power, the appearance of freedom. But this is only the appearance; clearly, the fulfillment of this promise is not within the domain of art."[56] That is, we can't measure the effectiveness of art as we can a piece of legislation, or a demonstration, or a political campaign for candidates or for issues. But I do believe that the experience of performance, and the intellectual, spiritual, and affective traces it leaves behind, can provide new frames of reference for how we see a better future extending out from our more ordinary lives. Seeing that vision, we can figure out how to achieve it outside the fantastical, magic space of performance.

Reanimating Humanism

Utopian performatives usefully point us toward redefinitions of concepts and values once held dear but more recently exhausted under the terms of postmodernism and the political ascendancy of a hardly compassionate American conservatism. In cultural criticism, postmodernist thought meant mistrusting the possibility of originality and insight, and abandoning belief in the transcendence of meaning and truth for a more cynical relativity. The related arguments of poststructuralism, a theoretical method in literary studies that dismantled so-called master narratives and canonical texts and belief systems, usefully allowed commentators to deconstruct the inculcations of conservative ideas about gender, sexuality, race, ethnicity, and other identity markers, as well as to instill doubt as a generative mode of thinking. Partially through the effects of postmodernism in culture and poststructuralism in criticism, democracy and humanism somehow became bankrupt concepts in the progressive American imagination, driven to disrepair and disrepute by the cynicism of late capitalist globalism.[57] Part of my argument, in trumpeting the progressive potential of utopian performatives in performance, is that reanimating humanism and seeing, through performance, more effective models of more radical democracy might reinvigorate a dissipated Left. Through the power of affect, usefully explored and even harnessed at the theater, perhaps progressives can once again persuade one another that a better world doesn't have to be an out-of-reach ideal, but a process of civic engagement that brings it incrementally closer. Political theorist Mary Dietz says that "democracy [is] the form of politics that brings people together as citizens," that "democratic citizenship" is a relation of "civic peers; its guiding virtue is mutual respect; its primary principle is the 'positive liberty' of democracy and self-government, not simply the 'negative liberty' of noninterference."[58] How might a radical notion of democracy allow us to see it as a structure for liberation, rather than restraint?[59]

Part of the power I see in utopian performatives is the way in which they might, by extension, resurrect a belief or faith in the possibility of social change, even if such change simply means rearticulating notions that have been too long discredited. A desire to revitalize humanism or democracy doesn't have to be seen as naive and idealistic; Turner suggests that such belief, through "exposure to or immersion in communitas seems to be an indispensable human social requirement. People have a real need, and 'need' is not for me a 'dirty word,' to doff the masks, cloaks, apparel, and insignia of status from time to time even if only to don the liberating masks of liminal masquerade."[60] While Turner's suggestion seems at first most apt for performers who participate in generating communitas or utopian performatives, perhaps such need describes audiences, too, who might find, in performance, necessary ways to release themselves from the inhibiting restraints of the "as is" for the more liberatory possibilities of the "what if"; that is, a common human need to hope.[61]

The revised humanism I imagine doesn't devolve into the transcendental sign of "man," and doesn't become omniscient and omnipotent. This reanimated and reenvisioned humanism is contextual, situational, and specific, nothing at all like the totalizing signifier it once described. This wiser humanism has learned from the difficult work of identity politics and absorbs those lessons into its belief system. This reconstructed humanism is multiple, respecting the complexities and ambiguities of identity while it works out ways for people to share and feel things in common, like the need for survival and for love, for compassion, and for hope.

Referring to the events of September 11, 2001, leftist commentator Todd Gitlin says, "Terrorists remind us, you and I, that we share the common condition of citizens, that we are subject to all they are subjected to, that we cannot secede."[62] Lest his emphasis on citizenship appear too nationalist (with its danger of xenophobia and blind, uncritical patriotism), Gitlin says,

> I'm not complacent about how far we've come toward securing a human future, yet the growth of institutions such as the Hague human rights court tells me that we might be on our way; if not toward a federal world government, then at least toward a sort of Articles of Confederation in which we collectively agree that the enforcement of the collective good trumps the national boundaries that were the great political achievements of the eighteenth and nineteenth centuries.[63]

Gitlin proposes, then, a postnationalist expression of humanism to replace the fractures of identity politics and to gather citizens of the world together in a common search for equality and freedom. I very much still identify as a feminist, and still feel community with people who call themselves "queer"; my perspective remains steeped in feminism, queer theory, and critical race studies. But I also want a more capacious form of response and address. While noting how the performances I discuss position the politics of identity, I find myself equally interested in how, through their particular performance styles and genres, these performances address something we might call our common humanity.[64]

In chapter 6, I search through performances, looking for models of reanimated humanism in moments of breathtakingly clear and hopeful interactions among performers and between performers and spectators. In Deborah Warner and Fiona Shaw's production of *Medea*, for instance, I find an argument for love and faith, even amid the tragedy of infanticide. An overarching humanism seems to steer the performers in Mary Zimmerman's *Metamorphoses*, as they enact historical myths and cajole us with their continuing resonance. The "universal," viewed through moments of utopia in performance, loses its insistent, transhistorical charge, and becomes, like communitas, like "society," like "utopia," a point of process moving toward what political theorist and philosopher Martha Nussbaum calls a more "human core."[65] As Nussbaum admits, "Many universal conceptions of the human being have been insular in an arrogant way and neglectful of differences among cultures and ways of life."[66] But, she suggests, "We do not have to choose between 'the embedded life' of community and a deracinated type of individualism. Universal values build their own communities, communities of resourcefulness, friendship and agency, embedded in the local scene but linked in complex ways to groups of [people] in other parts of the world."[67]

Is it too much to ask of performance, that it teach us to love and to link us with the world, as well as to see and to think critically about social relations? As I note in chapter 2, I know I risk sentimentality with this work; I know I risk emptying even further overused signs like "peace" or "love." Yet I find myself wanting to take back these words, to refill them, to ground them not in naïveté or troubling innocence, but in concrete, material conditions that give rise to empathy (and more) for others.[68] How can we use sentimentality as something positive instead of abandoning it?[69] Neoconservatives know how to use powerful, emotional images; witness, for example, the efficacy of antiabortion activism. Pending legislation in Texas will require waiting periods for those choosing to have an abortion, during which these women will be offered vividly photographed images of fetuses at various stages of development in an attempt to anthropomorphize a collection of cells and microbes.[70] Prochoice progressives can't seem to agree on what counterimages to use that would encourage women to *feel* differently about their choices. We're fearful of hegemony; some progressive scholars have internalized the lessons of poststructuralism too thoroughly to be able to settle unambivalently on one effective counter-representation.[71] In *Utopia in Performance,* I suggest that utopian performatives can accommodate the Left's fear of prescription, while at the same time engaging languages of emotion and images, of passion and fervor as part of a necessary, crucial representational counterdiscourse.

The Performances

Chapter 2, "'A Femme, a Butch, a Jew': Feminist Autobiographical Solo Performance," begins to address such productive emotional entangle-ments and effects. I mine for my examples the "Throws Like a Girl" series of women's solo performances I curate for an Austin theater collective called the Rude Mechanicals that produces new work at the Off Center, a converted warehouse on the city's East Side. In the series' first installment in fall 2001, the Rude Mechs and I brought Holly Hughes, Peggy Shaw, and Deb Margolin to Austin to perform. They also led public workshops on generating performance for students and the University of Texas and Austin communities and visited classes and shared their insights in question-and-answer sessions with students and local artists and audiences. Their residencies reconnected me to deceptively simple but profound experiences of performance practice and theatergoing. The stories Hughes, Shaw, and Margolin told reanchored me to my own feminist, lesbian, and Jewish histories, while enabling me to feel an enhanced and broader sense of community that didn't stand on the ceremony of identity politics. I supported the series as the curator, as the link between the solo artists and the producing theater collective; as a teacher, explaining the significance of this work to theater and to American politics for my students; as an artist, participating in the performance workshops and generating my own keen, heartfelt images; as a spectator, participating in breathless moments of utopian performativity with the rest of the audience; and as a facilitator, helping to translate political and performative languages back and forth across perceived divides until communitas felt—even momentarily—achieved.

The localness of the series and its embeddedness in the everyday work and emotion (what the late French sociologist Pierre Bourdieu would call the "habitus")[72] of my then-new hometown let me play these multiple roles in relation to these performances. Moving back and forth between the East Side theater and the theater building at the University of Texas, my curating and teaching, facilitating and discussing became as creative for me as performing. These practices carried their own utopian performatives out into the local community. The wide, rich context created around the performers' work allowed other people also to experience themselves through various affiliations—as spectators, as workshop participants, as critics, as a community that hosted three generous, warm, inspiring artists. These communities of citizens created a wide public not just of feminists, Jews, and queers, but of people who care about the ideas and issues that these feminist, lesbian, and/or Jewish performers addressed, as well as about the pleasure provided to them as witnessing, active spectators. Gitlin says, "You don't need identity politics to condemn racial bigotry or hatred of gays. You can—you must—condemn them *as a human being*."[73] To paraphrase his injunction, it wasn't necessary to *be* a feminist, or lesbian, or Jew to respond to these performances; being a human being was enough. "Throws Like a Girl" brought University of Texas people and Austinites into various temporary communities, all of which highlighted us for ourselves. We saw ourselves as our "higher selves," as a critic once said of Lily Tomlin's *Search for Signs of Intelligent Life in the Universe,* which I discuss in chapter 3. During the three months the series first organized my experience, I found intense moments of inter-subjectivity not just between performers and audiences, but also among members of the audience. The residue of those visits, nearly four years later, galvanizes me still.[74]

Similar experiences resonate in other performances I discuss in this book, several of which also developed from artists' residencies at the University of Texas in Austin. For example, in January 2003, the Department of Theatre and Dance cosponsored with Mark Russell, a graduate of the department and then the artistic director at P.S. 122 in New York, a five-day festival of international performance art called "Fresh Terrain."[75] Seven performances, each presented several times through a tightly scheduled few days and framed by roundtables of invited critics and local faculty, anchored the concentrated event. The emotional intensity of "Fresh Terrain" felt much like what I'd experienced in the "Throws Like a Girl" series. The festival provided a site for people hungry for affective and aesthetic social experiences to nourish themselves with performance art in a range of styles and genres and facilitated focused attention on performance practices and their reception. Groups of spectators—students, faculty, local people, other artists, presenters from around the country— found community in the particularly intense, carefully defined experience of moving through several theaters in a single University of Texas building to see performances and of taking time to talk, together, about what we'd seen and felt and what it might mean. I discuss Ann Carlson's *Blanket* (in chapter 6) as an exemplary moment in "Fresh Terrain," one that generated utopian performatives by catching the audience in its generous, provocative embrace and by knitting us close together, even temporarily, in rapt attention to the simultaneous past/present/future of our own lives. *Blanket* asked us to help each other and help Carlson mark time, to acknowledge history, and to admit that a common mortal future waits for us all.

The festival or series format extends the temporary public the audience constitutes across a longer period of time, a condition that facilitates utopian performatives. Although I saw most of the productions I discuss in this book on a single night, with a usually anonymous audience, some of my examples derive from these extended periods of communal spectating, which created more opportunities for critical and affective discourse around performances that a familiar group of people shared. Does it matter when the audience becomes familiar to itself? What happens when an audience reaches a level of comfort that dissipates the tension of strangeness that often charges spectators settling down so close to each other for an hour or two? Perhaps these more intimate audiences become micro civil societies

> sustained by groups much smaller than the *demos* or the working class or the mass of consumers or the nation. . . . They become part of the world of family, friends, comrades and colleagues, where people are connected to one another and made responsible for one another. Connected and responsible: without that, "free and equal" is less attractive than we once thought it would be. [Civil society] requires a new sensitivity for what is local, specific, contingent—and, above all, a new recognition (to paraphrase a famous sentence) that the good life is in the details.[76]

An ongoing audience is perhaps a more receptive audience, attuned to the vocabulary of the theatrical moment and attentive to the responses of its fellows. Theater scholar and critic Martin Esslin says, "At its best, when a fine play in a fine performance coincides with a receptive audience in the theatre, this can produce a concentration of thought and emotion which leads to an enhanced degree of lucidity, of emotional intensity that amounts to a higher level of spiritual insight and can make such an experience akin to a religious one, a memorable high-point in an individual's life."[77] Esslin describes what I'm calling a utopian performative; does the "receptive audience" create the necessary condition for such moments?

For instance, the critical symposium at the "Fresh Terrain" festival at the University of Texas provided instances for the receptive audience to speak alongside performers about their mutual experiences. At one of the symposia, Canadian artist Daniel MacIvor said performance is about "teaching people empathy and how to listen." He said that when he's on stage, he feels like there are "people out there who become one thing, breathing together," which is perhaps another way of speaking of communitas.[78] Ben Cameron, the executive director of Theatre Communications

Group, who served as a visiting critic, said performance "helps someone inhabit their skin boldly." Mark Russell, the event's curator, said performance "is something done very well."[79] I was struck by how this language imagined performance as a practice in which the individual balances his or her needs with those of community, one where human interaction is about sharing breath; it rejects the language of capitalist production that we tend to use when describing how performance is created. That is, during "Fresh Terrain," no one spoke of how performers were "used"; no one talked about the great performances directors "got out of actors." The metaphor of use and extraction was discarded for language that described the inter-subjectivity that makes theatrical magic, that harnesses desire to meaning making, and extends meaning making to a reinvigorated effort at world building. Madge Darlington, a core member of the Rude Mechanicals artistic collective, said on her symposium panel, "I *have* to see theater; I *have* to make this a society that *has to have* art."[80] That imperative drove "Fresh Terrain," since we moved as a spectatorial community from watching events, sharing our copresence as the motivators and makers of meaning, to discussing them, playing out the possibilities of how they felt and what they might mean.

On the other hand, how does the tension of proximity work for a more anonymous audience in the theater, whether or not it's a consistent one, when an armrest becomes a site of cordial negotiation? How do we feel each other's presences as reassuring or invasive, and what does performance do (what *can* performance do) to change the effects of those feelings? Can seeing performance teach us how to be physically intimate with strangers, in a culture that works harder to keep the space between us growing? As theater critic Eric Bentley comments about going to the theater, "Here one is, sitting down with total strangers to share experiences of considerable intimacy."[81] Something in the very liminality of theater, in its suspension from the common distractions of everyday life, allows even an audience of strangers to be receptive to emotion. Bentley continues his wonderings about theatrical intimacy:

> There are directors in the New York theatre who invite actors to pour out "love, *real* love" into the auditorium. The hope is that the audience will reciprocate. . . . Where in the auditorium does the amorous out-pouring actually land? If the actor's role is a ghost, an audience is a ghost of a ghost. At eleven o'clock, when the actor drops his role, he stands revealed as a man, but when the audience drops *its* role, it van-

ishes. These people leaving the theatre are not "audience": they are Smith and Jones to whom the actor did *not* address himself.[82]

Only in the temporary public comprised by performance does the audience's identity cohere. And in that coherence, spectators find themselves recipients of an "amorous outpouring" that would be impossible to receive without their peers surrounding them.

The third chapter, "Finding Our Feet in One Another's Shoes," investigates the potential for utopian performatives in solo performances that invoke multiple characters across the same person's body. Lily Tomlin, in *Search for Signs of Intelligent Life in the Universe;* Danny Hoch, in *Jails, Hospitals, and Hip-Hop;* and Anna Deavere Smith, in *Fires in the Mirror, Twilight, LA,* and *House Arrest,* provide keen examples of performers who use the forum of theater and the vehicle of their bodies to bring multiplicitous communities together for polemical discussion. Written by Jane Wagner, Tomlin's production joyfully bids for a reanimated humanism achieved through the specific social critiques of feminism. Hoch's performance evokes experiences and people from his multiethnic, multiracial home in Brooklyn's Williamsburg neighborhood, and presents for public discussion the complexities of lives typically not seen in front of audiences. Smith uses her own particular brand of ethnography to stage conversations among people too suspicious of, or hostile to, each other to talk in the same room. By bringing them together, for dialogic contemplation with the audience, Smith offers new, multiple perspectives that open up the meanings of historical events and material lives. All three performers conduct what performance studies scholar Joni Jones calls "performance ethnography," practicing the details of cultural difference at the most minute level of the body—gestures, physical positions, inflections of speech and emotion—to experience another from within a specific cultural location.[83] These performances offer spectators a way to see the potential of imaginatively walking, even if metaphorically, in the shoes of someone else.

The fourth chapter, "*Def Poetry Jam:* Performance as Public Practice," discusses how experiencing utopian performatives in performance might empower people to engage civically in participatory democracy. How can performance model—not just in content or form or context, but through the interaction of all three—ways of communicating in a public sphere that might encourage us to take mutual responsibility for reimagining social behavior? In this chapter, I recount my experience seeing a Broadway performance of *Russell Simmons* [*sic*] *Def Poetry Jam*, at which by renovating the conventions of audience/performer interaction, the old, hegemonically white theater became a forum for taking pleasure in and affirming experiences that Broadway theater typically erases. The young, multiracial, multiethnic, multigendered, pansexual cast of slam poets performed a reinvigorated image of American democracy, through which they expressed their patriotism, their claims to American dreams, without sacrificing their particular identities, passions, or social commitments. *Def Poetry Jam* modeled for a moment the potential of a nation built on pride in our differences, in which our mutual "otherness" explodes the horizon of American citizenship. The production reveled in what feminist philosopher Iris Marion Young calls "unassimilated otherness," in differences cohabitating congenially in a newly roomy "unoppressive city."[84]

In chapter 5, "*The Laramie Project:* Rehearsing for the Example," I compare the Tectonic Theatre Project's New York production of *The Laramie Project* with a production of the play at a professional theater in Austin. Both productions raised questions about how performance can prompt audiences to see themselves as citizens, to participate in a democracy that takes ethical responsibility for tears in the social fabric. The Austin production, in particular, represented how public spheres form around crises, and then are subject to media manipulation. This *Laramie Project* presented a struggle over the authority of discourse and its control. These productions used the occasion of performance to extend civic dialogue, creating a temporary public through the power of feeling the audience experienced together.

Chapter 6, "Militant Optimism: Approaching Humanism," suggests how we might reenvision the project of radical humanism through the affective and aesthetic potential of utopian performatives. How can theater make transformation material, rather than just metaphorical? By discussing the off-Broadway production of director-adaptor Mary Zimmerman's *Metamorphoses,* I argue that theatrical effects—like using water on stage, or asking actors to engage the full physicality of their bodies—can incite people to profound and creative responses that let us feel hope for the potential of our lives in human community. In Ann Carlson's solo piece, *Blanket,* also discussed here, those theatrical effects graced a soundscape that captured a private and public history of significant moments in the civil rights struggles of the last fifty years in the United States. Carlson used theatrical images and metaphors to ignite a very material emotional exchange between herself and the audience in the present of her virtuosic performance. Deborah Warner's Broadway production of *Medea,* with Fiona Shaw in the lead, used concise, incisive emotionality to insist that spectators experience the power of affect in theatricality. By telling a mythic Greek story, Warner and Shaw translated the magnitude of Medea's fury, pain, and grief into a commentary on contemporary gender relations, on corporate indifference, on the hypocrisy of community, and on the power of acting and design elements in performance itself.

Intersubjective Radical Amazement

In many of the performances I study in this book, the performers' charisma and virtuosity motivate the utopian performative.[85] I realize that spectators seduced by a performer's powerful presence run the risk of coercive persuasion; I've engaged and sometimes agreed with the post-structuralist critique of the metaphysics of presence, in which, some theorists suggest, charisma is a force for fascism. For example, critic Ann Wilson says, "nostalgia" for presence is a "longing for human authenticity," and critiques the belief that theater can create just the kind of communal experience I detail in this book:

> The simplistic notion that theatre makes some ineffable human quality present by tapping into an ahistorical human essence seems to me to be largely a counter-response to an awareness of the constructed nature of human identity. . . . I would suggest that the tenacious clinging to notions of presence and authenticity, to the essential human quality of theatre, probably needs to be re-thought if what it is to be human is to have a unified self which exists prior to technology. . . . It seems odd that we tend to see theatre as somehow removed from . . . technolog[y], as if it arcanely maintained a space in which some essential humanity can be rediscovered.[86]

She says, "As much as we might yearn for a theatre which affirms an essential humanity allowing us to forge bonds with each other that might serve as the basis of community, this position seems like a nostalgia for a world which doesn't exist, if indeed it ever did."[87]

I understand Wilson's resistance, and share her hesitations about nostalgia for old forms of humanism that suggested people cohere as recognizable, fixed subjects. But utopian performatives debunk notions of "ahistorical human essences" because they "do" community momentarily, in gestures of feeling that can't last long enough to become transhistorical or essentialist. Utopian performatives are themselves technologies, mediations in Enlightenment notions of authentic selves and coherent, static communities. Despite Wilson's reasonable cautions, I'm deeply interested in just how presence, in just how talent and magnetism, can be used as a means to progressive, rather than conservative, goals. Most of the performances I discuss here offered intense moments of electrifying presence: the intersubjective vulnerability of Hughes, Shaw, and Margolin in their solo performances; Tomlin, Hoch, and Smith, performing diverse communities of people on their own bodies; the def poets charging the audience with their powerful, seductive declarations of citizenship; *The Laramie Project*'s demonstration of community grief and redemption; Ann Carlson's solo yet somehow collective, cross-generational tour through felt American history; Fiona Shaw's violently devastated Medea; and the actors in *Metamorphoses* emerging transformed from a pool of Greek myths. All these work their captivating magic through the power of the performers' presence, not to insist on authentic experience, or essential humanity, or premodern primitivism, but to see, for a moment, how we might engage one another's differences, and our mutual human-ness, constructed as it is in these brief moments together.

Audiences often form community around a common present experience of love for a charismatic, virtuosic performer, not necessarily around their desire to be close to him or her, but through the performer, to be pulled into comfortable, more intimate proximity to each other. Intersubjectivity extends beyond the binary of performer-spectator (or even performers-audience) into an affective possibility among members of the audience. For example, Peggy Shaw moves into the house in a brilliant moment of communitas in her performance *Menopausal Gentleman*, taking individual people's hands and holding them for a soulful moment of eye contact while she sings Frank Sinatra's "My Way." If she holds your hand, the moment is exquisite, but communitas comes from watching fellow spectators witness and anticipate this shared exchange. The house lights, which come up for this moment, call attention to our mutual copresence as affectively moving and somehow both necessary and comforting. This moment acknowledges that we all came here to do this, to share our attention, to acknowledge our pleasure, and to hope for our mutual, collective transformation. Although for individual spectators, this moment may represent the apotheosis of fandom or fetishization, admiration or attraction (or actually, revulsion and repulsion), it allows the audience to see each other feeling, see each other reacting. When Shaw returns to the proscenium, the audience closes its ranks but is left a little nearer to one another, glowing with the remains of such public intimacy.

Tim Miller, in *My Queer Body*, pushes a similar moment even farther. He leaves the stage, nude, to sit in the laps of near-by spectators. Miller explains the moment:

> There is one point in the show where I wander out naked into the audience, exposed by the glare of the follow spot as I get close enough to see people. I look them in the eye and acknowledge them as the community occupying that theatre for that evening. . . . At a certain point, I sit on an audience member's lap and look into their eyes. My butt naked on their lap. I try to speak simply to them about this feeling of loss and craziness inside me. "I AM here with you. My body is right here. I'm sweaty. I'll probably get your pants all wet. You are right there. Here, feel my heart. I still feel alone. A little afraid of all of you."[88]

This moment of literal physical interaction and emotional intersubjectivity refuses the mutual protection of the mystic gulf between stage and house, making the spectator's and the performer's mutual vulnerability part of the equation worked through in performance. Miller insists on his present materiality (even while his performance of himself remains heightened, despite his physical vulnerability—after all, he still has to project, to be heard), on his own fears and anxieties, perhaps to demystify his own virtuosity and to increase the audience's comfort. Of course, a performer doesn't have to come down off the stage to break through the sometimes intimidating wall of his or her own charisma—Ann Carlson, for example, manages the same effect/affect in *Blanket* by simply speaking directly to the audience—but the way they call out to an audience visually or emotionally often makes it seem as though they have left the frame. The fact that Miller and Shaw do touch the audience underlines intersubjectivity and provides it, perhaps, with a limit-case; their brief moments of physical exchange stand metaphorically for the intimacy they establish emotionally for the duration of their performances.

To make my case for communitas and for the necessary reanimation of humanism through performative gestures of utopic hope, I'm influenced by performance historian and theorist David Savran's call for a "sociology of the theatre."[89] Savran suggests that we look at specific material conditions and modes of performance production to widen our frame of reference for how theater makes its meanings and interacts effectively in the public sphere. Following his lead, I chart here how geographic location, the economics of cities and of the arts, and contemporary discourses about identity and politics impinge on or delimit the possibilities for meaning in the performances I discuss. My aim is to see these performances as importantly material, as productions of history and ideology that suggest possibilities for a differently configured future.

As a result, I make a conscious choice, in *Utopia in Performance*, to write only about productions I liked, about performances that inspired me emotionally, intellectually, and politically. I'm committed to try to untangle how these performances "work," how it is that through some formula of form and content, context and time, they formed meaningful, moving, even transformational moments at the theater. I'm inspired by David Román's notion of "critical generosity," through which he argues that performance should be taken on its own terms, and read through the exigencies of a social moment, offering cultural criteria equally as important as more straightforward aesthetic ones. "Criticism," he says, "can also be a cooperative endeavor and a collaborative engagement with a larger social mission."[90] Part of my project here is to study the ways in which performance lets audiences see *as if for the first time* or *see anew*, through an alienation effect that's emotionally resonant, how to create moments of a future that might feel like utopia in the present of performance. Writing about the affective experience of theatergoing requires evoking the primary "stuff" of a moment of performance.

In this regard, phenomenology—the study of how objects are *perceived* by subjects, rather than what they *are*—provides a useful methodological launching point. As theater scholar Stan Garner argues, "[T]heater engages the operations of world-constitution . . . as spectator, actor, and character seek to situate themselves in relation to the world, both make-believe and radically actual, that confronts and surrounds them."[91] He says that "theatrical space is phenomenal space . . . in which categories of subject and object give way to a relationship of mutual implication."[92] I revel in my own love for theater and performance, and challenge myself to write from within that feeling, what Garner calls that "experiential 'stuff,'"[93] rather than masking that sustaining primary emotion behind a veil of abstraction or obfuscation. I want my writing to translate to readers those moments of intense affective response, to inspire them, too, to reconsider performance as a vital place for human connection and critique, love and respect. *Utopia in Performance* licenses spectators (from the most critically engaged to the most casual) to pay attention to what we *feel*. I intend my writing to bring readers as close as possible to the experience of being spectators of the performances I describe, to take you, the reader, along with me, through my own imaginative emotional, intellectual, political, and even spiritual re-creations, and encourage you to seek out those moments in the performances you go on to see. *Utopia in Performance* allows me to linger in those moments before the house lights go up, to ponder how, rather than ending with the curtain call, utopian performatives might ripple out into other forms of social relations.

chapter two

"A Femme, a Butch, a Jew"

Feminist Autobiographical Solo Performance

Somehow, during all the times she had thought about acting
before . . . [she] had forgotten that the audience was made up
of individual people, each one endowed with the capacity to
stare. . . . Their faces were embarrassingly attentive; and then,
at the end, they just left, emptying out into the street. It
seemed to [her] that there should be a parting ceremony for
leaving the theatre, some sort of solemn, deferential gesture.
That the audience was the one that should bow.
    —STACEY D'ERASMO, *Tea*

With the first notes a frisson runs through the house; the
hairs spring to attention on napes of necks; erectile tissues
stir unbidden beneath pearl-studded shirtfronts and
matronly bodies, and within the farthest folds of nuns'
habits. Two things can inspire such a shiver: a beautiful voice,
and someone walking on your grave. But only the former can
allow you to share the shiver with a packed house.
    —ANN-MARIE MACDONALD, *Fall on Your Knees*

What I describe as an audience is a gathering in the same
place of those brought together by the same need, the same
desire, the same aspirations to satisfy a taste for living
together, for experiencing together human emotions—the
ravishment of laughter and that of poetry—by means of a
spectacle more fully realized than that of life itself. They
gather, wait together in a common urgency, and their tears or
laughter incorporate them almost physically into the drama
or comedy that we perform to give you a stronger sense, and
a more genuine love, of your own humanity.
    —JACQUES COPEAU, *From Acting to Performance*

How can performance, in itself, be a utopian gesture? Why do people come together to watch other people labor on stage, when contemporary culture solicits their attention with myriad other forms of representation and opportunities for social gathering? Why do people continue to seek the liveness, the present-tenseness that performance and theater offer? Is the desire to be there, in the moment, the expression of a utopian impulse? Certainly, people are drawn to theater and performance by fashion and by taste, by the need to collect the cultural capital that theatergoing provides. Live theater remains a powerful site at which to establish and exchange notions of cultural taste, to set standards, and to model fashions, trends, and styles. Yet I also believe that people are drawn to attend live theater and performance for other, less tangible, more emotional, spiritual, or communitarian reasons. Desire, perhaps, compels us there, whether to the stark, ascetic "spaces" that house performance art, or to the aging opulence of Broadway houses, or to the serviceable aesthetics of regional theaters.[1] Audiences are compelled to gather with others, to see people perform live, hoping, perhaps, for moments of transformation that might let them reconsider the world outside the theater, from its micro to its macro arrangements. Perhaps part of the desire to attend theater and performance is to reach for something better, for new ideas about how to be and how to be with each other to articulate a common, different future.

I offer here a series of experiences, examples that moved me to begin to define utopia in performance. Many of my thoughts in this chapter are grounded in my work as a professor at a large state university. I teach in the largest theater department in the country (we enroll 350 undergraduate and 100 graduate students, and employ nearly forty faculty), a program from which most students focused on acting will gravitate toward New York, Chicago, or Los Angeles, since many see themselves as would-be stars. In my classes, I encourage them to imagine themselves as citizen-scholar-artists, as people who think about their art practices and their relationship to democracy, not just their fantasies of popularity. I try to encourage in them an attachment to theater's possibilities as a place of inspiration and vision, as well as a vehicle for leisure and entertainment. I want them to see a connection between their work as actors, designers, or critics and the state of our world, so that they'll feel they have something ethical and social as well as aesthetic to contribute. I want them to be moved by what they do, and in that emotion, to feel the potential of their art to reach people deeply. I want to train my students to use performance as a tool for making better futures, to use performance to incite people to profound responses that shake their consciousness of themselves in the world.[2]

Perhaps that, already, is utopian, the idea that theater can do any of those things. Yet that's the depth of reaction for which I long when I go to the theater—I don't think we should expect anything less. Theater remains, for me, a space of desire, of longing, of loss, in which I'm moved by a gesture, a word, a glance, in which I'm startled by a confrontation with mortality (my own and others'). I go to theater and performance to hear stories that order, for a moment, incoherent longings, that engage the complexity of personal and cultural relationships, and that critique the assumptions of a social system I find sorely lacking. I want a lot from theater and performance.

Theater scholar Dragan Klaic's book *The Plot of the Future: Utopia and Dystopia in Modern Drama* looks at plays that revive "interest in the future as a dramatic theme and as a chosen time setting of dramatic action."[3] But my contention is that performance—not just drama—is one of the few places where a live experience, as well as an expression, through content, of utopia might be possible. My concern here is more performative and more technical.[4] I'm interested in the material conditions of theater production and reception that evoke the sense that it's even possible to imagine a utopia, that boundless "no place" where the social scourges that currently plague us—from poverty, hunger, cancer, HIV/AIDS, inadequate health care, racial and gender discrimination, hatred of lesbians, gay men, bisexuals, and transgendered people, the grossly unequal distribution of wealth and resources globally, religious intolerance, xenophobia expressed in anti-immigrant legislation, lack of access for the disabled, pay inequity, and of course a host of others—might be ameliorated, cured, redressed, solved, never to haunt us again. I have faith in the possibility that we can imagine such a place, even though I know that we can only imagine it, that we'll never achieve it in our lifetimes. But that knowledge doesn't prevent me from desiring a theater in which an idea of a better future can be articulated and even embodied, however fleetingly.

Utopia means, literally, "no place" and was coined in the sixteenth century by Thomas More. As political scientist Lyman Sargent says, "Utopian thought construed more widely . . . is not restricted to fiction and includes visionary . . . and apocalyptic as well as constitutional writings united by their willingness to envision a dramatically different form of society as either a social ideal-type or its negative inversion."[5] Scholars point out that while a vision of a radically different (and presumptively better) future drives experiments with utopia, something coercive lingers about the term. Utopias can be enforced at the expense of liberty, general consensus achieved by limiting choice.[6]

But idealism draws me here; as scholar Roland Schaer says, "Utopia, one might say, is the measure of how far a society can retreat from itself when it wants to feign what it would like to become."[7] I find this notion very rich, the idea that in order to pretend, to enact an ideal future, a culture has to move farther and farther away from the real into a kind of performative, in which the utterance, in this case, doesn't necessarily make it so but inspires perhaps other more local "doings" that sketch out the potential in those feignings. As Sargent notes, in his extensive taxonomy of the genre of utopian literature, "Utopias are generally oppositional, reflecting, at the minimum, frustration with things as they are and the desire for a better life."[8] These definitions all point to the future, to imaginative territories that map themselves over the real. The utopia for which I yearn takes place now, in the interstices of present interactions, in glancing moments of possibly better ways to be together as human beings. Quoting philosopher Ruth Levitas, performance theorist Rustom Bharucha says, "What is needed are not better 'maps of the future,' but more 'adequate maps of the present,' which can inspire the most effective means of activating the desire for a more humane world."[9]

As scholars who study it demonstrate, most historical writings about utopia are futuristic tracts that describe social reorganizations or the redistribution of wealth and cultural roles. Especially the nineteenth-century socialist utopians, like the Oneidas and the Shakers, like Charles Fourier, Samuel Butler, and Edward Bellamy, concerned themselves with imagining and trying to implement societies founded on their own, uniquely devised utopian principles.[10] My goal here is not to propose a "real" utopia, if that's not an oxymoron. I'm not even sure I'd like to live in a utopia, a place without conflict or dissension, or that I'd like to see theater that describes such a perfect place. Klaic notes, "Utopia is, by its very nature, without conflict—a state of stasis, harmony, and balance. These are not ingredients for exciting theatre, which is always based on conflict, opposition, and contradiction, or at least tension." He says, "Theatre succeeds when it presents its utopian arguments as a blueprint, open to opposition, rather than depicting the consequences of their implementation."[11] Some scholars wonder if there would even *be* theater in a utopia.[12] We'll never know. But theater can move us toward understanding the possibility of something better, can train our imaginations, inspire our dreams and fuel our desires in ways that might lead to incremental cultural change.

I'm not interested in constructing a utopia, although many of us who engage politically with nonprofit organizations work to devise such systems through our memberships on boards of directors and through the idealism of social service groups that want to do things differently. My concern here is with how utopia can be imagined or experienced affectively, through feelings, in small, incremental moments that performance can provide. As film theorist Richard Dyer says, in his chapter on entertainment and utopia, "Entertainment does not . . . present models of utopian worlds. . . . Rather the utopianism is contained in the feelings it embodies. It presents . . . what utopia would feel like rather than how it would be organized. It thus works at the level of sensibility, by which I mean an affective code that is characteristic of, and largely specific to, a given mode of cultural production."[13] These feelings and sensibilities, in performance, give rise to what I'm calling the *utopian performative*.

How, then, can a utopic promise or possibility be advanced in the space of performance, in what Richard Schechner describes as the "gathering-performing-dispersing" motion of the whole performance event? It's worth quoting Schechner at length:

> When people "go to the theatre" they are acknowledging that theatre takes place at special times in special places. Surrounding a show are special observances, practices, and rituals that lead into the performance and away from it. Not only getting to the theatre district, but entering the building itself involves ceremony: ticket-taking, passing through the gates, performing rituals, finding a place from which to watch: all this . . . frames and defines the performance. Ending the show and going away also involve ceremony: applause or some formal way to conclude the performance and wipe away the reality of the show, re-establishing in its place the reality of everyday life.[14]

Seen through the lens of performance, the possibility for utopia doesn't only happen when the lights go down and the "play" begins. For instance, utopia can present itself in rehearsals, when a group of people repeat and revise incremental moments, trying to get them right, to get them to "work." The noted experimental theater director Anne Bogart, in fact, says, "I often see my rehearsal situation as utopian. Rehearsal is a possibility for the values I believe in, the politics I believe in, to exist in a set universe which is within the room."[15] Anyone who considers herself a theater person knows when something "works"—it's when the magic of theater appears, when the pace, the expression, the gesture, the emotion, the light, the sound, the relationship between actor and actor, and actors and spectators, all meld into something alchemical, something nearly perfect in how it communicates in that instance. We all rehearse for the moments that work, and critics look out for them, when they're still idealistic enough to believe in them. Through an itinerary of performance, we can enlarge the potential territory in which something might "work" to the whole gathering-performing-dispersing frame and look more widely for a moment of utopia.

Some critics debate this premise. Philip Auslander, for example, in his book *Liveness: Performance in a Mediatized Culture* explicitly critiques as sentimental the notion that performance remains the domain of the live, that intimacy and immediacy are possible there in ways unavailable in other media, such as film or television.

> Investigating live performance's cultural valence . . . I quickly became impatient with what I consider to be traditional, unreflective assumptions that fail to get much further in their attempts to explicate the value of "liveness" than invoking clichés and mystifications like "the magic of live theatre," the "energy" that supposedly exists between performers and spectators in a live event, and the "community" that live performance is often said to create among performers and spectators.[16]

Auslander believes these terms set up a false binary between live and mediatized performance, one he very persuasively proves doesn't exist.

But I must admit that I believe in all the things that Auslander disparages, mostly because as a onetime actor and sometime director, and as a writer, spectator, critic, and performance theorist, I've experienced them all. I've felt the magic of theater; I've been moved by the palpable energy that performances that work generate; and I've witnessed the potential of the temporary communities formed when groups of people gather to see other people labor in present, continuous time, time in which something can always go wrong.[17] But Auslander argues "against the idea that live performance itself somehow generates whatever sense of community one may experience. . . . [M]ediatized performance makes just as effective a focal point for the gathering of a social group as live performance."[18] Surely any gathering can promote community. But theater artist-theorist Herb Blau once said that watching live performance is watching the actor dying onstage; I think sharing that liveness promotes a necessary and moving confrontation with mortality.[19] The actor's willing vulnerability perhaps enables our own and prompts us toward compassion and greater understanding. Such sentiments can spur emotion, and being moved emotionally is a necessary precursor to political movement.[20] Performer and playwright Anna Deavere Smith says, "The utopian theatre would long for flesh, blood, and breathing. It would be hopelessly old-fashioned in a technical world, hopelessly interested in presence, hopelessly interested in modes of communication requiring human beings to be in the same room at the same time."[21] By clinging to the fleshy seductions of old-fashioned primal emotion and presence, Smith's work spurs political action by reminding us that however differently we live, our common, flesh-full cause is that in performance, we're dying together.

Let me give you a specific example of an event in which possibilities for utopia were performed in and around a theater, through a women's solo performance art series I curated with a local theater company, the Rude Mechs, in collaboration with the University of Texas, in fall 2000.[22] That fall, I taught a course called Performance Studies/Performance Art. My goal was to introduce students to the wider field of performance studies to expand their knowledge beyond the stricter limits of conventional theater. "Performance studies" takes a variety of forms in contemporary scholarship, but the strand in which I train my students comes from an interdisciplinary mixture of anthropology and sociology with the more traditional concerns of theater history. Performance studies scholars use ethnography and other extratextual methods to look far beyond the play as the center of a performance event, to study ritual ceremonies across cultures and geographies and histories, as well as aesthetic structures that ground and promote cultural interaction. They study audiences and how they receive performance; hermeneutics and interpretation; context and the ways and locations in which performance is produced.[23] Because this course was offered in a theater department to students I knew would be interested in practice, I paired performance art with performance studies so that students would see how performance artists—many, but not all, solo performers—use the ideas of performance studies to expand the possibilities of conventional theater work.

We addressed various theoretical issues, such as those Schechner poses in his description of performance structures as framed by gathering-per-

forming-dispersing, a model that can apply equally to dramatic performance or performance in everyday life, a key site of investigation in performance studies. We also read Marvin Carlson's survey of performance,
which describes performance art as a resistant cultural form that allows
oppositional and marginal identities to be expressed and explored. Once
we'd established these concepts, we looked at work by contemporary performance artists such as Guillermo Gómez-Peña, Robbie McCauley,
Adrian Piper, Marga Goméz, Luis Alfaro, Lisa Kron, Danny Hoch, and a
host of others, that exemplifies some of the ways performance can be
employed and experienced as politically activist as well as aesthetically new
and invigorating, as, perhaps, utopian.[24]

With funding from various departments across campus, I was able to
invite three nationally known performers to campus. Their extended visits
complemented the reading and video viewing we accomplished in class. I
also worked with the Rude Mechs, a local theater collective, to program
performances. The Rude Mechs are an Austin-based company who've
worked together for the last ten years producing original work and occasionally new scripts by other playwrights. The Rudes had recently taken
the lease on a converted warehouse on Austin's East Side, which they use
as their performance space. The East Side, across the interstate that bisects
Austin, remains relatively untouched by the gentrification that has
exploded the growth in Austin's north, south, and west, although a civic
organization is now exploring local development and expansion possibilities. The East Side is the Latino part of town, where taquerias and small
grocery stores line the streets, butting against national fast food chains and
liquor stores. The Rude Mech's theater, the Off Center, is located here,
squarely in the heart of Austin's most marginalized community.

The East Side houses small theaters and theater companies who represent the experimental avant-garde of the Austin performance scene; the
East Side would resemble New York City's Williamsburg in a geographical
analogy. The experience of driving to the one-hundred-odd-seat Off Center is different from going to, for instance, the twenty-eight-hundred-seat
Bass Concert Hall in the Performing Arts Center on the University of
Texas campus. Going to the Off Center differs from driving around
Austin's small downtown, trying to find parking to see a touring performer or a play at the Paramount or State theaters, two old vaudeville
houses that sit side by side on Congress, the avenue that originates in the
Texas statehouse and extends into Austin's southernmost reaches. Downtown and its environs, as in other cities, houses more conventional theater

fare. The Austin Theatre Alliance links the administrative functions of the Paramount and the State; the State tends to produce seasons drawing from the standard repertoire of modern and contemporary drama and the occasional new play, while the Paramount books performers like Korean-American-queer comedian Margaret Cho, the Ballet Trockaderos, and Laurie Anderson, and productions like *The Sing-Along Sound of Music.* The theater's elaborate, rather rococo design lends itself to campier or more aesthetically daring evenings of performance than the more staid architectural lines of the State Theatre.

The way cultural capital circulates in Austin, and its structure within the city's geography, mirrors its movement nationally. Many performances, of course, derive their cultural capital by virtue of their location, or from how closely they mirror the proprieties of high, low, or middle-brow culture, or by how enthusiastically they're sanctioned by critics and the theatrical marketplace as "must see" events. *The Producers,* for example, the theatrical adaptation of Mel Brooks's film, draws people (despite or perhaps because of its original one-hundred-dollar top ticket) through its Broadway success and critical approbation for its satiric irreverence toward "political correctness." When it toured to Austin in spring 2005, it played the Bass Concert Hall at the University of Texas, the city's premier producing venue. With its gaudy searchlights and its bus-and-truck tours of Broadway musicals, Bass stands as the local temple to the most commercialized of high and popular art. In addition to its Broadway series, the hall books Austin's symphony and ballet company, and international touring musical acts from Linda Ronstadt and Emmylou Harris to an array of Latin American musicians and dancers. Legend has it that the stage was built to match the dimensions of the Metropolitan Opera House in New York, but the auditorium design boasts an ascetic modern style that makes it feel cold and impersonal.[25] The orchestra seats extend fifty or so across with no aisle and beyond thirty rows from the stage. From the balcony's horrible sight lines, the stage looks like a speck of dust stirred up in another country. Yet spectators always dress up to see shows there; their sartorial choices mark them as suburbanites or people from Austin's environs, rather than habitués of the city's downtown arts scene. Attending productions at Bass provides a completely different experience of an evening out. A subscription to the Performing Arts Center's season, produced in Bass, represents a status ticket in Austin for a particular kind of spectator: wealthy donors to the university, city philanthropists and cultural mavens, and people from the suburbs and outlying areas who consider the PAC the local arbiter of cultural value.[26] The PAC's series develops its own brand of cultural capital, mixing touring shows with more highbrow music and dance and, to its credit, a multinational, eclectic array of world performance genres.

The Off Center and other alternative theaters in Austin like the Vortex or Salvage Vanguard accrue their cultural capital through their difference from these more elite, centered sites of culture in Austin. These theater companies attract audiences to spaces to see edgy, avant-garde, nonmainstream work, or performances that break through the enforced decorum of hegemonic whiteness or presumptive heterosexuality or constrictive notions about gender or race or ability or ethnicity. The Off Center's reputation made it a likely place to launch a women's solo performance series. The crowd it draws would be predisposed to find in the work a measure of fashion, style, or trendiness, as well as (and most importantly, for me) a gesture of commitment toward community, progressive politics, and resistant art.

Crossing the divide of the city moves you into a place of subaltern or marginalized culture, outside of what even a midsized city like Austin constructs as its cultural center. Cultural capital accrues here from seeing performance within a Latino community setting that's typically invisible to culture-mongers, even in Austin.[27] Pulling into the grass and gravel lot where spectators and performers park their cars outside the theater, finding the outdoor ticket kiosk, beside a table where you can buy candy and a beer before you head into the theater, or hang outside and talk and smoke and catch the breeze in Austin's warm night air while that huge Texas sky darkens into pinks then purples then blues—this signals a different experience of theatergoing, and it matters to what transpires inside. There's a landscape to Texas that's revealed, rather than hidden, at the Off Center, by the lack of downtown lights or traffic, by its uniqueness, by its distance from elite, white culture. While Bass Concert Hall, the Paramount, and the State mark themselves, through their locations, architecture, and season selection, as part of national or international culture, the Off Center acknowledges its localness and works with it rather than against it, which makes a sense of community easier to feel there. Of course, the programming at this offbeat, eclectic space aspires to a kind of hip legitimacy—the new plays it produces are rarely realist and more often nonlinear, postmodern explorations or other less conventional performance work. The Off Center's sense of the local, then, is marked by Austin's reputation for artistic experimentation and unconventionality.

The performance series on which I collaborated with the Rude Mechs at the Off Center was called "Throws Like a Girl: A Femme, a Butch, a Jew," and it showcased solo performances by Holly Hughes in September, Peggy Shaw in October, and Deb Margolin in November. Their visits to Austin and to the campus were structured identically: each month the performer came to the University of Texas to speak to my class, to do a free public question-and-answer session to which the community and the university was invited, to do a free three-hour performance workshop that was also open to the community, and to perform three evenings of their work at the Off Center, one of which was followed by a talkback, another by a reception. I'm describing the location and structure of the series at some length, because these are the material conditions that I believe fostered a sense of utopian possibility throughout our collective experience with the "Throws Like a Girl" series. And as I noted earlier, utopia, I think, is in the details. Dyer's taxonomy of utopia in entertainment includes energy, abundance, intensity, transparency (by which he means sincerity), and community, all of which organized the affective reach of the University of Texas performance series.[28]

The structural regularity of these events, for people who wanted to participate in everything, provided a ritual-like atmosphere, a framework on which people could rely, could hang their anticipatory energy and funnel their curiosity. As I noted in the introduction, serial events offer audiences a chance to breed familiarity and community. Some of my students had no prior experience seeing performance art, and were somewhat suspicious of what they understood as its unbridled ferocity. Others had perhaps seen performance art but had never crossed I35 in Austin, let alone gone to a performance space that didn't seem like a conventional theater. The series allowed students to acclimate to a genre with which many of them had been unfamiliar and to quickly learn to see differences among the performers in style, content, and address.

The series was also thematically linked by its focus on feminist solo performance. Each of the performers shared a common history. All three began their performance careers at the WOW Café in New York City, a community theater on the Lower East Side that became a hotbed of irreverent lesbian and feminist performance through the 1980s and 1990s, much of which borrowed popular forms like television sitcoms and variety shows and infused them with new and hilarious meanings.[29] All three performers had worked together at various times at WOW and now tour similar performance spaces across the country and internationally. All three performers have solidified their solo careers. This sense of affinity among them also threaded through the three-month Austin event.

I curated the series intentionally to showcase solo performance by women of a certain generation, a pedagogical strategy that allowed me to share with students my own urgent sense of feminist performance history. In some ways, feminist performance has always been utopian, trying as it does to create new meanings for gender, race, and sexuality through performance. The three performers I invited have always used their art to gesture toward a better world, whether implicitly or explicitly. Although the Performance Studies/Performance Art course was broad-based and diverse, I felt keenly my own desire publicly to honor women whose work had been foundational to my own writing in feminist performance criticism. This desire motivated me to bring Hughes, Shaw, and Margolin to Austin for weeklong residencies. I performed, as a middle-aged teacher, my own identification with these women, my own pride in the history they formed and in which I took part as a spectator and a critic. I also demonstrated my insistence that as a new generation of performance artists takes hold, we honor the women whose work in many ways founded the genre.[30] Still, I knew that my choices were a window into my own desires and my own web of historical identifications.

I also wanted to honor my own generation of women in their midforties and early fifties and older, who came of age at a time when we couldn't take for granted feminist or lesbian representations in the public sphere. Feminist and lesbian performance carried so much weight when it first began to appear, bravely and insistently, in subcultural spaces in New York and in communities around the country. People created it because they needed it to survive; it remains even now marked by this urgency, especially for lesbians, gay men, and queers. As playwright Sarah Schulman writes so poignantly,

[T]he gay audience at stake is principally my generation. We are a confused group of queers. In many ways, we are the ones who have experienced the most dramatic and traumatic shift in public depiction of homosexuality. We had such profound oppression experiences in childhood that they qualify as trauma. We are the last of the dirty-dark-secret generation. We are the last group that came of age in a time in which homosexuality was never mentioned, had no public representation. . . . [W]e have experienced changes that are too huge to digest and often too confusing to fully comprehend. So, when we walk into a theater and see two women kissing on stage after we've been humiliated and vilified by our own families for doing the same thing, we're thrilled. But in the context of contemporary culture . . . that kiss does not have the meaning we once dreamed it would. It does not mean that we are full human beings whose lives can now be truthfully represented among the selection of lives that make up the American experience.[31]

This generational sense of arrival and disappointment, tinged with the memory of very real, very material oppression for aligning your desires and your politics as feminist, lesbian, or queer, prompted me to invite this group of women to Austin.

Their residencies at the University of Texas and at the Off Center affected many of us in emotional ways. Holly Hughes visited first. Hughes has performed her solo work—including *World without End* (1984) and *Clit Notes* (1994)—around the world for the past twenty years, and was one of the founding presences of the WOW Café.[32] Hughes's plays, the notorious *Well of Horniness* (1983), a take-off on Radclyffe Hall's famous if dour classic lesbian novel *The Well of Loneliness,* and *The Lady Dick* (1985), a lesbian noir that parodies the potboiler style of 1940s detective fiction, set the tone for a generation of lesbian performance that claimed the power to twist popular cultural genres to its own transgressive ends, rather than simply critiquing oppressive representations of women in these forms. In the early 1990s, Hughes became one of the so-called NEA Four, solo performance artists whose individual grants were denied by the National Endowment for the Arts during a period of highly politicized and high-profile congressional outcry against what senators like the archconservative Jessie Helms called pornographic art. The press and the federal government demonized Hughes and her work, along with feminist Karen Finley and gay male performers Tim Miller and John Fleck, propelling her into high public visibility with deeply negative consequences.

Hughes remains an activist artist, whose performance work and public presentations insist on examining culture and politics through art. She was eloquent in her meeting with my class and in her public interview. She deconstructed the notion of "preaching to the converted," an issue that already concerned my students, who feared that political work reaches a too narrow audience of people already persuaded to think progressively. How, they wondered, could more people be persuaded, so that performance and its potential for social change wouldn't be ghettoized far from the notice of those who perhaps need to see it most? Quoting theater scholar David Román and performance artist Tim Miller's collaborative writing on this issue, Hughes proceeded to shake up some of these notions, suggesting that "conversion" is always unstable, that people are never, finally, converted to anything; there's always ambiguity, ambivalence, and doubt.[33] Performance, Hughes insisted, is a renewal of faith, and progressive politics are always faith-based.[34]

At the Off Center, Hughes performed *Preaching to the Perverted* (2000), which addresses her ten-year court battle with the NEA over the rescinding of her individual artist grant and the decency clause the agency subsequently appended to its funding awards.[35] Hughes's performance is invested with presence and intelligence, cut on the sharp edge of a wit that makes meaning from personal and political pain. With a series of rough but iconically full props—cardboard boxes, evoking the soapbox on which political artists are always accused of standing; a series of small American flags that Hughes waves and discards, celebrates and mourns through the course of the performance; confetti and streamers and the detritus of political campaigns, which litter the floor as her performance winds down—these and her body, dressed simply in black Capri pants and a wrinkled white shirt tell a difficult story of how American democracy marginalizes so many of its citizens. The piece exorcises, for Hughes, her experience as one of the NEA Four (or, as she says ironically, "Karen Finley and the three homosexuals"), detailing the censorship by the radical Right that prompted her first to lose her grant, then win it back on its first and second court appeals, and then to be dragged to the Supreme Court by the Clinton administration to argue the decency pledge. By interweaving her own family history with her future as a pariah at the Supreme Court, Hughes reveals the lies uttered in the name of democracy and the ways it keeps its dark side flapping on the back of the flag where you can't always see it.

The piece has a pedagogical function, teaching spectators how the Supreme Court works, from the perspective of a "bad" girl attending the proceedings to hear her own case argued. In Hughes's hands, the "Supremes"—as she calls them—become patriarchs (regardless of their actual gender) who punish bad children. She represents them, though, as identical miniature rubber ducks, stuck with toothpicks into their corrugated cardboard bench, symbolically diminishing their stature for the sake of her argument. "I'm not here because I'm a citizen / Participating in an institution of a democratic country," Hughes says. "I'm here because I have been bad / very very bad / And I am so lucky to be sitting here at all."[36] The court's architecture, she suggests, inspires intimidation and fear, and the justices seem predisposed in their judgments, rather than truly open to argument.

External voices drive Hughes's movement through the piece. The audience hears the tape-recorded voices of people who call to heckle or support Hughes, from commentators whose names are familiar from national radio and television spin shows, to friends, to agents, to editors calling to exploit her notoriety or to describe it back to her as a good thing. "There's no bad publicity," they chortle, while Hughes grows more and more helpless to control her own image as it explodes across the media, put to use according to ideological necessity and rarely matching what any of her performances truly meant or intended. Hughes paints the disjuncture between herself and the person whom (as she tells us in *Preaching*) the head of the NEA, John Frohnmayer, called "the self-avowed lesbian whose work is very heavily of that genre." This separation grows larger as the piece proceeds, and her alienation from the symbols of democracy that litter the stage becomes more painful to watch.

Preaching to the Perverted describes a world very much out of joint, blatantly discriminatory in its practices, cold and white and unresponsive to the needs of all of its citizens. Hughes's critique is not only of male, heterosexual dominant power but also of hegemonic whiteness. She describes the court's architecture as imposingly remote and marbled white, its racial biases written into its facade. The piece informs, editorializes, entertains, and moves the audience to a kind of righteous anger not just on Hughes's behalf but on behalf of all of those whom the flag waves away from democracy, from queer artists to the African American mother in the piece who tells her daughter the flag isn't hers and not to salute it in school.

Art historian Richard Meyer, in his analysis of Hughes's performance, says, "Hughes extends the narrative of her defunding into that of the culture wars more generally and from there into a free-wheeling story of the ways in which private memory rubs up against public controversy."[37] The force of Hughes's memory and her reading of the controversy, and the ways in which it offers points of personal or social identification for spectators, provides what Meyer believes is a call to action. Hughes reminds us that performance, while a "space apart," is an active space, one tied to a public sphere in which the mutual agency of performer and spectator might have meaning. Meyer writes, "Each time I see *Preaching to the Perverted,* whether in a university classroom, a conference hotel, or a community-based theatre, I visit this 'space apart.' In reenacting the history of her own censorship, Holly Hughes defies the silencing of art and sexuality that history sought to enforce. And she invites me—along with everyone else in her audience—to do the same."[38]

Critics of Hughes's performance in other locations seemed bemused by the ways *Preaching to the Perverted* stretched genre conventions. Rather than extending critical generosity, these critics tried to fit Hughes's performance into preexisting categories that might help contain, rather than explain and appreciate, the work. For instance, Dennis Harvey, writing in *Variety* about the show at the New Conservatory Theatre Center in San Francisco, says, "Hughes often adopts a standup comic's brassy tone to underline the trivialization of gay (as well as feminist and ethnic-minority) issues in our culture."[39] Robert Nesti, writing about Hughes's performance in the Out on the Edge Festival at Theater Offensive in Boston, says, "In a style similar to comedian George Carlin and Dennis Miller, she deftly exposes the absurdity of her situation, one in which the rhetoric obscures all reason. And does so with a tireless energy that keeps the piece fresh despite its nearly two-hour length."[40] Once established as conventional comedy, the performance becomes intelligible to these critics as slightly more than the agit-prop diatribe their reviews imply provides the show's theatrical lineage. As stand-up comedy, *Preaching to the Perverted* can be heard as social critique framed within a safe space of entertainment, a place where audiences come to laugh with, and sometimes at, the comedienne and her foibles. While such a frame might allay critical anxieties, it also robs the performance of its critically utopian performative gesture— Hughes's insistence that by studying the anatomy of power in the United States, we can intervene to change it. Such genre categorizing also robs the piece of its force as feminist autobiographical performance by explicitly depoliticizing the work.

The experience of watching Hughes's emotionally vulnerable, insightful performance galvanized many spectators at the Off Center. After the performance on opening night, most of the audience remained for a talkback. Staying in the theater after a performance provides a moment of what Schechner calls "cool down," when together, the performer and spectator relax and shift from the "ecstatic" moment of performance back into the grooves of more prosaic life.[41] Staying together in that space can be a time of shared subjectivity. The performer—spent but made euphoric by her experience as the utopian performative's delivery system, still under the aura of her charisma, the afterglow of her theatrical performance now infusing her performance in everyday life—can look back, can speak directly to spectators, and can be addressed in kind.

Each of the performers was unstintingly generous in these moments. They worked hard to connect with people, to answer questions honestly and openly. In these exchanges, the performers, too, were fed, buoyed by the responses of an audience of students and community folks educated about their work and committed to providing it a responsive cultural context. The talkbacks and the public question-and-answer sessions at the University of Texas were intersubjective moments, when the performer shared insights not only into her process but also into the multiplicity of meanings the performance and her larger body of work might generate in cultural history. In these moments of talking, the spectators' labor, their gesture of what David Román has called "critical generosity," opened a window onto utopic possibilities for the performers.[42]

Perhaps because of the tendencies of the artists we invited, their remarks refused the separation between their theory and their practice, between their art and their politics, or even, in most cases, between their private and public lives. They embodied a resolution of the vexations that dog us all: how to maintain an artistic practice when you're learning or using an academic vocabulary; how to stay attached to your most deeply felt beliefs about culture when you're working in a form that sometimes militates against their expression; how to create work of your own when the commodification of culture, and the lack of an alternative counterculture, closes off avenues of access for all but the most formally and politically conventional work. Hughes, Peggy Shaw, and Deb Margolin, by sharing their experiences and their beliefs, inspired me and my students to keep working at these awkward dualities, to believe that they can be resolved, however transiently.

For instance, Shaw captivated us all during her visit to our class by spinning an hour-long tale of how she became a performer. With all the easy charisma that makes her magnetic in performance, Shaw told us the story of her life, one full of hope and coincidences and happy accidents that led her to be briefly married, very young, to have a child (who has now borne Shaw's grandchild), to stumble upon the drag performance troupe Hot Peaches in Sheridan Square in Greenwich Village, to tour with them to Europe, to hook up with the feminist troupe Spiderwoman and, through them, with Lois Weaver, and then to form the Split Britches Company with Weaver and Deb Margolin. Split Britches created some of the most stimulating, intelligent, moving feminist performance in the last two decades of American history.[43] As a solo performer, Shaw tours and performs three different shows—*You're Just Like Your Father* (1994), *Menopausal Gentleman*

(1997), and *To My Chagrin* (2001)—all of which address her life as a middle-aged butch lesbian. Shaw's story makes something from nothing; hers is a tale of unbridled faith, freedom, and possibility. Shaw's utopian vision pictures a world where people commingle, where there's plenty for everyone. And that vision starts in her performances, which she calls "theater of necessity," culled from the depths of what her soul has to say to others.

The danger of theater, she says, is in the power of presence, in the power of the transformations it makes possible. Against Auslander and other critics, who discredit presence as a function of a metaphysics they no longer value, Shaw inhabits her charisma seductively. Like Auslander, I don't want to mystify the notion of presence, although I believe in its influence.[44] I think that certain performers evoke and use it better than others, but it's through technique and precision that presence gains power, comes to point us toward those other, better worlds. If utopia, in performance, can only happen through the performative, through an action that makes it appear, then performers' technique is quite important. In Peggy Shaw's presence, through her charisma, she reveals her generosity as a human being. In that generosity, I see utopia. It comes from the transparency, or sincerity, that Dyer marks as utopian in entertainment.

Shaw's performance *Menopausal Gentleman* details her experiences as a fifty-three-year-old grandmother (her age when she wrote the piece) passing as a thirty-five-year-old man. The piece is full of such contradictions, ambiguities, and ambivalences, as she describes the tiger of hormones pacing through her veins, breaking through her skin in sweat that becomes her "own private summer."[45] She choreographs each movement and gesture in a sharp, incisive, emotional, and physical arc. Like Hughes's piece, Shaw's builds through association—the nonlinear text works by accretion and accumulation, rather than progressing through a more typical narrative full of conflict and resolution. In fact, each of the three performances, Margolin's included, refuse the kind of narrative closure and coherence that marks more conventional theater. Instead, they share insights, emotions, and political critique through vignettes, anecdotal evidence, and exquisite images that gather force through their momentum.

Those moments in *Menopausal Gentleman* call attention to Shaw's handsome, aging, hormonally crazed body, as she stands center, posing in her glorious navy blue suit, cut in a 1940s retro style, double-breasted, pin-striped, graced by a sharply folded handkerchief angled out of her breast pocket. The suited pose recurs throughout the piece, always marked by adjustments—of her cuffs, her neck, her crotch, simulating the settling of a male body into the clothes that adorn his masculinity. Knowing that underneath the artifice are the bindings that hold Shaw's breasts, and the flesh of a woman who's borne a child, loved other women, and performed gender on and off stage in a multitude of ways, makes the image of Shaw's gentleman compelling and poignant, full of desire, longing, and loss.

Only a low wooden bench shares the stage with Shaw. The movement of the piece is accomplished with lighting that isolates her body, her face, her hands, accompanied by a sound track of Nina Simone, Toni Childs, Screamin' Jay Hawkins, and Frank Sinatra. If Hughes is haunted by the sounds of dominant power, invading her private world with their public pronouncements, Shaw's ears ring with the noise of her body, making her private sounds into public nightmares. Her heart beats noisily, like an engine echoing out of its hold. Nina Simone plays while Shaw dances in the dark, with mini-flashlights strapped to her wrists and ankles, shining pointed light on her hands and feet. The light makes her skin translucent, shining on the lines of her skin and her veins. Dancing in the dark like an apparition with no body, only limbs, Shaw isolates her parts but evokes the absence of the whole, somehow embodying the condition of all performance as both presence and absence. In her choreographed physicality, she demonstrates the labor of gender, even if she insists she's "so queer [she] doesn't have to talk about it." What she performs is the sweat required not only to flush hormonal changes through an aging female body, but the hard work of "being a gentleman in menopause."

Menopausal Gentleman is full of grief, replete with images of leaving, loss, opportunities missed and irretrievable, lovers saying good-bye and not turning back, where once they stood and waved until they could no longer be seen. The piece attempts to incorporate such losses, to feel them as present, even while the ghosts recede. "I fall to pieces in the night," Shaw says. "I'm just thousands of parts of other people mashed into one body. I am not an original person. I take all these pieces, snatch them off the floor where they land before they get swept under the bed by the light, and I manufacture myself." Time passes, written on the body: "I wish I could hold time still, just lift it up to that tube of bright fluorescent light to examine it. . . . I'm going to feel all the emotions I've postponed so far in my life. I'll just go slow, there's time." Shaw's reassurances are rueful, lingering in the space between us as questions, not truths. And because we know that only theater-time is simultaneous, "now" time, we recognize Shaw's insistence that she can hold time as wistful, impossible.

I referred in the introduction to the moment in *Menopausal Gentleman* when Shaw talk-sings to Sinatra's "My Way." She begins leaning against the downstage left wall, then slowly moves out into the audience, up the narrow center aisle of the small space, shaking people's hands, speaking directly to them, patting them on the back. This is an intersubjective moment; they often become utopian performatives. Shaw leaves the space marked off for performance to approach the audience, to mingle freely, empathizing, greeting, allowing for moments of identification, curiosity, desire, even love to extend through the audience. Her presence moved through the house like a current; she electrified the audience, bound her to us, and brought us close to the complexities of her longings and our own. Is this not a glimpse of utopia, the generosity of the performer in sharing her hands, her heart, her desire, with an audience of friends and strangers? Shaw moves through the audience as though she knows everyone, leaving the comfort of theatrical distance to mingle, house lights up, among people who have been watching her, some, no doubt, with desire and longing. In this moment, she makes herself attainable as the object of such desire, and shares her own longings as a desiring subject, wanting the connection, the temporary break with anonymity that shaking someone's hand, looking into her eyes, allows.

There's a similar, but different, scene in *Preaching to the Perverted* when Hughes announces a "dreaded moment of audience participation," in which she invites two different spectators to read hate mail she received during the height of the culture wars. Yet Hughes's and Shaw's moments of venturing into the audience, hailing them into the space of performance, aren't coercive or ridiculing, as is so much of what passes for audience participation in more mainstream theater. With her assistants, Hughes creates coparticipants in the production of her performance's meanings. The spectators invariably read the hate mail with the proper self-righteous tone, but their personal affinity is clearly with Hughes (they are among, that is, the "perverted"). They perform bigotry and join her in undermining its threat. Shaw's seductive mingling likewise levels the performance field. By pressing the flesh, she humanizes herself, brings herself down to size, and refuses the awe her own charisma inspires.[46]

Part of what appeals to me here is Shaw's romanticism, an affective address that, like love, has been perhaps banished too long from our discussions of performance or research.[47] Dyer, this time writing in defense of disco, notes that "romanticism is a particularly paradoxical quality of art to come to terms with. Its passion and intensity embody or create an experience that negates the dreariness of the mundane and every day. It gives us a glimpse of what it means to live at the height of our emotional and our experiential capacities—not dragged down by the banality of organized routine life."[48] This intense, utopic romanticism is what creates those moments of magic and communion in performance.

Yet again, as with Hughes's performance, the more mainstream reception to *Menopausal Gentleman* for the most part misses the keen sense of community and the intimacy that founds Shaw's work. Genre anxiety—perhaps a displacement for gender anxiety—influences critics in the popular press, who characterize Shaw's work as "[c]ombining stream-of-consciousness monologue, stand-up comedy, and blues lounge act," an "entertainingly disturbing . . . one-person revue," and as a "ready-for-prime-time spellbinder."[49] The words they use try to place Shaw within entertainment traditions that can explain and diffuse the power of her gender ambiguity and its transmutation into poetry in her heart and body. Her poignant vulnerability and the winsome hope that drenches *Menopausal Gentleman* are somehow reduced by descriptions that call her a "resplendent . . . original, with intimations of Chaplin and the great clowns."[50] The *Boston Globe* reviewer suggests that "if she were to move up the theater chain like Lisa Kron [one of Shaw's comrades from the WOW Café days, who now performs at more visible venues like the Public Theater in New York] she might need a little more in terms of a set and a little less in terms of playing to the audience."[51] He implies that in "real" theater, theatricality and a safe remove from the audience necessarily implies professionalism. He implicitly denigrates the value of intersubjectivity and would disallow the direct communication that often prompts utopian performatives.

Audiences less anxious about gender ambiguity perhaps stand to gain the most from the potential of communitas in Shaw's performance. Anthropologist Victor Turner's notion of "communitas" in social drama describes what I'm calling utopian performativity in performance. He says, "Spontaneous communitas is 'a direct, immediate and total confrontation of human identities,' a deep rather than intense style of personal interaction. 'It has something "magical" about it. Subjectively there is in it a feeling of endless power.'" Turner asks, "Is there any of us who has not known this moment when compatible people—friends, congeners—obtain a flash of lucid mutual understanding on the existential level, when they feel that all problems, not just their problems, could be resolved, whether emotional or cognitive, if only the group which is felt (in the first person) as 'essentially us' could sustain its intersubjective illumination?"[52]

These moments of communitas, which rippled through all three performances and the performers' residencies, offer springboards to utopia.

Our last visitor of the series, Deb Margolin, was part of the infamous Split Britches trio with Shaw and Lois Weaver. During those years, Margolin performed as the foil for Shaw and Weaver and wrote much of their material, from *Beauty and the Beast* (1982) to *Little Women* (1988) and the Shaw-Weaver duet, *Lesbians Who Kill* (1992). When the trio stopped performing together, Margolin, like Shaw and Weaver, embarked on a solo career, touring her fanciful, articulate, and affecting monologues. During the series, Margolin spoke eloquently of art and desire. In her talk in class and in her public interview, Margolin insisted that passion matters, that "desire is our dramaturgical force." She said that for a woman, standing up in front of people is a radical political act, expressing, as it does, the desire to speak. At that moment of speaking, she says, you're one point at which the universe expresses itself, at which you "grab a fistful of experience and redistribute it through theater." Performance, she believes, is the last communal experience, a place in which she no longer feels alone with her observations, no longer has to feel that she's the only one who's noticed something—something strange, something moving, something vital. As the late feminist performance theorist Lynda Hart notes in her introduction to her edited collection of Margolin's work, "[T]his is what you can seek and expect to find in Deb Margolin's work, these small moments, these most innocent and ordinary exchanges, that are nonetheless the very warp and woof of what constitutes our lives, and makes our deaths meaningful."[53] Margolin's performance, *O Wholly Night and Other Jewish Solecisms,* is all about noticing, witnessing together moments that otherwise might pass into oblivion, moments that might signal, if you look at them properly, the advent of a utopia when, for Margolin, the Messiah comes.

O Wholly Night, evoking as it does the Jewish Messiah whose mysteries infuse daily life, presents perhaps the most overtly utopian content of the three performances in the series. Margolin is an elegant storyteller, never losing sight of the people she's addressing, that is, those in the theater with her, always acknowledging our presence by a nod, by a conspiratorial look, by a knowing "take." As Hart says, "[S]he holds us. The present happens in rooms that she is in."[54] She begins the piece by telling the story of the torn and beautiful silk dress that hangs upstage throughout the performance. She acquired it from a Mrs. Friedman, a friend of her parents, on the occasion of Mr. Friedman's death, and holds onto it longingly, knowing that at some point, the garment will fulfill a totemic function in performance.

When she's commissioned to write a piece for the Jewish Museum for its "Too Jewish?" exhibition, she calls Mrs. Friedman to ask her again about the dress's origins. But the older woman denies the garment and its history. Exasperated, she says, "Look, Debbie, I never gave you a dress. And if you need a story, MAKE IT UP!"[55] This is the benediction for her performance, one that instantly rubs fiction against truth and that throws into doubt stories that in their fantasy, their phantasmatic fullness, ring utterly true.

Margolin's performance concerns waiting for the Messiah, trying to summon the utopia he or she will bring along. The Messiah's identity is a mystery. "It's like a big Halloween party," Margolin says. "Life is a costume party in which anyone may come forward from behind a mask and reveal themselves as Moshiach. And since you never know who or when, it's best to be as graceful as you can to everyone and to try to dress reasonably" (143). Waiting for utopia to reveal itself requires grace, provides an ethic for living that Margolin models in performance. Her emotional generosity, Shaw's seductive physical generosity, Hughes's intellectual and political generosity, and the vulnerability all these acts entail—aren't these rehearsals for utopia, in a gesture, in a way of living, in an address to an audience that converts strangers into community?

The night of Margolin's first performance in Austin, it rained, much harder than usual, a torrential downpour that didn't stop for hours. On the Off Center's tin roof, the pounding water sounded like cacophony, a gathering of drummers who couldn't follow the beat. And because the space is essentially jerry-rigged, the roof leaks; puddles formed over the playing area. It appeared that the show couldn't begin because of the noise and the damp. But at 8:30, after waiting fruitlessly for a letup, during which she wandered through the audience talking to people and taking opinions about what we should do, Margolin moved downstage center, acknowledged the weather and the challenge it might present to her performance, and began *O Wholly Night*. She strained to project over the noise from the roof, and we strained to hear, and in the process, we were brought even closer, in a performance that's all about intimacy and immediacy. Through the night, as we watched Margolin perform around the growing puddles, and cupped our ears to hear, the rain came to sound like applause, its rhythm a recognition of the presentness of the moment we shared and its uniqueness. The show will probably never be played quite that way again. Yet those of us watching that night were stirred by the intimacy, by Margolin's vulnerability, by her courage and refusal to let the environment silence her, by the urgency of what she had to say.

Margolin describes holding her young daughter as a utopic moment: "We are Messianic in each other, my daughter and I . . . her sleep is like Moshiach [the Messiah] to me: quiet, effortless, a true relief at the end of a long day . . . as I hold her, I realize with certainty that a part of what defines Messiah for me is relief" (144). Perhaps utopia, too, is about relief, presented performatively in gestic moments of clarity: Margolin holding her daughter; Shaw unbinding the flashlights from her wrists and ankles, calling out to a lover not to leave; Hughes removing the silly rainbow wig she donned to dance to the gay anthem, "I Will Survive," finally dropping all hope that her hand could ever genuinely wave the flag. These performances all describe a kind of loss; Hughes won the battle with the NEA but in some ways lost the war when the Clinton administration instituted the mandatory decency pledge, and attached it to all its grants; Shaw loses her lover, who finally does leave; and despite her hopeful waiting, for Margolin, the Messiah never comes. But perhaps these aren't moments of defeat; perhaps they're moments of relief, messianic moments that herald the arrival of a new and better world. Or perhaps the seeds of utopia are only present at times of failure and apocalypse. Michael Loewy, writing on Jewish messianism and utopia, says that "in many Talmudic texts the idea appears that the Messiah will only come in an era of corruption and total culpability. . . . Only the revolutionary catastrophe, with a colossal uprooting, a total destruction of the existing order, opens the way to messianic redemption."[56] If this is so, then the performative moments of loss, despair, grieving, and absence might, in fact, herald the new.

Margolin "sees Messiah where he refuses to see me" (150), in the quotidian, unnoticed details of people's lives. She describes prosaic moments in which people are called upon to "act as Messianic stand-ins," moments when Margolin says she's "lifted out of myself into the soiled robes of Moshiach" (155). It's this affective quality of utopia that performance can draw for us—ordinary people lifted from our lives to form connections that in utterly simple ways make the world better. This is utopian performativity, in which the deed makes the doer the Messiah. And because, as Dyer notes, "everyday banality, work, domesticity, ordinary sexism, and racism are rooted in the structures of class and gender in this society, the flight from that banality can be seen as a flight from capitalism and patriarchy as lived experiences."[57]

Such flights from banality into an intense, sincere, generous romanticism pointed toward utopian performatives in all three performances. For instance, Margolin and Shaw's performances included moments of utter silence, moments in which I felt utopia rising with the hairs on the back of my neck. In *Menopausal Gentleman,* two-thirds of the way through the performance, after Shaw has finished a particularly vigorous physical scene, the lights dim, and she returns to the edge of the bench to retrieve a bottle of water that's been there, waiting, the whole time. The blue light is focused so that her face is in shadow, but the bottle, as she raises it to her lips, is translucent, brilliant, bubbles moving through a tube that seems crystalline under the theater lights. She stands, and she drinks; she's silent while music plays in the background. She drinks until she's sated. But it's the moment of the performer's silence, the performer's rest, the performer's replenishment that draws attention to her labor, her sweat, and the intensity of the hour we've spent with her. The water, draining out of the bottle almost rhythmically, down her throat to cool her, is a palpable reminder of her body and its needs. That she could meet her needs, take her time, take her moment, while we watched, seemed an act of utter faith and utter trust and utter peace. I felt such yearning, in a moment that probably didn't last a minute; a yearning to be with, to suspend this moment out of time, while one hundred people sat together breathlessly, watching Shaw drink.

In Margolin's performance, there's a moment in which she simply sits in the chair stage right. She's just finished relating a story, and she looks out at us with a pleasant, expectant, ruminative expression on her face. It's a pause, a break, a moment inserted between things, another moment of rest. Her silence was an instance of exquisite vulnerability, one in which rather than be unnerved by the absence of speech, I felt the audience wanting to take care, to extend our presence to her as she had hers to us. Hart says, "One of the many ways that I experience the beauty of Margolin's work is in the feeling she creates of waiting *with* rather than waiting *for.* A waiting without the anxiety of forward movement, without projection. A looking about, a keen attention."[58] Perhaps in these moments of communal, almost loving rest, when the flesh stops and the soul pauses, we come together, at attention and relieved, to feel utopia. In these moments, we feel the simultaneity of time; we revel in the "now."

I'm not suggesting that every spectator will find feelings of utopia in performances by Hughes, Shaw, or Margolin, or for that matter any feminist or queer performance artist. Their performances inspire me, move me toward such feelings of possibility, hope, and political agency. These three white women begin their address to the public sphere from outside its enforced norms, and through the critical stories they tell, help to dislodge its assumptions. As theater scholar Hilary Harris writes, "The imaging and the performing of an anti-racist white womanhood" requires rejecting the politics of respectability. "Shaw and Hughes . . . perform consistently and distinctly disreputable 'femininities.'"[59] Their queerness distances them from the politics of respectability, instantiating the "threat that a white womanhood might actually choose distance over proximity as its desired relation to the hegemonic public body and that it might do so in the service of an anti-racist whiteness specifically."[60] Rejecting the "whitespeak" that passively evades accepting responsibility for racism, Hughes and Shaw name ideology and the exclusivity of dominant discourses. *This,* they say, is whiteness; *this* is how it works.

Margolin, the "brainy Jew who talks too much,"[61] is already marginal to white womanhood, although her performances mime a kind of respectability that betrays it from within. By talking too much, and using such obsessively elegant language, Margolin removes herself from white privilege and power. She performs a kind of Jewish excess that marks her as affectively outside normative whiteness. Her insistence on charting her own desire, and on calling attention to her own body as a locus of sexual, emotional, and spiritual feeling, also rejects a respectability that would disallow her to speak in the first place. Margolin's reference to the Holocaust, to the marginalized and oppressed status of Jews in European history, also allows her to address time in what Walter Benjamin would call a messianic way, in which all time is present in the moment of "now."[62] Feminist performance theorist Vicki Patraka says, "Margolin, an American whose parents are Jews but not Holocaust survivors, but whose childhood was mapped by film images of atrocity, portrays the live Jewish body in the present as it grapples with the history of slaughtered Jewish bodies from the past."[63] Margolin's engagement with this sense of time as past, present, and future all occurring in the moment of "now," also helps us toward the utopian performatives her performances call forth.

All three performers could be accused of talking too much, of telling stories out of school. Storytelling, in fact, lends all three performances their power and works structurally to draw the audience closer and to offer them models for agency, for transformation and change. Literary theorist J. Hillis Miller writes, "The human capacity to tell stories is one way men and women collectively build a significant and orderly world around themselves. . . . Narratives are a relatively safe or innocuous place in which the reigning assumptions of a given culture can be criticized."[64] Hughes, Shaw, and Margolin all participate in this dual function of storytelling, creating order and criticizing underlying assumptions. Their stories are utopian performatives because, as Miller suggests, "[a] story is a way of doing things with words. It makes something happen in the real world: for example, it can propose modes of selfhood or ways of behaving that are then imitated in the real world."[65] To see women onstage, alone, telling stories is still, for me, a political moment, one I can't (or won't) take for granted. Hughes says she tells stories out of utter need, "a craving to tell a story, that's balanced by a hunger to listen." She says,

> All I can think is: thank God, I've got an audience. At least one pair of eyes are on me as I stumble through the story (stories) of my life (lives). And they're paying attention. I can tell they're following me, even though I'm plainly lost, because there's a light shining out of their eyes. I make my way along this light, knowing I'm being watched. Not in an Orwellian sort of way but watched in the sense of being watched over, guarded. Having an audience is a form of protection. It's like having the light of a hundred tiny private suns helping me find my way from one side of the story to the next.[66]

Through telling her story, she creates an attentive, listening public. I once asked Hughes why she needs to perform, given that her performances are so writerly, that they read so well on the page. She insisted that it's the social space of performance that gives her hope, that motivates her forward, the desire to see others listening, to be guided by that light shining from their eyes. Her stories, she writes, also offer the audience maps, ways of answering their questions, showing them where they've been and where they might go. "As far as I can tell," Hughes says, "everyone can always use a story."[67]

I agree with Hughes, and would only add that everyone needs to see a story performed, live. This need propels us to performance; as Sarah Schulman says, theater is raw,

> [r]eal people in front of you, wanting something, showing their desire. I think that's why theatre has a better reputation than it deserves. The people who make it are so vulnerable. Their desire is so palpable. Their lives are filled with struggle. Almost no one gets rich on the theatre. That's why we think of it as a place for progressive ideas, as a progressive force on the culture at large, something hopeful and somewhat pure.[68]

Schulman describes the community-based theater work that she most admires, a description that suits the context and contours of Hughes's, Shaw's, and Margolin's work over the last twenty or so years. While she bemoans the lack of grants, the lack of professional training, the lack of facilities and technical expertise, the grueling lack of money, and the insulting lack of attention from powerful presses, Schulman boasts that what "precommodified" gay and lesbian theater—and I would add, feminist—work had was a "passionate audience."[69] The passion of the audience explains why live performance continues; the desire to see it, to participate in its world-makings persists. People in my generation must instill such desire in people in the next. I want to perpetuate experiences of utopia in the flesh of performance that might performatively hint at how a different world could feel.

I know I'm risking sentiment here; I know that community and theater, like utopia, can be coercive, that nothing is outside of ideology, and that nothing is ever, truly, perfect. But I believe in the politically progressive possibilities of romanticism in performance, what Dyer calls "the intensity of fleeting emotional contacts . . . and the exquisite pain of [their] passing."[70] I believe that during the "Throws Like a Girl" series we achieved moments of spontaneous communitas, which Turner says "is sometimes a matter of 'grace.'"[71] "Communitas," he says, "tends to be inclusive—some might call it generous."[72] This, for me, is the beginning (and perhaps the substance) of the utopian performative: in the performer's grace, in the audience's generosity, in the lucid power of intersubjective understanding, however fleeting. These are the moments when we can believe in utopia. These are the moments theater and performance make possible.

chapter three

Finding Our Feet in One Another's Shoes

Multiple-Character Solo Performance

When explicating the dysfunctionalities of the present, a critical social theory should always do so in the name of a better future and a more humane society. The purpose of critical theory is not crisis management, but crisis diagnosis such as to encourage future transformation. A critical social theory views the present from the perspective of the radical transformation of its basic structure, and interprets actual lived crises and protests in the light of an anticipated future. In its *anticipatory-utopian* capacity, critical theory addresses the needs and demands expressed by social actors in the present, and interprets their potential to lead toward a better and more humane society.

—SEYLA BENHABIB, *Critique, Norm, and Utopia*

The spirit of acting is the *travel* from the self to the other. . . . If we were to inhabit the speech pattern of another, and walk in the speech of another, we could find the individuality of the other and experience that individuality viscerally. . . . Learning about the other by being the other requires the use of all aspects of memory, the memory of the body, mind and heart, as well as the words.

—ANNA DEAVERE SMITH, *Talk to Me*

Utopia can be a placeholder for social change, a no-place that the apparatus of theater—its liveness, the potential it holds for real social exchange, its mortality, its openness to human interactions that life outside this magical space prohibits—can model productively. In the last chapter, I found these feelings of utopia in Holly Hughes, Peggy Shaw, and Deb Margolin's interactions with their audiences. Their stories directly addressed spectators and modeled an ephemeral but powerful intersubjectivity that let spectators experience affectively, if fleetingly, what utopia might feel like. This chapter considers multiple-character solo performances by comedienne and film and stage actor Lily Tomlin; by downtown New York solo performer and hip-hop theater festival impresario Danny Hoch; and by performance ethnographer and solo performer Anna Deavere Smith. I investigate how performing across cultural identities in the formalized space of theater might provoke utopian performatives that offer glimpses of how people might *be* together in a more respectful, care-full, loving human community, however small or large those configurations might be.

My goal in prodding people to see performance practices as effective and pleasurable methods for contemplating visions of a better world is to reanimate a humanism that can incorporate love, hope, and commonality alongside a deep understanding of difference. As leftist historian Robin D. G. Kelley remarks in his book on the civil rights movement,

> Progressive social movements do not simply produce statistics and narratives of oppression; rather the best ones do what great poetry always does: transport us to another place, compel us to relive horrors and, more importantly, enable us to imagine a new society. We must remember that the conditions and the very existence of social movements enable participants to imagine something different, to realize that things need not always be this way.[1]

In Kelley's sense, feminism, for example, as a social movement has always been utopian, and so, I would add, has the feminist theater criticism that attempts to implement its goals, looking to performance for methods to reconstruct new, more fluid and powerful ways of being gendered, raced, and "classed" people. One of feminist performance theory's first moves was away from content into an analysis of form. Theorists asked if realism was too proscriptive for new understandings of gender, race, and sexual relations. How might more postmodern forms, with less coherent and insistently linear narratives, more fluid, fragmented plots and characters, and less fixed determinations of location and space, allow spectators to see gender in more expansive, progressive ways? How might new forms allow us to understand race, ethnicity, and sexuality beyond white heteronormative models (that is, understandings of relationships that presume heterosexuality as the only normal version)?[2] Feminist performance theory's next move, into reception studies, allowed scholars and critics and theater makers to think about how spectators are interpolated into or invited to identify or affiliate with performance texts, to ponder the various modes of address that differentiate how meaning is made and might be made differently.[3]

The utopian performative moves me into the theoretical and experiential realm of affect, into the live, present-tense relationship between performers and spectators in a particular historical moment and a specific geographic location. This work tries to describe the most ineffable, most difficult aspect of performance to capture, to manipulate and to "prove": how it makes people *feel*. Yet as I remarked in chapter 2, theater and performance studies scholars speak too rarely about how theater moves us and inspires us in our public and private worlds. Performance scholar David Román says, "The fear that our love of theatre will call into question our critical capacities follows from our field's efforts to credentialize itself against the charge of inconsequentiality. . . . We are bullied into keeping our love of theatre outside of our scholarship."[4] Why are we so reluctant to talk about what we love? How can we even *make* theater without hope and love? Canadian artist Daniel MacIvor, of the performance group da da kamera, says that he could only imagine making work with people he loves.[5] Why isn't love a value consistently articulated in our critical and creative work, especially if "love is a privileged site for the experience of utopia"?[6] In my effort to track the trace of utopian performatives in performance, feeling and explicating love provides an indispensable methodology.

Marxist cultural critic Raymond Williams provides another route through which to examine the social impact of emotion. He writes that what he calls structures of feeling "defin[e] a social experience which is still in process, often indeed not yet recognized as social but taken to be private, idiosyncratic, and even isolating."[7] I might find this kind of social experience at the theater, noticing emotion that's difficult to confirm outside of my own subjective response, but that I can feel, in those moments of inarticulate spontaneous communitas, among the audience. We create these moments in the perpetual present of performance. As Williams says, "[T]he making of art is never itself in the past tense. It is always a formative process, within a specific present."[8] A structure of feeling is "a kind of feeling and thinking which is indeed social and material, but each in an embryonic phase before it can become fully articulate and defined exchange."[9] This is where the utopian performative might be found: in feelings of pleasure and hope that often come before the security of articulation, that require a process of arriving in speech, the sense of possibility for something never before seen but only longed for, that glimpse of the no-place we can reach only through *feeling,* together.

As I watch and unravel the meanings of actors constituting themselves and their characters or subjects in performance, and of directors and designers organizing the spatial aesthetics and the temporal flow of the stage, I feel myself reconstituting my own subjectivity and my own sense that time and space can be fluid and malleable. Those moments make me want to take my partner's hand, or catch the eye of the stranger sitting next to me, to acknowledge that we're here together, that we need and deserve that physical, as well as emotional, connection. These are examples of structures of feeling that can't be accommodated by more official systems of language and meaning making.

> [S]tructures of feeling . . . is [a term] chosen to emphasize a distinction from more formal concepts of "world-view" or "ideology." It is not only that we must go beyond formally held and systematic beliefs . . . it is that we are concerned with meanings and values as they are actively lived and felt . . . we are talking about . . . specifically affective elements of consciousness and relationships: not feeling against thought, but thought as felt and feeling as thought: practical consciousness of a present kind, in a living and interrelating continuity.[10]

Williams describes a kind of mindfulness, a critical, hopeful presence of people open to each other in the present. Such feelings aren't outside ideology; Williams's "structure of feeling" relates intimately to social structures, but looks at the gaps, the aporia through which feeling can be prearticulate, with a liberatory patina of potential. Audiences and performers, as cocreators of meaning in performance, might strive together to imagine the potential for radically altered social communities in the momentary suspension of disbelief that constitutes theater.

This chapter looks at solo performers who create a multiplicity of characters through a transformational performance style that performance scholar Michael Peterson calls "monopolylogues": a theatrical entertainment in which one performer plays several parts or characters.[11] My inquiry here focuses on Tomlin, Hoch, and Smith, three performers who've created very different performances using the monopolylogue form. I'm interested in several aspects of their performances: (1) how they address their audiences—that is, how they locate the act of *listening,* for performer and for spectator, in different spheres with different political

inflections; (2) how they create transformations between their characters—using only iconic props or costume pieces and virtually no sets—
toward different performative and political effects, in a way that allows
"performers and audience members [to] enjoy the dynamic oscillation
between corporeality and signification in the embodied images they have
constructed together in the theatre,"[12] and finally, (3) how they, like Shaw
and Hughes and Margolin, tell stories that criticize conventional political
assumptions and work to reorder a world out of joint.

Solo performance, or "monodrama," takes many forms in historical
and contemporary performance practice.[13] Epic poems told by traveling
storytellers in the ancient western world fit this definition, as well as contemporary solo performers like Hughes, Shaw, and Margolin, whose stories address personal experience transformed for public presentation.
Monodrama includes a long tradition of Western performers enacting historical figures (Hal Holbrook, for instance, as Mark Twain, or Pat Bond as
Gertrude Stein), in conventional theater productions or in the more edu-
cationally oriented forums of Chautauqua performances. Solo performance categorized as monopolylogues also stretch across history, from
Ruth Draper in the 1930s to Eric Bogosian in the 1980s or John Leguizamo
in the 1990s, among others. Productions with more than one performer
also can and often do contain glimpses of utopia—I discuss several examples in subsequent chapters. But the monopolylogue form seems particularly suited for investigation as a site of utopian performatives because it
models the fluidity of cultural identities and offers a method through
which performers and spectators might experience them. As theater
scholar Harry Elam says, "The unique conventions and inventiveness of
the theater allow for provocative explorations of identity not possible in
the outside social environment";[14] this seems especially true for multiple-
character solo performers, who can stage various cultural identities on the
same body in ways that highlight difference but also perhaps point toward
commonalities among people. Elam, in fact, says, "For theatrical criticism,
attention to the performance of cultural identity can help illuminate the
complexities of difference at play."[15]

The metaquestion, which Peterson suggests any monologue performance poses, is, "Why are you listening?"[16] What is it that draws us to a
form in which the actor introduces us to people we're asked only to imagine? Why are we listening and what are we listening for? What do we want
to hear? What is it we hope to see? What does it model of the political
potential of the utopian performative? What features of utopia does it let

us glimpse or appreciate, if only imaginatively? Is there something in the very act of taking on the other in a way that's not possible in the real world a utopian performative? Why does this form seem so suited to exploring the fleeting, ephemeral dynamic I've made my quest? Is it because the simple complexity of the solo performer's presence and transformation across multiple identities asks us to suspend our disbelief in particular ways that let us see and hear other people with more empathy and understanding? Because we're willing to look, through the solo performer as shamanic guide, at subjects we would otherwise avoid? How is this form different from crude parody or mean satire, which sets out to belittle its characters, asserting the hegemony of dominant power? How does the monopolylogue form, in socially progressive hands, allow a more hopeful dialogue about difference, one that leads, perhaps, toward a more generous, compassionate sense of common humanity?

Performance studies scholar Joni Jones's work on performance ethnography and the role of embodiment in cultural authenticity also provides a useful theoretical frame through which to address these questions. Jones says, "Performance ethnography . . . is, most simply, how culture is done in the body. . . . If people are genuinely interested in understanding culture, they must put aspects of that culture on and into their bodies."[17] Tomlin, Hoch, and Smith model this practice, by writing onto their gestures and vocal inflections the cultures through which they move, the people whose voices they echo, so that they might resonate through an audience that has never heard them, in quite this way, before. Jones discusses identity as *practice;* to "authenticate" identity (a project Jones undertakes with postmodernist, rather than essentialist, goals that allow her to think of identity as fluid and changing rather than transhistorical and static) requires, she says, "a tireless striving for physical details that make up cultures."[18] Jones describes the quotidian processes of taking on identity that performance demands.

Jane Wagner's monopolylogue *Search for Signs of Intelligent Life in the Universe,* performed by Lily Tomlin on Broadway in 1985, then revived for Broadway again in 2000, provides one example of how a performer might strive for specific cultural details that practice identity and provide utopian performatives.[19] Tomlin creates a world with only her body as corporeal resource and as sign. On a stage that's bare, except for a step unit or stool and Tomlin's black-clad, lanky, always moving body, Tomlin and Wagner weave a universal human story. The play's deft political gesture begins with feminism as a way into a revised and reinvigorated humanism. The particularities of gender and sexuality and race politics remain, but the play's reach is inclusive from its own perspective, the way that universality, too, is only inclusive through the particular.[20]

The metatheatricality of *Search for Signs* authorizes its political commentary. With a light self-consciousness, the text refers to Tomlin as the dark-haired actress who's performing an "uplifting" show on Shubert Alley (23). Tomlin presents herself shortly after she introduces Trudy, the crazy-smart bag lady who will be the audience's "cock-eyed optimist" guide through the complicated, both familiar and surprising meanings and feelings toward which *Search for Signs* yearns.[21] Although it's Trudy who wears the umbrella hat that transmits human emotions and situations to share with aliens looking for intelligent life on earth, it's Tomlin who's always there, guiding the audience, reminding us through her initial confession of anxiety how much there is to worry about in the world. Tomlin shares her wry, ironic fears, while reassuring the audience that being with them, in this temporary community in this particular theater, reassures her. Of course, it's no accident that the space aliens finally find intelligent life at the theater; *Search for Signs* implicitly argues that it's through practicing the identities and social locations of other people that the "goose bump" moments—what we might call certain "structures of feeling" or utopian performatives—are found and sustained.

Tomlin models ways to practice identity through social gestus made both familiar and strange.[22] In a 2002 interview, she remarks, "Do you think my characters are not real? They're out there somewhere. I just imitate them."[23] The crazy bag lady is a recognizable type, even a stereotype. But Wagner and Tomlin imbue her with wisdom that makes the audience listen harder, that cajoles spectators into regarding with admiration a denizen of what middle-class Broadway audiences would usually disregard as an undesirable underworld. Trudy offers the audience a view of life from the margins. Through her encounters with aliens, the audience sees life on earth from an estranged, Brechtian position that leaves nothing safely ensconced in common sense. This strategy allows Tomlin to use Brecht's notion of the alienation effect, which he believed would keep audiences attentive to the political meanings of his plays by preventing them from losing themselves in identifications with characters. In Tomlin's hands, however, the estrangement of the A-effect breeds both critical attentiveness and affection for her characters and their poignant foibles.

Tomlin performs the gestus, marking each character with a gesture that defines her, while her words and her relations to the carefully self-contained social world Wagner creates unsettles bourgeois presumptions. Transformations between and among these social spheres happen in split-second adjustments of posture, gesture, and voice, which materialize on Tomlin's face and body through her hard performative (and *performed*) labor. Tomlin's body orchestrates its microcosmic world with what a reviewer of the 2000 revival called "symphonic grandness."[24] Watching that labor, too, models a utopian performative, which only exists as a doing. Tomlin's transformations, fast as they are, show us what can be done to practice, physically, interpretations of culture that might model radically altered social communities and point, through utopian performatives, to a revised and reanimated understanding of humanism. Tomlin performs unhappy, discontented Paul, who, after a quick fling with the feminist flower shop owner Marge, congenially becomes the sperm donor for Marge's lesbian friends Edie and Pam. Tomlin performs Kate, the bored, disaffected New York socialite, whose hair is done in an off-balance, avant-garde style by Bucci, a gay hairdresser put through styling school by Tina and Brandy, two African American prostitutes who ride with a reporter who's writing a story on their lives. As Tina and Brandy cruise through Hell's Kitchen, the sex workers pass Agnus Angst, the alienated punk rock teenage runaway, daughter of Janet, the lesbian performance artist, granddaughter of Lud and Marie, who sit patiently at home in their Early American–furnished living room, trying to understand and tolerate their granddaughter's difference. The interconnected world Tomlin and Wagner create represents its own utopian performative, as it illuminates the ways very different people's lives constantly touch each other. We live, the production suggests, not in separate worlds, but in adjacent ones that touch each other—and us—in unexpected ways.

Tomlin performs Lyn, whose early 1980s garage sale prompts the second act's meditation on feminism's evolution from radical political consciousness-raising groups to self-actualization movements for upper-middle-class Yuppies. Sifting through the detritus of a life that tried to balance holistic ecology and capitalism, feminism and corporatism, Lyn/Tomlin/Wagner becomes in act 2 another guide through contemporary politics and its contradictions. Through pungent one-liners and poignant situations, Tomlin and Wagner affectionately parody a generational politic through which they lived, with its celebratory moments—Geraldine Ferraro's nomination as vice president on Walter Mondale's presidential ticket in 1984; its trials—building a geodesic dome home from a kit advertised in the leftist *Mother Jones* magazine; and its fashions—the changing political slogans on T-shirts, and the Indian cotton drawstring pants and Birkenstock sandals that signal the devolution of politics into style. The use of history in the second act is much more specific, as it casually seduces the audience's attention away from the odd characters that adorn the human universe in the first act to the more specifically drawn feminist characters whose lives people the second, in a story that follows a more conventional plot structure.

Throughout the piece, Tomlin's characters talk both to each other and to the audience, maintaining the changing address characteristic of the monopolylogue. Playing Lud and Marie (Agnus Angst's grandparents), Tomlin alternates between the characters, staging conversations to which the audience listens. Transforming between Tina and Brandy (the prostitutes riding in the reporters' car), Tomlin's dialogue addresses the imaginary journalist, while the audience listens. Lyn's long second-act monologue is shared with the various characters she plays, in conversation with their personal trials and the historical moment that helps interpret them. A reviewer of the revival says, "[H]er performance remains virtuosic, bordering on the heroic, as she switches from one character to the next with the speed and alacrity of a light going on and off."[25] What her virtuosity requires, though, is an audience willing to listen intently, to pay attention to the shifting signs of culture Tomlin and Wagner ironize, and to reflect with fond solicitude on what it all might mean.

Tomlin and Wagner imagine a world that's by no means utopian; many of the characters suffer the pain and frustrations of historical change and several contemplate ending their lives. But hearing their stories, embodied with such grace, such care, such imaginative detail, offers the audience a utopian performative, an example of what it might feel like to regard friends and lovers, strangers and those most different from ourselves with respectful, intersubjective consideration and thoughtfulness. In addition, Tomlin's physical virtuosity brings her closer to the audience; it's hard not to love this chameleon-like talent, who works so hard and so happily and affectionately to bring people such an admirably interconnected, humane, and loving theatrical universe. Tomlin's performance encourages love for her characters, but since they play out across her own body, it's hard not to transfer the feeling she evokes to Tomlin, too. Tomlin performs with her heart as well as her miraculously flexible, expressive face and limbs; it's difficult not to respond in kind.

Trudy, the bag lady, and Tomlin in her appearance as herself in the first act, always speak directly to the audience, inviting us in through their utopian performatives and allowing Tomlin to sacrifice none of the "confessional closeness that goes with being a solo performer."[26] Trudy describes her interactions with her space chums, offering us an outsider's (an other-worldly) perspective on American idiosyncrasies, like fried clams at Howard Johnson's, or IHOP, or vibrators (sold by Tomlin's extratextual character Judith Beasley [familiar from Tomlin's turn on the 1970s television show *Laugh-In*] on a commercial Lud and Marie watch with a kind of tolerant shock and interest), or nondairy creamer, which one of the aliens quips is "exactly what we're made of" (77).

The aliens' philosophy helps frame and explain the audience's experience of the world they search. Trudy reports that the aliens believe that "everything is part of everything" (115). Their guide is the "Quantum Inseparability Principle," in which "every particle affects every other particle everywhere" (115). The principle is borne out by the story *Search for Signs* weaves. The world Wagner and Tomlin create is a densely connected system, in which characters pop up in each other's lives, whether on the center or the margins, to prove the inseparability theory, which finally, is a form of humanism. Tomlin demonstrates this "oneness" by performing all the characters that comprise this self-contained world, by acting out the social gestus of complicated relationships on her own body, voice, and soul. Asked if the work is draining, Tomlin says, "No, it's invigorating. Because first of all, I truly am elated that I'm doing it. And I think it's respectful. The material is respectful of the audience's intelligence and their spirits."[27] If the play finally arrives at humanism, its foundation in feminism deftly prods the audience toward a change in political perspective, encouraging us to glimpse a better world by using the perspective of gender identity to describe a potential social condition that would benefit any and all human identities.

I saw *Search for Signs* several times when it premiered on Broadway in 1986.[28] I recall, almost physically, how moved I felt to be in an audience addressed as feminists, as people assumed to be concerned with social justice who desire a better world. I remember my own goose bumps at hearing Geraldine Ferraro's vice presidential nomination acceptance speech played over one of the memory scenes, and my joy and amazement at hearing Cris Williamson's song "Sweet Woman"—one of the iconic songs of the 1970s lesbian feminist movement—played under a description of a character's lesbian encounter. Seeing *Search for Signs* on Broadway was the first time I ever felt my experience directly addressed or my emotions frankly solicited in the theater, the first time I saw a mainstream performance that, as Marilyn French wrote in her afterword to the play, "takes it as a given that a mass audience will accept feminist attitudes, that proceeds on the assumption that these attitudes are shared and that therefore does not lecture, hector, or even underline."[29]

Each time I saw the original production on Broadway in New York—once was with an invited audience, who witnessed Martha Swope, Annie Liebovitz, and other photographers capturing the production for what would become the published script—I could feel the largely female crowd around me gasp with delight and recognition at the moments that moved me, too. Hearing Ferraro's acceptance speech was so new, then, and not yet tinged with knowledge of her husband's financial corruption; the moment was still idealistic despite the Democratic ticket's loss in the 1984 election, still a moment we all thought heralded real gains for women in public life. We didn't know, then, that Ferraro's nomination was just a stray blip on the screen of party politics. Hope buoyed those audiences, along with a real sense of arrival; our story (however partial, however mostly white and middle class), took center stage, performed with such insight and feeling by a woman who was clearly one of us. Feeling such empowerment, such belonging, at a Broadway performance was rare and wonderful and infrequently repeated in my lifetime.

While in 1985 the play's explicit feminism was one of its hallmark values, in 2000, according to Tomlin's remarks about the revival and based on the bulk of the critical response, Search for Signs called us toward a reinvigorated, more inclusive humanism. Although very little of the text was changed, American cultural history had changed around the play. While some of the goals of feminism remain out of reach (such as equal pay for equal work, child care as an entitlement, the dismantling of glass ceilings across professions, to name just a few examples), the social movement for women's equality has become a more acceptable, ordinary part of the American vernacular. Since its feminist principles are no longer new, even though the play's interpretation of feminist issues still remains acute, the insistent humanism in Search for Signs is highlighted instead, especially at a historical moment in which a belligerent, bellicose "us versus them" mentality has infected United States politics and its antiterrorist rhetoric.

The Broadway revival was still running on September 11, 2001. Asked how she thought the show would play after the tragedy, Tomlin, invoking her own sense of communitas and her own commitment to humanism, said, "I didn't have any doubts about the show, because I know the show is so affirming and really talks about issues and themes that would be rele-

vant. It's really an embrace of the human family."[30] To another interviewer, Tomlin says, "The real beauty of it, to me, is that the audience is
theoretically, metaphorically, looking at itself. My favorite thing that was
ever written about it was, 'At the end,' this critic said, 'we were on our feet
applauding our higher selves.' When it's working at its best, the collective
experience in the audience affirms that connection—the connectedness
between all of us as a species."[31]

The show ends with several utopian performatives that gesture toward
a future in which people build alliances through their common humanity,
facilitated, rather than hampered, by their differences. Trudy's space
chums want to know about goose bumps: "Do they come from the heart?
Do they come from the soul? Do they come from the brain? Or do they
come from geese?" (201). To help them experience this new affectivity,
Trudy takes them to Shubert Alley to see a play:

> We were at the back of the theatre, standing there in the dark, all of a
> sudden I feel one of 'em tug my sleeve, whispers, "Trudy, look." I said,
> "Yeah, goose bumps. You definitely got goose bumps. You really like
> the play that much?" They said it wasn't the play gave 'em goose bumps,
> it was the audience. I forgot to tell 'em to watch the play; they'd been
> watching the audience! Yeah, to see a group of strangers sitting together
> in the dark, laughing and crying about the same things . . . that just
> knocked 'em out. They said, "Trudy, the play was soup . . . the audience
> . . . art." (212)

Even Kate, the New York socialite who is the play's most cynical character, is finally persuaded toward feminist humanism and to see possibilities for utopia in the serendipitous, poignant, fleeting encounters of everyday life. She says, after a concert she heard at Carnegie Hall, "I saw these
two prostitutes on the corner . . . talking with this street crazy, this bag
lady. And I remembered something I think it was Kafka wrote about having been filled with a sense of endless astonishment at simply seeing a
group of people cheerfully assembled" (210). *Search for Signs* honors the
audience as such an assembly. Tomlin and Wagner's humble gesture
makes the audience magic, makes the audience the origin of the utopian
performative, who can gesture toward a better world by showing up to
watch, to listen, to be together, to be moved, to watch each other respond
to a performance that creates history from our various experiences. An
interviewer reports, "[W]hat matters most to Tomlin is the ripening of her

art laced with a peaceful, egalitarian ethos. 'If I have an agenda,' says Tom-lin, 'it's that all of us as humans have been ridiculed; all of us as a species—we're so debased, that there must be some kind of human embrace that makes us worthy of something.' "[32]

Still, as performance theorist Sonja Kuftinec cautions, "[T]he inclusive nature of performance does not necessarily erase differences in percep-tions and beliefs."[33] *Search for Signs* works as a utopian performative because it creates community—however temporary—on the basis of exactly those differences. *Search for Signs* proposes, as queer theorist José Esteban Muñoz suggests in a different context, "an identity-in-difference," which "is one that understands the structuring role of difference as the underlying concept in a group's mapping of collective identity."[34] One of the theoretical justifications for pronouncing the end of humanism was its Enlightenment baggage, its insistence on centering universal "man" as the origin of meaning and rejecting a more complex, divided, multivocal view of human identity or subjectivity. But in a contemporary moment that even progressive artists and scholars are calling "postidentity politics," I'd like to suggest that realigning a new humanism with our hard-won nonessentialized understandings of how race, class, sexuality, and other identity vectors make us different as well as similar lets us work together to imagine a more just world.

No one can argue that predominantly male, white, heterosexual, mid-dle-class, Christian culture doesn't exist, or that identity differences don't matter. But they are no longer necessarily attached to a prescriptive stand-point theory. As geographer David Harvey says, "[T]he long-lost tech-niques of empathy and translation . . . across sensory realms is reconsti-tuted as a vital way of knowing to supplement (and in certain instances to transcend) introspection . . . '[W]here and who we learn it from and how we learn it' overrides the contemporary postmodern fascination with 'where we see it from' as the basis for intellectual arguments."[35] We've once again moved the axis of categorization—the perspective from which we understand our world—not to reparticularize it, but to incorporate within it our more nuanced perceptions of how people might stand together, as well as the social barriers that continue to keep us apart.

Danny Hoch's performances *Some People* (1994) and *Jails, Hospitals, and Hip-Hop* (1998) interpolate a different kind of spectator into the potential for utopian performativity, mapping a different collective iden-tity.[36] Hoch, too, transforms himself into a multiplicity of characters, none of whom would ordinarily hold center stage. Just as Tomlin and Wagner come at the question of intelligent life by telling stories from the margins—whether those of sex workers, bag ladies, or runaways—Hoch's stories are edged sharply in an experience of the street that comes from his own history of being born and raised in a multiracial and multiethnic urban neighborhood in Queens, New York, where, he says, "You had all these foods being cooked, smells ingested, languages spoken, and points of view."[37] The texture of these multiple cultures provides the foundation for his characters. Critic Laurie Stone says, "Danny Hoch belongs to the street. . . . His mimicry doesn't condescend . . . he can slip into otherness, because it's not *so* other."[38] Like Tomlin's, Hoch's characters are fictional, created from observations and relationships, from his experience of locality and geography. But like Hughes, Shaw, and Margolin, he bases his stories in his own experience with people and layers them with the shimmering complexities of art. Hoch told the *Revolutionary Worker* that he focuses on "untold stories that I [feel] needed to be center stage. . . . I [have] a responsibility to the humanity of each of these characters. But at the same time, I also [have] a responsibility to the imbalance of whose stories are being told and how."[39]

Jails, Hospitals, and Hip-Hop offers a more fragmented narrative of human experience than *Search for Signs*. Hoch represents various characters, who get entangled with the prison system or negotiate physical disabilities or are otherwise marginalized from dominant culture, including Bronx, a prison inmate on Riker's Island; Sam, a corrections officer; Gabriel, a young man with a speech disorder; Victor, a man who uses crutches; Peter, a street hustler in Cuba; and Emcee Enuff, a successful rapper. These characters never connect with each other, as they do in *Signs*. Hoch presents each persona directly to the audience, which substitutes for the presumed addressee, although occasionally he stages an exchange with an unseen interlocutor. Hoch's monopolylogues build a world in which cultural differences and the performed identities they shape are the stuff of the social, not the "natural." These characters spotlight the kinds of people whose lives are often lost in the interstices of dominant culture: maintenance staff, disabled people, minimum-wage workers, heavily accented immigrants, young and old women. Hoch tells each story from within the character he creates out of his own experience with cultural difference, covering transitions between stories with music and light cues that allow him to exchange a hat or a prop to signify someone new entering the scene of the stage.

Embodiment, for Hoch, means capturing the rhythms of the city; it's about northeastern American urban mythology. His work is textured with the sights and sounds and smells of a city life in which commonality and community means sharing an open water hydrant on a blistering summer day. Hoch is a one-man *Street Scene*, capturing, honoring, and conveying the multilingual immigrant culture of the twenty-first century just as Elmer Rice evoked those of the early twentieth. Hoch's work is funny but painful; he treads an edge that Tomlin and Wagner soften with wry observation and witty analogy. Hoch's insights are rueful; his characters unfold, showing their scars, along with their hope and resilience. Like Tomlin's, Hoch's personal generosity shines through his performances. Hoch himself is present alongside his characters, inviting us to love and respect them as he does. Like Tomlin, Hoch projects a charismatic personality that invites audiences to love him, too, to appreciate his virtuosity but also his ordinariness, the fact of himself as a middle-class white artist whose commitments to politics run deep. He purposefully turns our admiration for his performance into identifications with his politics, inviting us to align ourselves with his characters in a kind of truly progressive, meaningful coalition of the willing.

Just as Shaw, Hughes, and Margolin gave so generously of themselves during their Austin residencies, I've seen Hoch perform the same moments of kind and warm intersubjectivity with student and community audiences. Although he's now a major performer, deal-making with HBO and film studios to transfer his work to wider audiences, Hoch still takes time to talk to and talk the language of the young people who feel addressed by his work. The day after a performance of *Jails* that I attended at the University of California in February 2001, Hoch gamely showed up for a lunch discussion, talking openly about the challenges of moving his work from smaller, more targeted communities of spectators to larger, more anonymous audiences. His advocacy for the kind of performance work he does—a hybrid solo performance and community-based work—is as important to him as the performances themselves.

Hoch's stage set looks like Tomlin's, although he uses a few real props and costume pieces to more carefully particularize the characters whose lives he scans. Hats hang on a clothesline strung across the stage, and props like brooms and buckets rest discreetly across the bare back wall, the signs of people who labor with their hands and backs and continue to dream with their minds. Hoch presses his body into service as a corporeal sign in much the same way as Tomlin, performing the social gesture of a cultural moment or of a culturally recognizable character, but acting underneath the stereotype to find his or her contradictions, pathos, and dignity. Critic Bruce Weber says, "Hoch has a genuinely literary touch in his writing, and an unsentimental but aching sympathy for his characters."[40] Hoch's white rapper, Flip, for example, is a homeboy in the deep Midwest, looking into his bedroom mirror to rehearse the practices of hip-hop identity, imagining himself as a star chatting with Jay Leno on *The Tonight Show*. Standing in front of the mirror, he says, "I know what you're thinkin', Jay. You're thinking, like, 'How is it that this white dude could be such a dope rapper?' Well, the truth of the matter, Jay, is that I ain't white, man. I'm really black. . . . Like, check this out, see this birthmark, Jay? Well, it's not really a birthmark, see that's the real color of my skin, and the rest of me is a birthmark" (19). His (unseen) mother continually interrupts Flip's self-crafting performance to ask if he's finished his chores. He responds to her with polite irritation; he is, after all, a teenage suburban boy, even as he longs to adopt the posture of an urban hip-hop outlaw.

His fantasy is his own utopian performative: the rehearsal for an identity that will extend *his* from its constraints, the doing of gestures that unites him with the rappers whom he idolizes. The boy's prosaic life is charged with aspirations of being elsewhere, of being another. This juxtaposition offers spectators a chance not to pity or revile him, but to identify with the distances between a life lived and a *preferable* life imagined. Hoch's performance of the white rapper is detailed and respectful, both to white rural teenagers and African American urban rappers. The boy has only a few moments in front of the mirror to steal for his fantasy before his shift begins at a fast-food restaurant where he's a minimum-wage worker.

Like Tomlin's, Hoch's characters connect across race and economic levels; both performers tell stories of class that demonstrate its centrality, too, as a vector of identity. Hoch's profound empathy and understanding craft his characters, but he positions himself alongside his spectators. As Peterson describes Hoch's work, "[T]he 'successful' spectator must look through the words and actions of the character to the intention of the performer. The performance event involves both performer and audience in a collective observation of the character on display, and the cooperative spectator in a sense occupies the same position as the performer."[41] Peterson says that the audience is "clearly asked by the performance to identify . . . with Hoch's position as cultural critic."[42] He suggests that Hoch is different from other straight white male performance artists because of the "greater diversity of [his] characterizations, coupled with an attention to linguistics where some performers might concentrate on accent."[43] "[T]he multiplicity of urban speech controls Hoch as much as he shapes it. In other words, the typical act of the solo performer . . . is the performance of speaking; Hoch certainly performs this, but foregrounded as well is the performance of having listened. . . . [M]ultiple character work . . . is [usually] the performance of cultural virtuosity, while Hoch's is often the performance of cultural fluency."[44]

Theatre Communications Group executive director Ben Cameron has said that what distinguishes theater from other social activity is the intense listening it requires people do together.[45] Hoch performs the act of *having* listened as a kind of performative; the work he's done is presented in ways that let the audience do it, too—to listen hard, to learn, to feel. Still, Hoch's performance as Flip includes an empathic embodiment of a white boy's desire to be other, a performance that in some ways is only possible through Hoch's ability to secure his own real-life "authentic" experience with the boys in the 'hood. In the introduction to his published *Jails* script, Hoch says, "A few people think I am some anthropological/theatrical case-study guy. But I don't tape-record or interview people to then play them onstage. This is my world! These are my inner monologues, composites of stories and voices from me, my family, my neighborhood, my people. I think all the hoopla about my work comes from people simply not being accustomed to seeing traditionally peripheral characters placed center stage. Well, these characters are center stage in *my* world" (xiv).

Tomlin, too, secures her connection to realness through repeated autobiographical anecdotes that place her, like Hoch, within the 'hood. She tells *Backstage,* "I came from a working-class family. I lived in Detroit in a black neighborhood. I was exposed to a lot of different kinds of people, and I'm sure that formed my sensibility in some way, in terms of a certain kind of affection for almost everybody—for seeing their humanity. I'd see them in such vulnerable, frail, sometimes stupid circumstances, and then I'd see them do something so magnificent."[46] This sense of lived connection informs Tomlin and Hoch's work with respect and responsibility, even if they remain white griots whose race privilege allows them to bring stories of marginalized people to center stage. The form their monopologues use requires rapid juxtapositions between self and other that permit experiences to collide within the space of their own bodies. That is, Hoch juxtaposes Flip—a character whose whiteness seems closest to Hoch's own, even as Flip performs his desire to be African American—with his own story about being called to the *Seinfeld* television show to use his chameleon-like talents to perform a stereotype of a Latino pool attendant.

Hoch carefully places this personal anecdote to secure the politics of his impersonations. He relates how baffled Seinfeld was at his refusal to do the part with a Spanish accent: "Jerry says, 'But I don't get it. Is it derogatory? . . . Aren't you an actor, isn't that your craft, isn't that what you do, you know . . . little accents?' I said, 'Well, I play different characters, but why does the "Pool Guy" *have* to be in a Spanish accent?' And Jerry said, 'Because it's funnier that way. His name is Ramon.' . . . See, they didn't want the real thing, they wanted somebody that could do the real thing, but still be one of them" (39). Outside the monopolylogue form, Hoch's ability to perform the other is pressed into service by racist ideology to create a character of color isolated by the virulently white *Seinfeld* worldview. Hoch maintains his earnest racial politics by refusing the role, and implies that the kind of performing of others that he accomplishes is politically meaningful only when in the company of his other characters. In this case (although perhaps this is also true for Tomlin, as well as Anna Deavere Smith), the utopian performative requires an embodiment of community onstage as well as off.[47]

In addition to staging seldom seen experience, Hoch makes a conscious political effort to expand the audience for his performances. He gives free or reduced rate tickets to young people, hoping to attract those whose preferred cultural consumption tends to be musical, rather than theatrical, performance. An interviewer says, "He grounds his work in real communities, and he keeps his ticket prices low to attract young people and others who rarely see themselves—their experiences—portrayed. . . . Offstage, Hoch is a political activist who advocates the broadcasting of more accurate, positive images of people and communities."[48] When I saw him perform *Jails, Hospitals, and Hip-Hop* at the Public Theater in New York in the mid-1990s, and at University of Southern California in 2001, the audience was young, urban, multiracial, and extremely competent in reading the cultural signs Hoch transformed into and among. Already, the theater offered an altered view of the social, in which a diversity of people met to hear the margins talking, to listen to Hoch practice cultural identities.

Like Tomlin, a sense of immediacy and human need guides audiences through Hoch's work. In addition to his own solo work, Hoch has been instrumental in creating hip-hop theater festivals on the East Coast (especially in New York and Washington, D.C.), which are often described as theatricalized poetry slams. Hip-hop theater fits into the same hybrid genre category as *Def Poetry Jam*, which I discuss in chapter 4. Hoch says,

"What's great about hip-hop is how it has articulated the complaints of oppressed peoples, of people of color, in a way that's unprecedented. But it can't just complain anymore. If hip-hop is supposed to be the voice of change, then you can't just comment, you have to be constructive."[49] Where Tomlin looks to specific audiences to anchor her joyful moments of communitas, Hoch wants such moments to be effective outside the theater. He says, "What I need from my artists is a sense of urgency. I don't feel this in most of the art I see now. And I need a sense of collective responsibility, not just where the artist feels this, but where the artist makes the whole audience feel a collective responsibility sitting there together, even if we don't know each other."[50]

Although Tomlin and Hoch use similar methods to do work with similar political commitments, they work at different ends of a generational spectrum. I don't imagine empirical demographic research exists, but I think it's safe to say that audiences at Tomlin's revival were probably older and more homogenous racially than the generally young, racially mixed crowds Hoch's work attracts. Even though like Hoch, I'm white and Jewish, I'm typically a racial minority in audiences at his performances. And while I consider Tomlin's performance part of my own late-forties, early-fifties generation, I inevitably feel a bit old at Hoch's performances. I find the preshow music a little too loud and not melodic enough for me and the general hum of preshow talk and energy seems part of a new idiom of socializing that I don't quite speak. I enjoy a certain spectatorial bigenerationality because my tastes are eclectic and because I've been a spectator for a long time, so I don't feel uncomfortable so much as different, a healthy response to intermingling ages. But part of the project of tracking utopian performatives and their potential should be just such advocacy of multigenerational theatergoing, so that the communitas generated at performance can remain truly heterogeneous and coalitional. Hoch shouldn't be the only artist charged with attracting young and multiracial audiences to performance.[51]

Weber characterizes the program for the third annual Hip-Hop Theater Festival at P.S. 122 and the Nuyorican Poets Café in New York in 2002 as a "manifesto. And over all," he says, "the rhetoric is probably too indignant and too callow to preach effectively to anyone but the already converted. But the message is reasonable enough: that the contemporary theater has abdicated its role in addressing contemporary life, turning a blind eye to emerging generations of artists with new and different stories to tell and a new and different way of telling them."[52] Offering platforms to these new generations will provide more potential for moments of utopian performativity and the social change they promote.

Peterson says because Hoch's narratives aren't shapely, because they simply stop, without providing an end point, he minimizes the danger of audiences laughing *at* his characters, as some spectators at stand-up routines do. (Hoch, as far as I know, has never been compared to stand-up comics, as were the feminist solo performers I discussed in chapter 1, even though his work, too, trades at least partly in humor to make its case.) Instead, with Hoch as a critical guide, spectators are led to see his characters' quirks and their humanity. Hoch perhaps does his most political, performatively utopian work in just this refusal of closure. Peterson says, "Hoch seems to perform . . . the very desire for . . . transformation";[53] in that desire lies the utopian performative, an action that in its doing offers a glimpse of a better world. Hoch's transformations condense the differences between people so that they matter less. Peterson says that Hoch never aspires to a "universal body; he does realize that he 'can never fully walk in someone else's shoes.'"[54] Tomlin, too, avoids universalizing her body: she practices diverse identities, knit together in a fictional world where people are kind, careful, thoughtful, and compelled by each other's pain and by their dreams. Instead, their work offers the "performative production of political solidarity."[55]

David Harvey says that "we know a great deal about what divides people, but nowhere near enough about what they have in common. . . . Without translation, collective forms of action become impossible."[56] Both Tomlin and Hoch are translators; as a reviewer wrote about Tomlin, they express "the poetry of human behavior."[57] They use their ability to speak multiple languages, to embody multiple cultural identities, to bring more people into a discussion about difference and human commonality. Their liminal positions, at the threshold of social renovation modeled by the utopian potential of their transformational impersonations, allow them to see and help us to imagine, even just affectively, a better, more equitable world. Empathy gives them (and us) access, but finally, it's the aesthetics, the immersion of one subjectivity in the dreams of another, that calls forth the utopian performative, the performance of an identity not your own that allows you to build new worlds together. As the late performance studies scholar Dwight Conquergood said, "The aim of dialogical performance is to bring self and other together so that they can question, debate, and challenge one another."[58] Tomlin and Hoch perform a kind of hybrid-ity or sampling that borrows—with love, without stealing—to share a wider meaning.

Although the moment of identity politics now wanes—at least for those with enough power and political experience to take the long view of social relations[59]—they remain a reminder of the importance of naming standpoints, even as we move outward and onward into a more inclusive performance of culture. Likewise, authenticity still resonates as a criterion for measuring such performances. The difference now is that even the "authentic" is understood as performative, as a learned series of cultural artifacts that decode into a socially understood identity. Harvey says, "[B]y changing our situatedness (materially or mentally) we can change our vision of the world."[60] Hoch and Tomlin, then, stake their claim really only to a kind of "world traveling," to a cultural proximity and social empathy with common circumstances, above identity differences that are closer to the skin.[61]

Anna Deavere Smith, too, says, "In America, identity is always being negotiated."[62] "The discovery of human behavior can happen in motion. It can be a process of moving from the self to the other and the other to the self."[63] Yet Smith's working practice and effects differ in important ways from Tomlin's and Hoch's. Smith is African American; as performance scholar Dorinne Kondo asks, "What happens when the story is no longer one of black passing for white . . . but people of color performing each other?"[64] The fact that Smith does play white, as well as performing people of color, complicates Smith's performances, and allows her to address what Kondo calls "the utopian hopes and tensions animating what might better be characterized as a politics of affiliation emblematized in such terms as Latino, Asian American, women of color, people of color, queer, and others for which we may not yet have names."[65]

Where Tomlin and Hoch use comedy and hip-hop wit as social critique in the monopolylogue genre, Smith uses the drama of actual human enactment. Where Tomlin and Hoch establish their authenticity through biographical claims to nearness, to a particularly receptive ear, and to a facility for empathic performative mimicry, Smith theatrically reports on communities in crisis, finding "American character in the way people speak."[66] Her commitment to her own objectivity cloaks her cultural interpretations in the performance of presumptive authenticity, captured through speech patterns that she suggests tell the truth of an individual's emotions and their life experiences.

Smith always stands outside of the communities she enters, visiting

Crown Heights, New York, or East Los Angeles to gather stories, to listen to rhythms in language, to watch repetitions in gestures through which she then rebuilds for performance the real people whose lives she mines as well as mimes. In *Fires in the Mirror* (1992), Smith tacks between Hasidic and African American perspectives on the tragic accident in Crown Heights in which a Lubavitcher rebbe's motorcade struck and killed an African American child named Gavin Cato. Enraged by what they saw as a reckless display of power and entitlement and a disregard for other lives, some members of the local African American community fatally stabbed Yankel Rosenbaum, a yeshiva student visiting from Australia. Smith's performance ethnography recaptures, reperforms, on her own body, the speech and gestures and something of the essence of the people with whom she spoke. Some people were closely involved in the tragedy—for example, an anonymous Lubavitcher woman, a neighborhood woman named Rivkah Siegal, two anonymous young men, and Carmel Cato, among others—and some observed and commented on it from other locations—such as playwright Ntozake Shange, Public Theater artistic director George C. Wolfe, the Reverend Al Sharpton, journalist Letty Cottin Pogrebin, activist-academic Angela Davis, and others. The performance becomes an embodied chronicle of ever-shifting positionality, of the impossibility of seeing such a moment and its consequences from an omniscient point of view. Likewise, in *Twilight: Los Angeles* (1994), Smith performs the speech and gestures of people in the East L.A. community she interviewed shortly after the violent reaction of community outrage when a jury acquitted the white police officers who were videotaped gratuitously beating motorist Rodney King. *Twilight* lets Smith embody a range of ethnic and racial identities and to offer even more multivocal, competing perspectives on the same socially scarring event.

Smith's performances do important political work, interrogating unresolved, festering conflicts. Rather than being couched in the subcultural language codes of hip-hop—which Hoch's audiences might or might not "get"—and instead of relying on jokes, puns, and allusions to feminism and history—which Tomlin's audiences may or may not "get"—Smith's work appears transparent, as though she gives her audiences everything they need to know about what law professor Lani Guinier calls, referring to Smith's work, "the tough issue of race at the height of racial conflagration."[67]

In some ways, Smith's monopolylogues reinstate a conventional dramatic agon, as she attempts to balance her representation of competing interpretations of deep social conflicts. Critic Theodore Shank says, "The power of Anna Deavere Smith's performance is that she allows us to relate to her as well as the characters. She's present simultaneously with the characters. . . . Our relationship with the performer is deepened by the fact that she presents many characters. What they have in common is Smith's humanity."[68] Because all the language of the people she summons on stage in both performances was originally spoken to her, by her request, Smith is centered in her performances. She's the invisible interlocutor whose eyes, ears, and mimesis give the audience access to these racially divided communities.

Introducing a snippet of Smith's work in the collection *Extreme Exposure,* Guinier shares a telling anecdote about being interviewed by Smith at the Ninety-second Street Y in New York City. Nervous before going on stage, Guinier asks Smith how one makes an entrance. Smith responds, "I have no idea. . . . I have not gone on stage before simply as myself."[69] Smith in some ways uses the building of character, rather than the intermingling of selves, as her gesture toward a politics of complex inclusion. Smith chooses not to perform her presence as interlocutor, but to let it haunt the characters she mimes, letting the audience imagine the prior moments of preperformance, the metaframe in which Smith enters people's lives with notebook and tape recorder, then edits their conversations together across her own body, modeling what they might sound like if they were in the same room. Performance theorist Ann Pellegrini says Smith "effects a talking cure."[70] Theater becomes her utopia, a no-place where such intercommunity dialogue is possible.

Unlike Tomlin and Hoch, Smith's presence doesn't beam love into the audience or necessarily see it reflected back to the stage. Love becomes a question in Smith's work, rather than an answer: how would social arrangements need to shift for the African Americans and Hasidic Jews in Crown Heights to love each other? What must shift for a multiracial, multiethnic audience to be able to love any of the polemical, controversial people Smith brings together on stage? Perhaps Smith's gesture toward radical humanism comes through a politics of coalition that admits to the pain and the suffering of difference before love can be entertained as an emotion. As activist Bernice Johnson Reagon said in a foundational feminist text, "You don't do no coalition-building in a womb. . . . Coalition work has to be done in the streets. And it is some of the most dangerous work you can do. And you shouldn't look for comfort."[71]

Fires in the Mirror and *Twilight: Los Angeles* invite audiences into deeply conflicted, rage-full communities, but with Smith always as the key, always as the interpreter to whom each character reveals his or her truths. Guinier calls Smith "a fluent translator" who "[uses] the stories people tell her. . . . She is not simply observing and documenting events—she becomes the people who are the events."[72] While Smith herself disappears into the real, the performance boasts her material access to it, demonstrating her cultural virtuosity, rather than cultural fluency.[73] "Mimicry," says Smith, "is *not* character. Character lives in the obvious gap between the real person and my *attempt* to seem like them. I try to close the gap between us, but I applaud the gap between us. I am willing to display my own *unlikeness*."[74] If Smith's work exemplifies social mimicry, she implies that rather than *becoming* another, we might more productively use the specific details of a separate life to walk for a moment in another's shoes, to speak for a moment in another's voice, not to become and not to mock but, as Joni Jones suggests, to feel what it might be like to *be* the other over an inevitably unbridgeable gap. Smith performs mimicry instead of mimesis, never pretending to hold a mirror up to life but only to mimic it, pointing to the images she creates of identity as separate from her and from each other, as surrounded by gaps that shouldn't be closed but with which we must always grapple.[75]

Another difference between Tomlin, for example, and Smith, is that along with character, Tomlin also performs the audience. Smith enacts character, and simply shows the audience a possible future in which different bodies inhabit the same space without violence or mutual hostility. The form Smith creates gives the audience a way of seeing the incidents she documents through real people's lives. Tomlin loves her audience as much as her characters, while Smith's relationship to both her spectators and her characters is more dispassionate and distanced, more pedagogical. While Tomlin says her characters are "out there somewhere," and Hoch's characters are composites of people he knows, Smith's performances are replete with real people whose stories, words, and gestures refer back to a particular, historical body in time and space. Alluding to the gradual development of her trademark acting practices, Smith says, "I could then create the illusion of being another person by reenacting something they had said *as they had said it*."[76] Rather than fictionalizing the spirit of their truths, Smith sticks to the letter of the selves into whose shoes she puts her feet. This contrasts her work with Hughes, Shaw, and Margolin as well; their autobiographical performance, although based in some sort of truth, also fictionalizes, using fanciful images and metaphors that come from their stories, rather than how they're edited, as in Smith's performances. *Fires* and *Twilight*, for example, insist on the real, and although Smith's presence resolutely centers each performance, she's also absent from them.

Smith's political gesture is to turn these diverse monologues, these discrepant points of view about irresolvable tragedy, into a staged conversation that in itself becomes a utopian performative, a momentary "doing" of a world in which such interracial, cross-gender, cross-faith, cross-cultural dialogue might be possible. As feminist media critic Tania Modleski says, Smith gets her characters to act on new common ground—the stage.[77] The utopian performative here is perhaps more metatheatrical; the "doing" of conflict in a wider public forum, embodying it for people who've probably only read about Crown Heights or East L.A., makes of the *theater,* the stage itself, a doing where a more equitable, if still complicated dialogue can be maintained. Philosopher Cornel West says, "*Fires in the Mirror* is a grand example of how art can constitute a public space that is perceived by people as empowering, rather than disempowering."[78] He says, "As a citizen, Smith knows that there can be no grappling with Black anti-Semitism and Jewish anti-Black racism without a vital public sphere and that there can be no vital public sphere without genuine bonds of trust. As an artist, she knows that public performance has a unique capacity to bring us together . . . human art can triumph in the face of a frightening urban crisis."[79]

The experience of intersubjectivity might not be felt as keenly between performer and spectator in Smith's woven social tapestries, but through the example of her body, she models the potential for intersubjectivity across radically polarized social groups. Smith herself says, "What we keep forgetting is that when a public person presents a persona, he or she is simply offering 'It's as if I were.' That 'It's as if I were' is an invitation for us to begin to behave 'as if we were' a group. That 'as if' is very important for civic action."[80] Smith doesn't need to love her characters to present the "as ifs."

Perhaps some of the important political work of her pieces is that she's not trying to get audiences to love the characters, either, just to make them willing to hear these lives and perspectives juxtaposed against each other in the no-place that's the stage. At the end of *Search for Signs,* Trudy says wistfully of her space chums, "I like to think of them out there, in the dark, watching us. Sometimes we'll do something and they'll laugh. Sometimes we'll do something and they'll cry. And maybe one day we'll do something so magnificent, everyone in the universe will get goose bumps" (213). Trudy's resolutely humanist wish affectively evokes the kind of utopian performative I'm trying to describe. Through practicing identity in performance, and by creating variable structures of feeling, a different kind of cultural fluency might be learned, one that begins to offer a fleeting glimpse of humankind united around common difference. These monopolylogues create a more radical humanism, and gesture toward a world that's more socially just. As performance scholar Linda Kintz says, "[C]ommunity and hope should not have to be argued so rigorously, while individual isolation is taken as absolute truth. . . . One presumes intersubjectivity, connection, and hope; the other presumes loss and separation."[81]

Perhaps the monopolylogue form allows us to listen differently, from a position of embodied imagination in which other people's lives become meaningfully detailed alongside our own. Perhaps the form allows us to hear the cacophonous discourse of American culture as harmonious, rather than as unintelligible. Perhaps the act of taking on another on stage models a hopeful method for living near others with respect and affection, with grace and even love. Tomlin, Hoch, and Smith listen hard to the coursing, conflicting voices of culture, using their bodies, their imaginations, their souls, their gifts to assail the gaps between self and other, to make an intersubjective community of connection and hope. They ask their audiences to listen equally hard, with the express aim of simply making the world better. Kondo says Smith, Hoch, and other documentary performance artists' "performative portrayals of event, place, and racial multiplicity intervene in the comfortable spaces of civic pride in place, of theatrical convention, of notions of art as transcendent and universal, of art as the product of individual creative genius, and of a liberal humanist politics that would recuperate their work under the sign of a power-evasive multiculturalism."[82] Tomlin, Hoch, and Smith practice social identities to capture the fluent details of cultural difference. They move me to experience an inarticulate structure of feeling, and prod me to make my own utopian performative gestures outside the theater. Discussing his own research, theater scholar Bruce McConachie says, "No performance by itself can alter the routines of everyday life, but . . . theatre can provide 'what if' images of potential community, sparking the kind of imaginative work that must precede substantial changes in customary habits."[83] Perhaps theater is by definition utopian—a successful, transformative performance is always a doing that catapults an audience into a no-place of possibility, where we might gladly expect the unexpected. Those transforming moments are themselves utopian performatives that imagine and embody the world in "what if" rather than "as is."

chapter four

Def Poetry Jam

Performance as Public Practice

For years now people who have been peculiarly aroused have
gathered in this place. The impulses that have led them to the
box office and into the windowless room vary. Some are
bored and want only to purchase a place for an evening that
will more or less be entertaining. A better part, which is
growing today and formed by the working people, does not
want to kill time but wants to use it. These theater-goers, too,
want to be entertained, hence loosened up and liberated, by
the performance, but not without more ado or to be merely
liberated from something but to be liberated for something.
. . . This need . . . is positively linked not only to the compli-
ant or hypocritical but to the tempting wish to undergo a
transformation.
—Ernst Bloch, *The Utopian Function of Art and Literature*

The world intended in art is never and nowhere merely the
given world of everyday reality, but neither is it a world of
mere fantasy, illusion, and so on. . . . As fictitious world, as
illusion, it contains more truth than does everyday reality. . . .
Only in the "illusory world" do things appear as what they
are and what they can be.
—Herbert Marcuse, *The Aesthetic Dimension*

From this "no place," an exterior glance is cast on our reality,
which suddenly looks strange, nothing more being taken for
granted. The field of the possible is now opened beyond that
of the actual, a field for alternative ways of living. The question therefore is whether imagination could have any constitutive role without this leap outside. Utopia is the way in
which we radically rethink what is family, consumption, government, religion, and so on. The fantasy of an alternative

society and its topographical configuration "nowhere" works
as the most formidable contestation of what is. What some,
for example, call cultural revolution proceeds from the possible to the real, from fantasy to reality.
—PAUL RICOEUR, *From Text to Action*

Performance, as I argued by discussing monopolylogue performers in the
last chapter, offers a way to practice imagining new forms of social relationships. I believe in theater's use value as a place to fantasize how peace
and justice, equality and truly participatory democracy might take hold
sometime in a near or distant future, as well as in theater's value as a place
in which to connect emotionally and spiritually with other people. Seeing
performance requires that we listen attentively to the speech of others, that
we hear people speak and feel their humanity and its connections with our
own. Performance creates ever-new publics, groups of spectators who
come together for a moment and then disperse out across a wide social
field, sometimes (hopefully) sharing the knowledge they gained, the emotions and insights they experienced at the theater. Chapters 4 and 5 ask
more specifically, How can performance model civic engagement in participatory democracy? How might performance let us rehearse truly
democratic public practices through a kind of social mimesis? That is,
instead of art imitating life, how might we bend life to imitate theater, with
its necessity for attentive listening, for dialogic reciprocity, for the company (and kindness) of strangers? Attending and creating theater is an act
of civic engagement that can illustrate other ways to "do" local and global
politics.

Theorists of the public sphere—Jürgen Habermas, Nancy Fraser, and
Chantal Mouffe, among them—see it as a site of discourse set apart from
the more institutionalized apparatus of the state, like the government or
the courts, or newspapers and the media. The public sphere is ad hoc and
spontaneous; its very informality keeps it free of the surveillance that con-
strains more structured, regulated systems. In Fraser's estimation, "The
idea of the 'public sphere' . . . is . . . theatre in modern societies in which
political participation is enacted through the medium of talk."[1] Through
discursive engagement (literally, through talking), people constitute themselves as citizens, subjects who both acquiesce to and dissent from the
mandates of the hegemonic (or more insidiously put, "leaderless") state.
Fraser says the public sphere "is not an arena of market relations but rather
one of discursive relations, a theatre for debating and deliberating rather

than for buying and selling."[2] Although she uses "theatre" metaphorically, the term seems appropriate for how it conveys a sense of public forum, for how it resonates with an aura of debate. And although this sphere of communal life is not a market for the exchange of goods, it is, following sociologist Robert Putnam, a place where people exchange ideas, where they promote and collect certain kinds of social capital and, when theatergoing anchors the public sphere, the kind of meaningful cultural capital theorized by sociologist Pierre Bourdieu.[3]

Thinking of performance as a public practice through which radical democracy might rehearse places it within a particular, grounded context, rather than an elitist or romantic one. People *do* performance, in both performative and material ways; publicly practicing performance makes it a tool of both expression and intervention, of communication and fantasy, of reality and hope. Performance is "an activity in which we engage," rather than "a thing or a collection of things."[4] Removing performance from contemplative Kantian aesthetics into the material realm of activity makes it accessible to a larger public, to people who can use it for leisure, for entertainment, or for intervening in the conduct of their lives. Thinking of performance as a social practice allows us to start, as theater theorist Alan Read suggests, "with those in mind who do not expect representation, who are nevertheless the cause of all writing and labor, a lay man and woman whose everyday lives are an infinite improvisation of making do, of making up and making theatre. Such broad statements serve to clarify that an understanding of theatre as 'conduct of life' has always been in tension with the notion of theatre as 'specialized activity.'"[5] The performances on which I focus in this chapter and the next, as well as elsewhere in this book, exemplify theater as a conduct of life, a place to rehearse our potentially full and effective participation in a more radical, participatory, representative democracy.[6]

Each of the performances I discuss in chapters 4 and 5 consider theater a vital part of the public sphere, refusing the conventional separation of audience and performers to reach instead across the footlights toward intersubjective intimacy and encouragement, respect and grace. Chapters 2 and 3 of *Utopia in Performance* looked at autobiographical feminist and then multicharacter solo performance as incubators for utopian performatives. Chapters 4 and 5 survey three performances that differ in form but display a common desire for using their enactment as an example of critical civic engagement. These pedagogical performances demonstrate how to be active citizens to audiences who might not regularly see themselves as agents in their own lives, let alone in their political systems. They also teach people how to be spectators for a particular event, and how to participate, perhaps differently than usual, in constituting an audience, a public. The experiences of theatergoing I discuss here fashioned utopian performatives from the urgency of their address, revising the terms of conventional theater and performance to invite citizen-spectators into a critical conversation about politics and oppression, about love and hope. In their utopic, performative enunciations and in their imaginative use of the physical space of the stage and the theater auditorium, these productions performed an alternative to present social relations by using metaphor, language, dialogue, images, movement, sound, presence, and desire to model what utopia might feel like. By focusing on the "now" of performance, on the affect and impact of the present moment, utopian performatives let us embody conditions of which we can otherwise only dream. Perhaps, in fact, performance is an act of public dreaming.

For example, *Russell Simmons Def Poetry Jam on Broadway* uses the language and structure of slam poetry to create a powerful evening of theatrical virtuosity in which the young cast speaks in their own words their urgent dreams, their fervent wishes, and their exquisite determination that their poems can make a difference in public life. *Def Poetry Jam* uses words and the charismatic presence of its multiracial performers to sound a fierce, sometimes anguished cry for respect, dignity, and difference in a culture that deeply suspects people because of the color of their skin. The performance opened the theater into a public sphere in which new ideas for social relations might be rehearsed.

Moisés Kaufman and Tectonic Theatre's *The Laramie Project,* which I discuss in chapter 5, is a play based on interviews conducted by company members with citizens of Laramie, Wyoming, shortly after gay college student Matthew Shepard was brutally beaten to death in a chilling incident of hate as crime in October 1998. My own complex response to the script and the two productions of the play I've seen—one the New York City production with the original cast, the other an Austin production at our professional, Equity theater—teases out the challenges of using the methods and metaphors of theater to consider how the play's subjects and its audiences participate in democratic local and national life. Although a documentary play about a heinous crime seems an unlikely site for utopian performatives, I want to suggest that through the idiom of performance, a collective, metaphorical redemption became possible in production, moments of utopian performativity that showed spectators possibilities beyond the degradations of the present. By underlining the audience's constitution as a public, or as an important part of the public sphere, these productions illuminated participatory democracy as a practice of speech.[7]

At each of these performances, I felt myself part of a different kind of public sphere, invited by the apparatus of production to engage a conversation about democracy at a historical moment in which constitutional rights were being flagrantly challenged. I saw these productions in 2002–3, a turbulent moment in American history. The George W. Bush administration was contemplating its strike against Iraq, pumping what turned out to be flawed intelligence propaganda into the American media to fan the flames of righteous warmongering. At the same time, U.S. residents felt particularly vulnerable to terrorism and germ warfare, not that long after the World Trade Center collapse and the anthrax scare. People opened their mail cautiously, and found themselves startled by any unexplained white powdery substances they came across in their workday lives. Racial profiling and the enforcement of the Patriot Act shrank civil liberties; citizens who looked Middle Eastern fell immediately under suspicion because of their facial features or skin color. Americans who demonstrated and spoke out against the war had to balance their criticism of the American government's tactics of distraction (after all, wasn't the disappeared Osama bin Laden, not Saddam Hussein, the more obvious evildoer in this post–September 11 landscape?) and their very real fear of potential bioterror or other fatal attacks.

While the grief over the World Trade Center's destruction brought the nation together, the zealous xenophobia of its aftermath quickly tore us apart. Chauvinism shrinks nationalism to the smallest possible definition, narrowing the presumption of citizenship to ever-smaller categories (like white, male, heterosexual, native-born, Christian). The never-firm membrane between religion and the state broke easily, allowing politicians like then attorney general John Ashcroft to determine and implement his own definitions of patriotism, citizenship, and treason.[8] The rush to consensus cancels dissent and vehemently marginalizes those who refuse to swallow official interpretations without careful analysis and healthy doubt.

This atmosphere threatens civil liberties. The United States holds political prisoners indefinitely in detention camps like Guantanamo Bay in Cuba without recourse to lawyers or the clarity of formal charges; conservative student groups blacklist university professors if their classes are too "political" (usually meaning if the instructors mention opposition to the war in Iraq or try to engage students in critical thinking about American culture at all);[9] and even the small increments toward gay and lesbian social parity achieved through the Supreme Court decision overturning *Bowers v. Hardwick* and the Massachusetts Supreme Court decision securing marriage as a constitutional right regardless of gender or sexual identity, cause uproarious backlash in the popular imagination. The social and the political, never distinct, entangle more and more complexly with chilling consequences. Taking a stand on the war in Iraq, on the cartoon-like capture of Saddam Hussein in December 2003, or on the abrupt curtailment of First Amendment rights can brand a citizen a traitor.

Each of the performances I address here seemed prescient in how they anticipated and engaged the vagaries of this complex present. *Def Poetry Jam,* through its poets' direct address, presumed an audience in its multiracial likeness and demonstrated how their concerns are part of what constitutes "America." *The Laramie Project,* especially in its Austin production, asked audiences to literally stand and be counted as residents of the town mulling over their responsibility (collective or individual) for Matthew Shepard's murder. Each production raised the question of citizenship, participation in democracy, and public accountability, though because of their different production contexts and their origins at different moments in history for different audiences, these questions fell differently on spectators' ears. *Def Poetry Jam* was a Broadway production of slam poetry, an art form popularized in urban communities and through the success of the HBO series of the same name; *The Laramie Project* was an off-Broadway production performed by the very actors who conducted the interviews with the townspeople of Laramie about a highly publicized tragedy; and the third was a regional theater's production, in Austin, of the Tectonic Theatre Project's play.

These productions offered different strategies for civic engagement through performance, which emerged from the relationship each established among content, form, and context. They offered different examples of dialogue and different forms for speech. They created different vehicles in which to experience the prelinguistic longing that's first shaped by structures of feeling, then actively articulated through theatrical performance, when speaking becomes a public practice of insurgent movement toward a truer, more inclusive democracy. These performances practiced with their audiences ways of being together that captured, however briefly, a process of striving, of imagining a more humane, less divisive, pleasurable, respectful relationship among us. They practiced making publics by discarding the conventions of theater that require distanced, polite, aesthetic contemplation, to actively and intentionally persuade spectators to acknowledge the moment and to share what they felt, to *talk* in the present of performance.

These performances also suggest how the experience of being at the theater can make us feel hope and possibility in the copresence we share with other spectators and performers. All three directly engage democracy and citizenship, even though these issues needn't be present for utopian performatives to happen. Utopian visions, in fact, can be defined "in terms of their function as inspiration . . . allow[ing] content and form to be more fluid."[10] Instead of "narrating stories about perfect social worlds, we [can] use the idea of utopia to challenge us to explore a range of possible human conditions."[11] Paul Ricoeur, a theorist of narrative and interpretation, also argues that the "specific contents of proposed utopias" need to be overcome. He writes, "This paradox provides us with a clue for interpreting the utopian moment in terms of a theory of the imagination rather than emphasizing its content."[12] In theater, we can experiment with these imaginative visions, breathe life into the golems of possibility, move bodies and create images and sounds in ways that let spectators feel the material potential of living in a social world rearranged by valuing peace and harmony, instead of war and strife.

Showing Up: Converging Publics at the Theater

Composing, enacting, and experiencing performance requires social optimism, and relies on faith in people's desire to come together in groups to experience an expressive, symbolic world, one that might open "the field of the possible . . . beyond that of the actual, a field for alternative ways of living."[13] Theater makers create performances and, believing deeply in the power and elasticity of community, advertise their work, tell and show people what they've done, and invite public response. People come to see and share theater with them, arriving at previously announced times and places. What an act of faith that is, to open the doors of a theater to an ever-changing public, a public that, as queer theorist and activist Michael Warner suggests, is only constituted in the moment during which it's addressed.[14] Imagine the nexus of overlapping social commitments and interests that constitutes any audience for any performance. Imagine numerous potential spectators, reading the local paper, circling something that piques their interest, making arrangements to drive, to walk, to take a bus or a subway to the theater, to have dinner beforehand with friends, or to go out after for conversation and a bite to eat, embedding their spectatorship in a larger process of sociable cultural engagement, the larger world of Schechner's gathering-performing-dispersing matrix.[15] Imagine all those potentially interested people converging at the same place and time, with the express intent to see a performance. The hope these practices enact sometimes amazes me, especially in an era when leisure has become ubiquitous and fluid, when cinemaplexes offer multiple starting times for films, and fitness centers are open around the clock. As one arts reporter notes, "Americans increasingly favor activities that enable them to choose the time they take their leisure—perhaps explaining in part the record levels of attendance at art museums, where audiences can attend whenever they choose during open hours, as opposed to a performance, where the curtain rises at a specific time."[16]

When I go to the theater, I'm invariably surprised that all these people have chosen to come, have acted on their interest or desire or need to be together for a few hours with relative strangers to witness the telling of stories, the creation of images, the magic of theatricality, the wonder of imaginations at work in this crucible of light and texture and sound. When I see people converge, and when I'm part of that convergence, I'm already moved by this demonstration of community, by the faith we've brought to the importance of gathering together. The act of coming, of showing up, signals to me that communities still constitute themselves around the importance of physical presence.

Sociologist Robert Putnam, in his popular book *Bowling Alone*, argues that community has disappeared in America, and that people need to reconnect once again through social networks of interactive contact. Putnam says, "'[S]howing up' provides a useful standard for evaluating trends in associational life in our communities."[17] Theater still depends on such a social contract, establishing a start time that requires us to make concessions to the temporal demands of our lives. Seeing theater and performance requires us to show up in the evening at eight o'clock or at two o'clock or three o'clock matinees, to put our bodies in a place where artists tell their stories and paint their pictures, where our *presence* is necessary to complete a loop of meaning. Films spool through projectors impervious to the liveness of their audience; people graze at filmgoing, fitting movies into the interstices of their lives. But performance (even more spontaneous street performances, or demonstrations, or other performances in everyday life) require the presence of bodies and the act of showing up to perform or to witness.[18]

Theater also requires attentive listening, which models a mode of civic discourse that our sound-bite society often precludes. Ben Cameron, the executive director of the professional organization Theatre Communications Group, says that going to see theater demands an intensity of listening unlike other forms of media or arts or entertainment. In fact, when I attend a performance, once the lights go down it takes me a moment to accustom myself to this different form of concentrated listening. If the play is exposition heavy, it takes me a moment to catch up with the narrative events because my mind is too busy absorbing all the visual and emotional and aural stimuli and situating myself in the presence of the "not real." Gertrude Stein describes this experience at the theater as "syncopated time"; she says it takes us a moment to settle into the very different rhythm of the live actors' speech and their embodiedness in front of us. Stein says, "Your sensation . . . in relation to the play played before you . . . your emotion concerning that play is always either behind or ahead of the play at which you are looking and to which you are listening."[19] Theater theorist Kate Davy, explicating Stein's idea, says that "syncopation occurs whenever the spectator stops (whether to remember, reconsider any number of variables, doze, or check the program for an actor's name), while the play continues. Having stopped or paused, the spectator must then 'catch up,' emotionally, in an effort to match the emotional movement of the event on stage."[20]

Spectators come to theater not only to witness, not only to passively consume, but also to participate by actively imagining other worlds. Performance remains an incomplete form, whose address is only fulfilled in the moment of reception. As director Mary Zimmerman, whose production *Metamorphoses* I discuss in the last chapter, says, "That's the pleasure of the theatre: the slippage of difference between what you're seeing and what you know you're seeing. That square box [the stage] can fill up with almost anything. In movies, it's a special effect. Here, it's achieved by an act of faith."[21] In that present, live moment, the synergy of the actor's embodiment and the spectator's willing imagination creates possibility, the potential for new understanding and insight charged by the necessity of intersubjectivity.

The German Marxist philosopher Ernst Bloch, writing on the utopian function in art, says the process of imagination itself is "expectant and has an objective presentiment of the not-yet-developed as well as something not-yet-well-developed. The awareness of the frontline position is the best illumination for it; the utopian function, as the comprehended activity of expectation, of a hopeful presentiment, keeps the alliance with everything dawning in the world. . . . [T]he utopian function is the unimpaired reason of a militant optimism."[22] By bringing such militant optimism into the public sphere, performance presents another way to dissent from state regulation and ideological fixity.

Warner suggests that a public is a "cultural form, a kind of practical fiction" necessary to the circulation of discourse through a "social imaginary," by which he means that publics are really fictions we imagine through how we participate in them.[23] By attending any given performance, I become part of the public it addresses. A public is a "relation among strangers," a combination of anonymity and intimacy organized through a laserlike attention in the moment of discursive connection.[24] Warner says, "The act of attention involved in showing up is enough to create an addressable public. Some kind of active uptake . . . is indispensable."[25] *Def Poetry Jam* and *The Laramie Project* solicit active uptake by inviting their audiences to sing, to speak, to discuss, to stand and honor, as well as using the more conventional uptake mechanisms of performance, which prompt audiences toward respectful applause at the curtain call, and toward questions during postshow discussions if spectators or performers care to stay. The audience's self-declared interest in these performances perhaps guarantees their success; as theater scholar John Fletcher says, "The work of converting strangers into a community able to share a utopic moment is made possible by virtue of the fact that these performances aim at a conversion of those 'strangers' who are *in a larger but nonetheless significant sense* already converted."[26] The act of showing up proves them receptive, converts already to the effectiveness of performance as a public practice; their presence at the theater signals (hopefully) their willingness to think, to feel, to engage.

I always remember who accompanied me to a certain play or performance. My memories of performance begin materially: "I saw . . . with . . . at . . . in . . ." I recall almost palpably the energy between us as we absorbed the moment together, the discussions we had afterwards, the tendrils of emotional connection growing between us as we watched. The localness of theater and people's spectating practices means that we often know someone else in the audience, especially those of us who return with commitment to certain theaters, or who regularly follow the work of certain companies, playwrights, actors, or directors. Many theatergoers return to the same theaters again and again, and comprise, with other spectators (strangers or friends) a faithful audience for the work.[27] Warner would suggest that when we know some of the people in the audience with us, and when we're addressed together from the stage, such intimacy enables the public we create to be a "scene of practical possibility"; what he calls the "unknown" element in a public—the strangers who surround us in temporary community—offers a "hope of transformation."[28] Experiencing a utopian performative perhaps requires both—friends or acquaintances and strangers—to create the conditions in which utopia might be "done." Perhaps this is what draws me to theater with such belief in its transformative powers—the new worlds it creates with each showing, the potential, each evening or afternoon in the dark auditorium, of feeling myself part of a public newly constituted, held together in the moment of performance by a filament of faith. That common faith exercises itself through the active imagination necessary to flesh out the meanings of performance. Since performance is only a liminal, temporary locale, a no-place like utopia, it brings us to the threshold of change, offering a purchase from which to look over into an alternative—even if inaccessible—version of social relations.

Theater scholar David Román, for example, recalls attending Tony Kushner's *Angels in America* in its Los Angeles premiere, just before the 1992 presidential elections. Román describes the social practice of going with his friends to see Kushner's very long two-part play as an act of endurance founded on the need for community and on their mutual respect for the actors' labor and for their own work to make meaning. "On the eve of the elections," he writes, "the hope of *Perestroika*, rekindled in the play through love and kinship, announced a shift from the utopic to the possible."[29] Telling his story, Román says, "We return again and again to the space of performance."[30]

Def Poetry Jam Writes America

Imagination is the bridge between
the things we know for sure
and the things we need to believe
When our world become [sic] unbearable. . . .
I believe our lives are often shorter

Then [*sic*] we expect
So for as long as we can, I believe
we should believe in some things
we don't know for sure
Acknowledge the range
of possibilities not limited by what we see
move reality with imagination
we decide what our destinies will be.
—Staceyann Chin, *Def Poetry Jam*

Russell Simmons Def Poetry Jam on Broadway accrues its social capital by calling into existence a more diverse public than those that usually gather to see theater on Broadway. The production enters the public sphere as a forum of what could be, discarding political pieties to encapsulate experience in a vivid, present sense of "now." Queer theorist Lauren Berlant says, "[P]oliticized feeling is a kind of thinking that too often assumes the obviousness of the thought it has, which stymies the production of the thought it might become."[31] On the contrary, instead of being didactic, in *Def Poetry Jam*, the poets unhinge politics and feeling from obviousness to engage the audience imaginatively with what might be. The show's nine poets demand attentive listening. Their generosity with their vivid stories and their beautiful words creates a public audience buoyed by intersubjectivity, one that reciprocates by talking back, by letting the poets know, in the moment of performance, that they are seen and heard.

Def Poetry Jam was the brainchild of Russell Simmons, the hip-hop entrepreneur who cofounded Def Jam Records, established a clothing line called Phat Farm apparel, and produces two HBO series, *Def Comedy Jam* and the made-for-television version of *Def Poetry Jam*. Simmons also runs the Hip-Hop Summit Action Network, which he founded in 2001 to promote economic and social justice.[32] Simmons used the network to head a voter registration drive among his fan base for the 2004 election. Although entrepreneurship and progressive politics sometimes seem strange bedfellows, Simmons insists that in his case one enables the other. "My Phat Farm sneakers?" he told an interviewer. "They underwrite the economic-justice campaign that traveled around the country. . . . I give to 50 charities," he remarked.[33] When Simmons sold his share of Def Jam Recording, he made an estimated $130 million.[34] Clearly, Simmons's wealth, acquired by cashing in on a cultural form mostly associated with underprivileged, poor young people, makes him a target of political suspicion as well as social admiration. But after all, Simmons isn't Philip Morris; his products popularize a cultural genre and capitalize on a moment that's riding the wave of fashion. That he puts money and attention into the political process and uses his clout to encourage young people to vote lets him lend his power to progressive causes and to intervene in conservative discourses. By bringing *Def Poetry Jam* to Broadway, for example, Simmons ushered slam poetry through a cultural circuit from the small urban coffeehouses in which the form was born in the mid-1980s (most commentators say in Chicago, where a local poet organized a weekly competition)[35] to the popular (if limited, subscription-only) audience of HBO to the forum that Broadway represents in the national imagination.

The show, created explicitly for Broadway, rather than moved from an off- or off-off-Broadway theater, presents poems performed solo, in duets or trios, or sometimes in chorus. Underscored by music played by an onstage DJ using two turntables, the solos are punctuated with moments of group poetry in which the performers thread their own ways through a common theme. While conventional slam poetry is solo, performed consecutively by single poets for the same audience, *Def Poetry Jam* as a theater performance makes slam dialogic, rather than monologic, and exemplifies how democracy might work, as well as revitalizing its content. The production models a practice of speaking that creates a public sphere through its address to a large audience, and by the conversation it stages among poets around similar political, as well as aesthetic, concerns.

Def Poetry Jam presents its poets in direct address to an audience filled with young people, many of them people of color.[36] The poets speak to each other occasionally, but the audience serves as their primary interlocutor, which opens the stage to the zeitgeist rather than closing it off as an observed, pristinely preserved museum. The performance constitutes dialogue by assuming a very specific "you" as its spectators; from that "you" can be constituted what Marxist political theorist Chantal Mouffe calls a "political community," in which "what makes us fellow citizens . . . is not a substantive idea of the good, but a set of political principles specific to [liberal democracy]: the principles of freedom and equality for all."[37] Staged as part of such a conversation, *Def Poetry Jam* becomes a vehicle for radical democratic citizenship.

The production's graceful theatrical lighting and the schematic, geometric set enhance the presence and talent *Def Poetry Jam*'s performers extend into the house. They would be resplendent without any theatrical apparatus, as many of them were in their original slam performances, but performing in a conventional theater empowers them to make a social statement, to take a public forum and claim it for their own. Their presence on Broadway makes their words precious, valuable, and inspires moments of communitas among strangers, moments when people sense themselves in sync with the group in a common sentiment of wonder, magic, and possibility. Theater scholar Shannon Baley describes the way in which, for the HBO version of the show, a kind of "authenticity" is manufactured; that is, the production is carefully geared to appear street-wise and unrefined, even though its very presence on the network already marks it as commodified, slick, and, she suggests, compromised.[38] On Broadway, however, something of the live, the "raw" (although clearly mediated), is restored to the performances, whose very lack of theatrical polish and discipline makes the poets' words seem more immediate and "real." Stan Lathan, the production's director, says, "I try to keep it as spontaneous as possible. . . . We try not to over-rehearse. The key is that the poets come out and there's honesty. They try to convey what they felt as they wrote the poem and what it does to them now."[39] The production commandeers authenticity, while at the same time, the performers obviously had to manufacture the polish and precision required for a relatively long run in a Broadway show: they had to learn to be an ensemble; to share the stage with each other; to listen and react to the others' speech; to produce a group ethic around common themes; and repeat their poems and make them sound fresh night after night. This contradiction between the poets' supposed spontaneity and their carefully produced, professionalized collective ethos helped give the production a complex edge, and contributed to its fruitfully uneasy habitation on Broadway.

Much of the press around the show and commentary in the published script underlines the producers' pride that the poets actually appeared for every show. Their remarks emphasize that slam poetry is usually a one-off event, and that the repetition of performing the same show each night on Broadway, hitting their marks and observing lighting and music cues, is alien to the culture of slam. For example, the introduction to poet Black Ice's biographical poem in the published script says, "Broadway was a hard routine for an ex-hustler to crack, but 'Ice' never missed a show; a testimony to how much he's turned himself into the messenger of the Earth he was destined to be. 'Every night I had to reinvent those poems because there is someone out in that audience that needs to hear what I'm about to spin.'"[40] The poets' challenge was to keep it real in its repetition; they did so by keeping their listeners, their interlocutors, clearly in mind and by considering themselves public prophets, messengers of and for the people.

The fact that the performers consistently "showed up," which Putnam underlines as so important for community, secures the utopian performative as a "doing" of performers, as well as spectators.

The performers in *Def Poetry Jam* speak urgently to the audience, with torrents of words that resound like anthems to the necessity for social change, whether they're describing lives lived in shame or in anger, in glory or in fear. Their love poems are sweet, drenched in the now, and lift their subjects with a kind of reverence into the fullness of hope that outlines the possible. Jack Zipes, in his introduction to Bloch's *The Utopian Function of Art and Literature,* says, "Literature and art [and I would add performance] contain the anticipatory illumination of that which has not yet become, and the role of the writer and artists is similar to that of a midwife who enables latent and potential materials to assume their own unique forms."[41] *Def Poetry Jam* performs such midwifery, eagerly illuminating how radical democracy might feel, in a celebration of agency that values each individual voice in this panoply of identities and imagines them harmonizing. The performance collectively argues for reenvisioning the nation as fully inclusive, and invites the audience to revel in the power, beauty, compassion, and necessity of this speech. The performance reverses the national dystopia of, for instance, Holly Hughes's *Preaching to the Perverted,* by insisting on the right of queer people and people of color and poor people to define themselves as American. Where in their solo performances, Lily Tomlin, Danny Hoch, and Anna Deavere Smith embody in themselves a multiplicitous citizenry and perform the "as if" of its social dialogue, *Def Poetry Jam* gathers people across difference and uses the forum of the stage and the vehicle of performance to actually rehearse speaking to and with each other. As Beau Sia, one of the poets, says about slam in general, "[I]t has brought a lot of kids together around the things affecting their world, who might not have even spoken to each other" (110).

The evening's structure exemplifies a slam poetry performance more than it does a conventional theater event.[42] The night I saw *Def Poetry Jam,* the DJ warmed up the crowd before he introduced the poets. He taught us to respond to this performance as we would a rock concert or a religious service. By playing music, he helped spectators relax into their occupation of the Great White Way, transforming a theater not typically associated with hip-hop style into a place where young people could feel comfortable. In many ways, in fact, the most unusual, potentially radical part of the performance wasn't the multiracial identity of the ensemble, but the generational difference from the median age of the typical Broadway audience that their relative youth, and the youth of the audience they attracted, brought to the theater.[43]

Def Poetry Jam's slam poetry and its hip-hop style defamiliarizes the theater and signals that all conventions will be suspended. That sense of discarding rules, of spontaneous speaking from the heart, lights the way to what Bloch calls the hopeful function of art as "anticipatory illumination." The critical reception to *Def Poetry Jam* in fact emphasized its rule-breaking, pioneering presence, without always seeing this as positive. Tony Vellela, writing for the *Christian Science Monitor,* says, "On a street map, it's a short 10 blocks from hip-hop mogul Russell Simmons's office on Seventh Avenue to Broadway's Longacre Theatre. On a cultural map, it can seem like a million miles. His latest vision, *Russell Simmons Def Poetry Jam on Broadway,* has made that journey, landing like a meteor in the middle of a theater scene more known for *Cats* and cartoons than cutting edge. While Broadway has seen other nontraditional offerings in recent years, . . . *Def Poetry Jam* breaks new ground."[44] Mimicking hip-hop "attitude," Ed Siegel, writing in the *Boston Globe,* begins his review, "Yo, dude. Got somethin' to tell ya. BROADWAY RULES!" He goes on to say, "When was the last time the Great White Way was so welcoming to other skin and hair colors?"[45] Elysa Gardner, writing in *USA Today,* says, "To say that *Russell Simmons Def Poetry Jam* isn't your grandmother's Broadway show would be an understatement."[46] In *Variety,* the industry standard, Charles Isherwood says of the show that Broadway has "seen nothing like it before."[47] Jon Pareles of the *New York Times* was one of the few writers in national newspapers to describe the event more neutrally, writing, "For the first time on Broadway, poetry with hip-hop roots is at centerstage." He noted, "While other Broadway theatres are filled with *Les Miserables,* revivals of old musicals and revues based on familiar songs, *Def Poetry Jam* is up to the minute. . . . 'This show is not going to be engraved in stone,' Mr. Lathan [the production's director] said. 'The poems are constantly being updated.' "[48]

Taken together, these comments underline *Def Poetry Jam*'s radical unfamiliarity to its august context, while at the same time, they express a certain anxiety about what the production's arrival on Broadway means. Rather than applauding the show as a milestone, as an important breakthrough for identity groups who haven't before wielded the power of such a visible public forum, some of these writers try to contain the show's potential interventions, reassigning it to familiar categories of cultural work that can be more easily dismissed. Gardner, in *USA Today,* for instance, says that the show's "more stringent social commentary tends to strike one note, and it's a predictable one. However superficially contro- versial their views, all adhere neatly to the rules on which political correct- ness is founded: 1) Insults are most acceptable when directed toward your own social or ethnic group or, even better, a group perceived as more empowered. 2) Preaching is easiest when you're facing the choir."[49] What Gardner neglects to take into account is that this "choir" is newly consti- tuted at this site; as her own review notes in her lead, this is not "your grandmother's Broadway show." Implicit in her comment, in the "your" to whom she addresses her review, is the reader's presumptive whiteness, middle-classness, and his or her comfortable remove from what another critic called "another popular injection of 'urban' culture into mainstream entertainment."[50] "Urban," in these reviews, comes to stand for multira- cial; "urban" is shorthand for "inner city," which is shorthand, in the national imagination, for African American, and government housing, and drugs, and poverty, and crime. These images juxtapose tacitly with "your" implicitly white grandmother, who presumably owns Broadway.

These critics' anxiety, then, comes from their sense of displacement from a center typically held by elite white audiences. This anxiety seeps into some of their writing on the show's content; Siegel, the *Globe* writer, tries to deflect the importance of the diversity he sees not just by mocking its dialect in his review's lead, but by declaring, "The nine poets follow one another onstage, forming a kind of victimization-on-parade."[51] The accu- sation of "victim art," flung so disdainfully into American culture in the mid-1990s by *New Yorker* dance critic Arlene Croce against gay African American dancer Bill T. Jones, continues to provide a silencing and con- tainment strategy.[52] If the potential radicality of *Def Poetry Jam* can be neu- tralized under the terms "victim art" and "political correctness," then per- haps its incursion into territory usually secured for whiteness can momentarily be tolerated and quickly dismissed.

The beginning of *Def Poetry Jam* works explicitly against such disap- probation by making the theater familiar for the young, multiracial audi- ence that might not know its conventional rules.[53] Once he secured the generationally coherent public community, the DJ asked the audience to sing songs that were obviously familiar to many of them, and most of them did. Their voices rose spontaneously in unison, and at the end of each refrain, they laughed at their own commonality, at the cultural markers and lyrics and melodies they knew together, even though most of them didn't know each other and few of them probably knew the conventionally polite and silent, mostly white, middle-class codes of mainstream theater-going. I saw the show with my friend Vicki Patraka; we're both white, both middle-aged, both professors, both Jewish, and both chewed on ginger candies to soothe our throats and stomachs after our pretheater dinner. While much of the audience sang, we looked at each other wide-eyed, at once impressed and moved by the singing and at a total loss about the melodies or the lyrics of the songs. The music didn't hail us; we're outside its intended generation. (Clearly, we're of the generation and the demographic most of the anxious reviews meant to address.) But we appreciated the suspension of the theater's imposing rules, and enjoyed the sound of strangers singing spontaneously in unison.[54]

The DJ spun songs that not only inspired an interactive, pleasurable, and appreciative mood, but also established a shared sense of cultural place. He encouraged the audience to make noise, to take control of their evening instead of sinking into reactive passivity. He addressed us generically as "New York," a multiplicitous geography by which everyone in the audience seemed hailed, a gesture reminiscent of touring musicians and comedians who say, "We love you Austin," or "Pittsburgh," or "Madison," or wherever they happen to be, signaling their acknowledgment of the audience as a specific public constituted by this particular occasion, while also calling forth civic community and perhaps even pride.[55] Such hailing also imported the codes of concert-going to a theater event, and perhaps reassured spectators less accustomed to attending a Broadway show.

The audience at *Def Poetry Jam* became a public called into being by the DJ's direct address, by the language of hip-hop (which circulates as community discourse well beyond the confines of the stage), by the music's call for a response, and by our knowledge of the conventions of our own various cultural expressions (since not all of us were so young and some of us appeared to be white), made pleasurably elastic by sharing music together in this old Broadway house. After he played a few preparatory songs, the DJ introduced the poets like athletes being announced on to the field, which, in addition to the concert-going codes, also emphasized the performance traditions of leisure and sports that might resonate with young audiences. He called out each performer's name and hometown as they ran out to center stage, and ended with the triumphant announcement, "This is *Def Poetry Jam*."[56]

The set, framed by flats of metal that looked like the back of garage doors, signaled a no-place, a space of utopic vision and imagined possibility drawn mostly by words.[57] Simple abstract shapes framed the actors when they performed, and lights sculpted their faces, etching the contours of bodies whose lived experience and fiercely outsiders' perspectives was integral to the words they shared. The set's lack of specificity evoked a moment out of time, suspended apart from the banality of daily life, which cultural theorist Richard Dyer suggests is key to the utopic undertones of entertainment.[58] The intertextuality of the slam poetry genre refers to other cultural forms and other social practices, making the production not an isolated, elite artistic expression, but one that's intimately and emphatically connected to larger cultural life and other social worlds.

In their performances, in fact, the poets became social prophets, heralding the possibility of an elsewhere where generosity graces vulnerability, where pride replaces pain, where the stuff of daily life becomes transformative rather than constraining. As historian Robin Kelley says, "[T]he most radical art is not protest art but works that take us to another place, envision a different way of seeing, perhaps a different way of feeling."[59] The essence of such art, and the social movements it supports, is what Kelley calls the "collective desires of people in motion, freedom, and love."[60] The poems in *Def Poetry Jam,* which often sounded like manifestos, were delivered like prayers, for freedom, for community, for a new harmonious nation that starts here, now, in this theater and then through its doors, outside.[61] The performance suggested "utopia can be an ongoing task rather than a resting place," a process of discovering and imagining other ways of finding common cause.[62]

The poems moved from solo pieces to collective riffs, choral sections that spoke of desires filled in by the specifics of each poet's experience or dreams. These collective moments, too, raised the performance out of banality into the beautiful. As sociologist Robert Schehr says, writing about the operations of new social movements that showed utopian potential, "Individuals acting collectively frequently broke with the routinized mundanity of daily behavior, vigorously confronting that semipermeable membrane comprising [normally] accepted prescriptions for [valued, moral] behavior. In doing so they created a social space necessary for innovative thought and action."[63] Likewise, in *Def Poetry Jam,* the poets break through the membrane of convention and the banal, rejecting everyday oppressions and constraints. Adding their own verses to the refrain, "I write America," they imagined a wider, more capacious notion of citizenship, one in which young people of color and queers and other marginalized people subvert dominant language by making love with its words, making the "master's tools" erotic and empowering rather than deadening or oppressive.[64]

Steve Colman, the only white man in the production, riffed on Langston Hughes in his poem, "She":

> What happens to a rhyme deferred?
> Does it dry up
> while you're raising a son?
> Or does it expose
> the closed fists
> and broken dishes?
> What happens when
> you meet the genie
> but you can't make the wishes?
> When your hands demand an object
> that your fingers can't reach
> When the pot of gold
> is a promise
> that the rainbow can't keep.
>
> (45)

Heralding the power of words to describe the intensity of such personal and political pain, he said, "I wanna hear a poem / where ideas kiss similes so deeply / metaphors get jealous" (3). Biracial Mayda Del Valle declaimed about "descendancy" [*sic*], about the complexities of identities too numerous to be checked off neatly in census boxes:

> when the day is done
> the color of my skin still
> marks me as an alien in the country of my birth.
> I can't check myself into a box.
>
> (83)

Several of the poets spoke about body image, comparing their own self-impressions to the cultural stereotypes they know Americans bring to them. Georgie Me, for instance, an African American woman, in "Full Figure Potential: A Fat Girl's Blues," said, "With haste I race to the destruction of my waist" (7).

You might look at me and see lazy and weak giving
no second thought that
before you an angel may speak. . . .
Now we're supposed to respect everyone with
Different choices beliefs and hues
But who gives a damn about a fat girls blues.

(8)

Me moved easily from humor to critique, pointing to the stereotypes that "fat girls" (and fat African American girls, in particular) suffer.

Poetri, a full-figured African American man, in "Krispy Kreme," said,

This black militant fella once told me
that Krispy Kreme
used to be called Krispy Kreme Kroissants . . . AHA!!!
Kroissant spelled with a K . . .
Just like the rest of their names
meaning KKK!
They were started to keep the black man
down and round
so when the revolution comes back around
all the black men would be too fat to fight.

(37)

The poem is at once a self-mocking anthem to one man's inability to resist the siren song of fat-laden donuts and, at the same time, a rebuke of corporate cynicism and personal, political paranoia and a fairly reasonable (if ironic) assessment of counterinsurgency tactics. Poetri politically tempers his wry impression of his own body image, too; in another poem, he said, "I want to act like couples don't grab each other / when I walk by. / I like to fake like the police actually wave to me when I drive by" (10). Regardless of how Poetri feels about himself, he's seen through white people's eyes that read his skin color first and make instant presumptions about his intentions and their safety.

On stage, the poets seemed nearly on fire with their energy, with their urgent need to speak to the crowd, with their hope for the efficacy of words to help people think and see differently. The collective ode didn't valorize victimization—although many of the performers reported suffering under oppressive ideologies—but rallied the audience to the possibilities of a future. The poets called for hope and determination ("Can I get an amen?" one of them continually asked).[65] In the stirring finale, they passed a microphone among them for a moment of poetry staged as a gesture of community, of sharing amplified speech urgent to be heard. "I write America," each poet joined in on the refrain, adding their vision to their common promise: Suheir Hammad, a poet who refers to herself as a "Palestinian of African descent" (189), said, "I rewrite America" (103). Jamaican-Chinese-American lesbian Staceyann Chin said, "For the voices who broke the silence / I write America" (104). Georgia Me ended the poem and the production with, "Speak only the truth / so the blind can see / WE MUST MAKE AMERICA / A TRUE DEMOCRACY" (105).

As writer Arundhati Roy says, "What is happening to the world lies at the moment just outside the realm of common human understanding. It is the writers, the poets, the artists, the singers, the filmmakers who can make the connections." She continues, "[The world] offers opportunities for a new kind of art. An art which can make the impalpable palpable, make the intangible tangible, and the invisible visible. An art that can draw out the incorporeal adversary and make it real."[66] The civic gesture of *Def Poetry Jam* brings that incorporeal adversary to the stage, where the poets stand up to its realness, taunt it with imagination and strength, outlast it with their individual souls and with the community they call into being with their words.

The def poets created a dissenting public, one whose attention is lavished with love and care. Toward the end of the first act, when all the poets were onstage, they witnessed each other's solo moments from various perches on the garage-like set. They watched each other through complicated gazes of admiration, jealousy, and competition; the production, after all, originated in the vernacular of poetry slams, which are like intramural sports for writers. But the performers also honored one another's speech; they modeled an attentive community. Lemon mouthed the words of most of the others when they spoke, as though he could only remember *his* words as part of what for him became a seamless whole.[67] The intensity of the poets' listening was as strong as the spotlight that outlined each soloist; their attention brought almost physical support and laid claim, in those moments, to the utopian performative they shared together onstage. I could feel their energy straining toward each other, holding each other up, cheering each other on, picking up the cues, keeping the pace going, because ultimately, this show belonged to all of them, and they presented it to the audience not like an offering, not in humility, but as a declaration of their own reenvisioned independence, their own claim to citizenship, as a subaltern national anthem of fierce pride, as oppositional world-building, and as an insistent, cacophonous, hopeful march of dissident sound.

These moments of performance build by accretion into what Jewish theologian Martin Buber, describing the utopian element in socialism, calls "fantasy-pictures." Buber describes how these fantasy pictures might propel us into a more utopian reality:

> What, at first sight, seems common to the Utopias that have passed into the spiritual history of mankind, is the fact that they are pictures, and pictures moreover of something not actually present but only represented. Such pictures are generally called fantasy-pictures [that] center with architectonic firmness on something primary and original which it is [their] destiny to build; and this primary thing is a wish. . . . What is at work here is the longing for that *rightness* which, in religious or philosophical vision, is experienced as revelation or idea, and which of its very nature cannot be realized in the individual, but only in human *community*. The vision of "what should be" . . . is yet inseparable from a critical and fundamental relationship to the existing condition of humanity. . . . The longing for the realization of "the seen" fashions the picture.[68]

Seen from within the utopic gestures of a performance like *Def Poetry Jam*, our longing to realize a world rich in equality, social justice, and love, and without fear of terror, is made palpable and visible, felt as well as seen, mutely and somatically understood as well as stated.

In *Def Poetry Jam*, the fantasy pictures worked a kind of invitational narrative magic that is "*inherently* dialogic, even dialectical, inviting readers [and spectators] into active participation in the text, rather than relegating them to the status of passive observers."[69] The poets' imaginations, their vision of the world and what it could be, propelled the affective magic of the utopian performative, inspiring spectators to *do* something to make the world better. The power of the performance's affect translates into political effects, in that it opens a possibility for action that spectators might not, before, have felt or seen. The performance works emotionally to create in its presence and in its present a desire to feel like this outside of the theater; it creates a palpable sense that the world *could* feel like this, if every quotidian exchange were equally full of generosity, compassion, insight, and love. The performance creates a need, a desire to strive for this affective measure of goodwill, so that the glow of intersubjectivity and community might extend not just through the rest of this night, but through many others, as well. By creating this hope, by engaging this anticipatory illumination and watching these fantasy pictures, the performance can change consciousness and move people to change social conditions. The performers' platform is not *just* this theater, this "now," but resides in this world, declared across geography and time. *Def Poetry Jam* engages the constitution of our country to stretch it wider, to let the umbrella of true citizenship cover more of its people.[70] Performers and audience that night seemed to share a wish, which offered a soaring arc of potential that we could all ride, at our own pace, in our own ways, together.

chapter five

The Laramie Project

Rehearsing for the Example

The Laramie Project uses the idiom of performance to construct a public with which to examine the flaw in the social fabric illuminated by the murder of Matthew Shepard. On October 6, 1998, the twenty-one-year-old gay college student, out searching for a semblance of a queer life for himself in Laramie, Wyoming, was picked up in a bar by two local toughs who robbed Shepard, pistol-whipped him nearly to death, tied his wrists to a fence beside an isolated rural road, and abandoned him. Shepard was found the next day by a bicyclist, who called the local police. He was rushed to a hospital, where he died five days later, prompting demonstrations around the country and a national outcry against hate crimes. The Tectonic Theatre Project traveled to Laramie to create a performance based on the events; their motivating question, according to director Moisés Kaufman, was, "How is Laramie different from the rest of the country and how is it similar?"[1] The play establishes a constellation of relationships, of kinship and strangeness, of proximity and distance, as the Tectonic actors-cum-interviewers resided temporarily in Laramie, sifting through its people's public lives and secret feelings.

The play puts people in relation to each other, identifying the locals by what they do—the actors interview doctors, law enforcement agents, waitresses, ranchers, and more—and the Tectonic company by their expertise in performance. Like *Fires in the Mirror* and *Jails, Hospitals, and Hip-Hop*, the play creates a conversation among people who might not otherwise have spoken to each other—or not spoken these words in this way—creating a new public sphere in which to scrutinize the events leading up to and following Shepard's death. The townspeople study their souls as they search out culpability for the murder; the performers, most of them based with the company in New York, study the townspeople. From this rather uneven distribution of social and theatrical power, *The Laramie Project* uses performance to attempt to create a "we"—from the odd collection of people who comprise the play's community to the performers and spectators who come to participate in its dialogue to the complex entity we call the United States.

In the process, it miscalculates some strategies, most flagrantly by maintaining the binary of rural/urban that keeps the tragedy distanced, "othered" from those who consider themselves more sophisticated big-city-dwellers. The play absents Shepard from its structural heart, if not its emotional one—the play's singular focus on what happened to everyone else, before and after his beating and murder, peculiarly displaces what happened to him. Although *The Laramie Project* could be called a performed ethnography, based as it is on interviews with real people in a real community, it doesn't quite perform "finding one's feet in the shoes of another" as effectively as Tomlin, Smith, and Hoch, whose work I discuss in chapter 3. But despite my hesitations about the text, borne out as they were in the original Tectonic Theatre Project production of the play in New York, I found utopian performatives in an Austin restaging of the play that kindled my admiration for what *The Laramie Project* tries to accomplish: to create a play as a place where the promise of human community and even democracy might be momentarily enacted.

"The Whole Thing Ropes around Hope"

> I think it's a scary proposition to assume more political and aesthetic responsibility for your actions onstage. I see it as part of a radical democratic process. . . . We can mobilize people and engage them in exercises of radical imagination and radical border-crossings.
>
> —Guillermo Gómez-Peña, "Navigating the Minefields of Utopia"

Like *Def Poetry Jam*, *The Laramie Project* tries to secure its attachment to a certain authenticity of identity and the truth of experience, to bring new audiences to the theater, and to use performance as a forum for rehearsing the practice of politics. Moisés Kaufman and his Tectonic Theatre Project had previously garnered critical attention for their New York production *Gross Indecency: The Three Trials of Oscar Wilde* (1997), a script devised from court transcripts and secondary sources that commented on the event. This next play began as an ethnographic project, when the company traveled to Laramie to interview townspeople in the wake of the media uproar and political outcries over Matthew Shepard's murder by Aaron McKinney and Russell Henderson.[2] The visiting ethnographer-performers found the town nearly shattered when they arrived shortly after the furor had begun to die down, and their discussions with locals caught the townspeople in ambivalent ruminations about what had happened to them and what had happened to Shepard. The Tectonic Theatre Project interviewers attempted to stay self-reflexive about their own complicated positions as outsiders in the western prairie town, and to record their own doubts about their abilities to truly do justice to the complexities of the conflicting, bruising stories Laramie called forth after Shepard's death and his murderers' trials. The resulting play is a fascinating example of performance as public practice with the potential for utopian performatives, while it also exemplifies the pitfalls of truly trying to embody another's experience.

In the introduction to the published script, Kaufman describes the Tectonic Theatre Project's work as focused on "moments in history when a particular event brings the various ideologies and beliefs prevailing in a culture into sharp focus."[3] In this way, the company's work resembles Tomlin's, Smith's, and Hoch's, in that it intends to use performance to practice a conversation about tense current events, a discussion that might not be possible in the reality of history. And, like the feminist solo performances of "Throws Like a Girl," which I discussed in chapter 2, it uses performance to reflect on and to share feelings about personal experience with political resonance. The conventions of performance permit conversations and, in *Laramie*'s case, musings about ideas that otherwise might have remained private. Like the monopolylogue work of the three solo performers I discussed earlier, poetic license allows *Laramie* to act as a mediator among communities and factions that might otherwise regard each other with suspicion or, worse, not at all. Kaufman's project is explicitly political. He wonders, "[I]s theatre a medium that can contribute to the national dialogue on current events?" (vi). He begins the company's inquiry with an eye toward understanding the conditions that allowed Shepard's murder to happen there in Laramie and implicitly toward wondering how such a crime might happen "here," in the place from and in which the reader/spectator sees and lives and to which the ethnographer-performers return.

This motivating "there/here" binary often dictates the perspective on the events the play reports from Laramie and entangles its productions in important questions about the ethics of ethnography and of performance as a responsible practice of participatory democracy, questions worth exploring in detail before I proceed to describe the moments of utopian performativity I found in the Austin production of the play. Kaufman describes their work simply: "A theatre company travels somewhere, talks to people, and returns with what they saw and heard to create a play" (vi).[4] His Brechtian strategy of presenting what the company saw and heard offers a creative alternative to theatrical realism, since *Laramie* explicitly questions the performers' ability to capture or relate the truth of the experiences they gathered in Wyoming. But at the same time, the notion of "return" implies that the company has journeyed *out* to bring something *back*. The Tectonic's approach differs from more community-based theaters like Cornerstone or Roadside, which stay in the communities with whom they build their work and invite the townspeople to actually create the work with them, to perform in it themselves, or even to be present to witness performances.[5]

In the Tectonic Theatre's model, the ethnographers transform themselves into duly self-reflexive reporters, but the audience is positioned to see through their outsider's eyes and to reflect implicitly from a distance on the events that the townspeople in Laramie suffered. A member of the company reads from his journal, "I have no real interest in prying into a town's unraveling" (10). And yet *The Laramie Project* enacts exactly such an invasion of privacy. The text tries to even the score by shining the white light of inquiry onto the performers as well as the people they interview; the company's journals, for instance, become part of the public record plumbed here for ruminative effect. The intermingling of public and private discourses becomes one of the production's major themes, as the townspeople's homes and lives are disrupted by national media determined to burrow their way into choice facts about the community that raised such brutal murderers. When *The Laramie Project* represents the media, a stage direction suggests that their "cacophony . . . should feel like an invasion" (46), but such an injunction begs the question of why the ethnographers' presence, too, shouldn't also feel like a breech in the rightful boundaries of townspeople's homes.

The Tectonic's humanist, anthropological guise means to bring sympathy to Laramie, to make the townspeople's voices part of a national discussion about Shepard's death that for the most part excluded them. But the action constantly moves across the there/here divide, and the actors inevitably filter their impressions of the townspeople's lives. Although its motives are sympathetic and benign, the play positions the people of Laramie as specimens to be amiably studied by an audience that's presumed to be from New York (like the performers) or from other sophisticated urban centers. The project proceeds from the perspective of outsiders *for* outsiders, with the danger of condescension to the local using such a technique involves.

The play positions spectators alongside the performers in its epistemological project of coming to know Laramie. While Danny Hoch adopts the same strategy, giving spectators access to his characters through his eyes, *The Laramie Project* somehow maintains a separation between the two populations, whereas Hoch works harder and more analytically to bring them closer together. Here, the townspeople serve as teachers; the company learns from them not just their complicated reactions to Shepard's murder (which sometimes, in fact, fades as the play's inciting event) but their idioms and their local practices. Because Shepard's murder happened in Wyoming and the company flew in from New York, the play appears to report from the "wilderness," bringing something of the "native" back to the civilized.[6] For example, when company member Greg Pierotti speaks with Marge Murray, a salt-of-the-earth woman, early in the play, she describes how much more rural Laramie used to be: "I could run around the house in my all togethers, do the housework while the kids were in school. And nobody could see me" (15). Pierotti responds, "I just want to make sure I got the expression right: in your all togethers?" Murray retorts, "Well, yeah, honey, why wear clothes?" And her accompanying friend, Alison Mears, scolds, "Now how's he gonna use that in his play?" (15).

Pierotti's urban naïveté about "country ways" lets the audience peek into Laramie with him, while at the same time, it makes Murray and Mears appear simple and somehow even more naive than Pierotti, since they appear not to know that talking about nudity in performance has long since stopped being risqué. Later in the same conversation, Pierotti asks the women, "What's SOL?" (16), once again playing the foreigner to a culture with its own particular vernacular (although I would guess that most audience members know that SOL means "shit out of luck." Are Pierotti's questions meant to disarm the townswomen, to give them a sense of superiority over this otherwise savvy city boy?). On the other hand, Pierotti says in an interview that what was "really amazing about this project [was] going back to Laramie . . . constantly being shaken up by what happened, meeting people I never would have ordinarily met and being stretched in ways that I never would have been stretched, plus confronting my own stereotypes about the West and being constantly surprised by the humanity I have encountered."[7] Comments from the performers' journals also reinforce their outsiderness and implicitly, the audience's knowingness: Kaufman reads an entry that says, "Today we are moving from our motel and heading for the Best Western. . . . My hope is that it is a better Western" (23). These jokes play well to lighten the mood of a play that could too quickly sink to pathos; but at whose expense are they calculated? Whom does this joke address? Because the play inadvertently exoticizes Laramie—sometimes belittling it and sometimes romanticizing it—*The Laramie Project* leads a sophisticated audience to think that such a crime "couldn't happen here," a wrongheaded and false understanding of hate crimes as a practice of only rural communities. Gay bashing happens in New York and other large cities every day.

At the same time, *The Laramie Project* probably succeeds as well as Smith's interview-based plays in staging a conversation about a deeply divisive public event. Here, however, the essential agon arcs between Laramie and the outsiders, rather than, as in *Fires in the Mirror,* for instance, two halves of the inside of a tension-filled, racially or otherwise fraught event. Much of *Laramie* introduces the townspeople and the performers, situating the process of the script's creation in several metatheatrical moments. A narrator introduces characters, providing a kind of captioning function that would be provided on screen if this were a documentary film.[8]

Although the townspeople fear what the theater company will do with their stories, a tenuous trust develops among them. Leigh Fondakowski, assistant director and head writer on *The Laramie Project,* says, "Many of us went to bars and hung out, talking to people and making connections that way. . . . By then, most of the press had left and yet the people didn't feel like they had had any closure. They were very upset with how they had gotten represented in the press."[9] Rebecca Hilliker, a theater professor at the University of Wyoming who's interviewed in the play, says, "When this happened they started talking about it, and then the media descended and all dialogue stopped" (11). The play jump-starts that dialogue, at least between the townspeople and these curious theater people. Zubaida Ula, a twenty-something Muslim woman in Laramie, says, "You know, it's so unreal to me that, yeah, that a group from New York would be writing a play about Laramie. And then I was picturing like you're gonna be in a play about my town. You're gonna be onstage in New York and you're gonna be acting like you're us. That's so weird" (26). Although Ula doesn't specify, perhaps what's weird is her sense that someone's impression of her, speaking her words, will travel without her, detached from herself while embodied in a stranger, performing for other strangers in a far-flung locale. Perhaps because the media treated them harshly and indifferently, the townspeople (at least as they're represented in the play) believe the more empathetic Tectonic actors will do them justice. Father Roger Schmitt, who serves as a voice of measured reason throughout the play, says to his interviewer, "I will trust you people that if you write a play of this, that you *(pause)* say it right, say it correct. I think you have a responsibility to do that. . . . You need to do your best to say it correct" (66). Schmitt's hope, he seems to know, can only live as a wish—he can't control how the Tectonic company will represent him or his town. But he trusts them to "say it correct."[10]

Perhaps in that trust, for utter strangers who will use his words and embody their interpretation of his gestures, Schmitt outlines the utopian performative potential of the play: that after a horrible tragedy, someone could represent it in a way that will "say it correct," that will set Laramie aright. Hope lies in Schmitt's trust that this rent in the human fabric might be mended by storytelling over which, ironically, he has no say. Even Marge Murray tells Pierotti, "To show it's not the hellhole of the earth would be nice, but that is up to how you portray us" (100). She does go on to say, "And that in turn is up to how Laramie behaves" (100), implying faith in the power of mimesis to get at truth. As they're getting off the phone, Pierotti reports, Murray tells him, "Now you take care. I love you, honey" (100). I'm moved by the trust she displays; that she can say she loves this stranger by the end of their interactions seems testimony to the possibility of people connecting across vast difference and distance. Kaufman, too, says, "In the end, it was a magical experience that fulfilled the purpose of theatre: for a community to talk about itself. In this day and age . . . it is unavoidable to ask oneself what theatre is needed for. The collaboration with the townspeople was a beautiful achievement in which we engaged in a kind of dialogue that would not have been possible any other way."[11]

If the townspeople and the performers established a warm intersubjectivity, one of the play's challenges is to invite audiences into this mutual exchange of respect and care. The most moving moments in the play, for me, are the ones in which other queer people in Laramie suddenly find themselves visible. In one story, for example, Harry Woods, a gay man, watches a homecoming parade from his apartment window and sees a group of people tagged to the end that's honoring Shepard's life. This group first appears as an afterthought to the conventional parade, but as he sees it grow very large in a short time, Woods feels that his life finally has substance. Harry Woods cries because it's the first time he sees his identity supported publicly, even if this parade honors a gay man who was murdered. Matt Galloway, the straight bartender who served Matt on the night of his death and speaks as the town's (or the play's) resident humanist, describes this group of marchers, of which he was a member: "A mass of people. Families—mothers holding their six-year-old kids, tying these armbands around these six-year-old kids and trying to explain to them why they should wear an armband. Just amazing. I mean it was absolutely one of the most—beautiful things I've ever done in my life" (63). That this march moves both of these men gestures toward a utopian performative—in that moment, for that short time, these two very different men feel deeply a sense of how things might change, if human differences could be honored. That they share their emotion with the audience gives us, too, something to feel; we're offered the potential to experience our own utopian performatives by these tellings that become doings.

Although *The Laramie Project* uses Matthew Shepard's murder as its starting point, the play doesn't spend much time talking *about* the murder.[12] In *Laramie,* the interviewers draw townspeople's sympathy for both Matthew and his murderers; the play's humanism chooses a kind of tolerance or fairness (what numerous reviewers called a "live and let live" message) over encouraging its characters or audiences to be angry about what happened to Shepard. For example, Dr. Cantway, the physician on duty at the emergency room the night of Shepard's murder, also treated Aaron McKinney, who was beaten up in a fight later the same night. Cantway moved between McKinney's room in the ER and Shepard's, without realizing the connection between the two men. He says,

> Then two days later, I found out the connection and I was . . . very . . . struck!!! They were two kids!!!!! They were both my patients and they were two kids. I took care of both of them . . . Of their bodies. And . . . for a brief moment I wondered if this is how God feels when he looks down at us. How we are all his kids. . . . Our bodies. . . . Our souls. . . . And I felt a great deal of compassion. . . . For both of them. (38)

Cantway's empathetic speech—and the notion that good and evil coexist and even coincide—ends the first act with a gesture of universality that frames Shepard's murder within a more religious than political discourse. Systemic homophobia and bigotry gets let off the hook, replaced with a morally inflected parable about the mysterious ways of god.

In fact, the play's conventional dramaturgy underlines the balance it strives to create between opposing points of view and its own emphasis on tolerance rather than anger at systematic inequity. The play uses Brechtian accents: the actors speak to the audience directly; they announce their characters before they perform them, highlighting the separation between themselves and those they play; the play is divided not into scenes but into "moments," which are carefully captioned in the text; the actors transform, visibly, among the various townspeople they play, always returning to themselves afterwards. But in *The Laramie Project,* the *Our Town* effect—with the narrator and subsequently some of the performers serving the stage manager's function as it's assigned in Thornton Wilder's text—works to create a folksy, friendly atmosphere, rather than a Brechtian, critical pose.[13] The narrative moves along a conventional exposition-crisis-resolution-denouement arc. Reggie Fluty, the policewoman who cut Shepard down from the fence where she found him already near death, shares the horrifying, upsetting details of freeing Shepard from the restraining ropes at the end of act 1, just before Dr. Cantway's speech about treating Shepard and McKinney at the same time. The structural choice to evoke the brutality of Shepard's death in gory detail, and then to throw the sympathy to one of his murderers, suffering from a fight in which *he* took a beating, undercuts any anger that might gather in the audience when they hear of Shepard's critical wounds. The play's structure balances spectators' identifications and lets us see, as Dr. Cantway does, from an omniscient and omnipotent point of view.

Likewise, the second act culminates in Shepard's death, and ends with the hospital spokesman remembering that he broke down when he read the Shepard family's statement, in which Matthew's mother says, "Go home, give your kids a hug, and don't let a day go by without telling them that you love them" (70). Sheepish about the tears he inadvertently shed in front of the media, the spokesman, Rulon Stacey, reports that he received an email from someone who said, "Do you cry like a baby on TV for all your patients or just the faggots?" (71). Stacey continues, "And as I told you before, homosexuality is not a lifestyle with which I agree. Um, but having been thrown into this *(pause)* I guess I didn't understand the magnitude with which some people hate" (71). Even after the announcement of Shepard's death, the play immediately underlines the town's antipathy for his "lifestyle" and begins to argue that Shepard wouldn't want his murderers put to death. Doc O'Connor, the local limousine driver who ferried Matt to the bar from which he was taken and killed, says, "I'll tell you what, if they put those two boys to death, that would defeat everything Matt would be thinking about on them. Because Matt would not want those two to die. He'd want to leave them with hope. *(Spelling)* H-O-P-E. Just like the whole world hoped that Matt would survive. The whole thing, you see, the whole thing, ropes around hope, H-O-P-E" (71). O'Connor's speech moves spectators quickly away from righteous anger toward the play's eventual resolution in forgiveness for Shepard's killers. The final act ends with the guilty verdict in Aaron McKinney's trial and Matt's father's (Dennis Shepard's) speech, which he delivered during the trial's sentencing phase. The judge and jury would no doubt be swayed by Matthew's parents' preference for life or death in McKinney's sentencing; Dennis Shepard announces that he has decided to "show mercy to someone who refused to show any mercy" and to "grant [McKinney] life," which provides a crisp denouement for the play's action (96).

Other subcrises crop up and resolve throughout the play. Characters recall their lives before Shepard's death, and over the course of the narrative, describe their growth in ways that mirror the progress of conventional characters in realism. For example, Romaine Patterson, Shepard's young lesbian friend, becomes an activist by the end of the play, organizing the "Angel Action" against Reverend Fred Phelps when he came to demonstrate against homosexuality outside the courtroom during Russell Henderson's trial. The Anti-Defamation League subsequently honored Patterson in Washington, D.C..

Reggie Fluty suffers her own crisis and resolution, when she finds out, early in the second act, that Shepard was HIV positive. She says,

Probably a day and a half later, the hospital called me and told me Matthew had HIV. And the doctor said, "You've been exposed, and you've had a bad exposure," because, you see, I'd been—been building—building a, uh, lean-to for my llamas, and my hands had a bunch of open cuts on 'em, so I was kinda screwed *(she laughs)* you know, and you think, "Oh, shoot," you know. . . . So I said to the doctor, "Okay, what do I do?" And they said, "Get up here." So, I got up there and we started the ATZ [*sic*] drugs. Immediately. (53–54)

Later in the play, when Fluty finds out she's HIV negative, she says, "I put my tongue right in my husband's mouth" (86).

This laugh line ignores Fluty's ignorance. Despite the discussion of homosexuality that Shepard's death theoretically prompted, she hasn't learned through this experience that HIV isn't exchanged through saliva; it appears that she's kept herself from kissing her husband from fear of contagion. Her attempt to save Matthew is ennobled in the play, but her ignorance ("ATZ" instead of AZT and the prohibition on kissing) is never contested. The scene when she learns she's HIV negative provides one of the play's redemptive, relieving, joyful moments, but as with much of the play's dramaturgy, it shifts the spectators' focus from Shepard to those townspeople affected by his death. And although the performers testify everywhere about what they learned from Laramie, why didn't these knowledgeable New Yorkers (many of them lesbian or gay) take responsibility for teaching Fluty the real routes of HIV infection?

In a peculiar way, Shepard and his HIV positive body disappears or is infantilized within *The Laramie Project*'s dramaturgy. Fluty, for instance, describing Shepard's appearance when she finds him, reports, "I seen what appeared to be a young man, thirteen, fourteen years old because he was so tiny" (36); in fact, Shepard was twenty-one years old. People in the play find Shepard's heroism in his struggle to stay alive after his beating; Fluty says, "The gentleman that was laying on the ground, Matthew Shepard, he was covered in dry blood all over his head, there was dry blood underneath him and he was barely breathing . . . he was doing the best he could" (36). This emphasis on his struggle against death at the godforsaken fence elides the fact that Shepard lived his life as an openly gay man in a very hostile environment, that his whole life, in fact, was heroic. The play works hard to move the characters and the spectators beyond the details of Shepard's daily life and beyond the tragedy, into the denouement.[14] Fluty says, "Maybe now we can go on and we can quit being stuck, you know?" (97). The narrative's chronology, interspersed with climactic moments, humor, and a certain amount of suspense that makes it generically familiar, promotes purging, an ultimately conservative catharsis to which the play arrives at its end.

Performance scholar Tessa Carr says of *The Laramie Project*, "We see a

community discussion occur that *did not happen.*" She says that the dialogue of the play functions as "a utopic moment of possibility for community interaction."[15] I wonder, though, if townspeople learned anything new
about themselves and each other (and not just how one contracts HIV)
through this play and its process, or if they only reaffirmed a vague notion
of their humanity, of the goodness they continually protest but never
interrogate. Eileen Engen, one of the townspeople, says, "The majority of
people here are good people" (49). The play promotes laissez-faire democracy, rather than radical, participatory democracy, because it refuses to
suggest that anyone should ultimately take responsibility for anyone else.[16]
Zubaida Ula, describing a candlelight vigil held for Matthew, reports with
frustration,

> And someone got up there and said, "C'mon, guys, let's show the world
> that Laramie is not this kind of town." But it is that kind of town. If it
> wasn't this kind of town, why did this happen here? . . . [I]t's just totally
> like circular logic like how can you even say that? And we have to
> mourn this and we have to be sad that we live in a town, a state, a coun-
> try where shit like this happens And I'm not going to step away from
> that and say, 'We need to show the world this didn't happen.' I mean,
> these people are trying to distance themselves from this crime. And we
> need to own this crime. I feel. Everyone needs to own it. We are like
> this. We ARE like this. WE are LIKE this." (60)

Ula, however, is a somewhat unreliable narrator for this truth, because
she's Muslim, and by her own admission she's an outsider, even though
she was born and raised in Laramie. Ironically, this outsider-insider Cas-
sandra character provides the play's clearest indictment of the hate crime
that caused Shepard's death.

Ula's speech receives relatively little airtime, compared to the script's
continual, repeated references to Shepard's "lifestyle" and the tacit disap-
proval the townspeople express that the play leaves unremarked. For
instance, Murdock Cooper, a rancher from a nearby town, says, "You don't
pick up regular people. I'm not excusing their actions, but it made me feel
better because it was partially Matthew Shepard's fault and partially the
guys who did it . . . you know, maybe it's fifty-fifty" (58). Other characters
express more explicit homophobia, repeating ages-old conditional statements about tolerating homosexuals as long as they keep their hands to
themselves and don't flaunt their preferences. Implicitly, the play blames

Shepard by giving Laramie's homophobes so many chances to express their disdain for him and by giving their speech so much credence.[17]

The play does, however, credit the theater with the potential for changing people's lives and minds, and its transformational style does provide something of a model for hopefully more progressive social action. Jedadiah Schultz, a University of Wyoming student, changes most over the course of the play, when finally, he's cast as the lead in Tony Kushner's *Angels in America* in the Theatre Department's production. Rebecca Hilliker, the department's chair, says, "[T]he question is, How do we move— how do we reach a whole state where there is some really deep-seated hostility toward gays? How do you reach them?" (85). To answer her own question, she decides to mount *Angels,* hoping, as I do, that performance can mobilize people to change their hearts and minds.[18] Through his experience in the production, Schultz changes his mind about gay men. He says, "I didn't for the longest time let myself become personally involved in the Matthew Shepard thing. It didn't seem real, it just seemed way blown out of proportion. Matthew Shepard was just a name instead of an individual. . . . I just can't believe I ever said all that stuff about homosexuals, you know. How did I ever let that stuff make me think that you were different from me?" (98). I find this recognition moment quite moving, in part because Schultz has come to this understanding not through direct involvement in politics (like Romaine Patterson, for example), but through performance.

Company member Amanda Gronich says, "I just hope we are doing justice to the people we interviewed. . . . And in any small way, if this play helps to prevent those kind of hate crimes from happening in the future, what a wonderful thing theatre can do."[19] The play argues that theater can and should participate in public dialogues, and this strategy in fact works to change Schultz's consciousness. Perhaps *The Laramie Project* doesn't "say it correct" (100), the way Father Roger Schmitt enjoins the company to report their lives. But perhaps theater can never "say it correct"; perhaps its utopian performative potential lies in its effort to say it at all, to speak into the public those things that might otherwise never be said. While I believe *The Laramie Project* is flawed as a political project, I support the work it tries to do and appreciate it as an example of the complexity of using theater to comment on and participate in national dialogues.[20]

I saw the original production of *The Laramie Project,* performed by the Tectonic Theatre Project actors, at the Union Theatre in New York in spring 2000.[21] I found it a rather complicated performance of ethnography. Though virtuosic acting helped the Tectonic troupe capture what the script describes as the essence of the town, the fact remained that we saw the actors' bodies, bending themselves to signify the citizens of Laramie. Their impersonations—each performer played multiple characters and transformed among them quickly—wound up condescending to the community whose pain and shame they captured. The characters read as little more than stereotypes taken from the contours of their lives and placed unsteadily within the theoretically aberrant event that was Shepard's death.

Why wasn't this production an example of "walking in the shoes of the other," as I suggested Tomlin, Hoch, and Smith did successfully, in chapter 3? Why didn't *The Laramie Project*'s production in New York work as such a detailed and ethical pedagogical investigation of cultural identity? The play's ethnography uses a method that should embody Joni Jones's theory of practicing cultural identity differences. *The Laramie Project* also usefully vies for spectators' emotional understanding by opening the story to multiple identifications. But the New York production of *The Laramie Project* represented the citizens in the play as a means to an end, rather than *ends in themselves*, which philosopher and legal theorist Martha Nussbaum argues is the hallmark of ethical liberal humanism. Nussbaum says, "Each human being should be regarded as an end rather than as a means to the ends of others";[22] the norm, she says, "should be the idea of being treated as an end rather than a means, a person rather than an object. . . . [T]he goal should always be to put people into a position of agency and choice."[23] I'm not sure that the Tectonic Theatre or *The Laramie Project* treated the townspeople of Laramie as ends rather than means. After all, the Tectonic Theatre received the kudos for making sense of the murder; the residents of Laramie remain scrutinized, but not truly engaged, leading to what performance scholar Dwight Conquergood calls "curator's exhibitionism," in which the person responsible for selecting and showing anthropological or ethnographic work receives the cultural capital it accrues.[24]

On the other hand, this polemic perhaps begs of the question of whether any performance can really present a human being as an end in his or her self. Because performance always stands in for something, perhaps it's always a means to another's ends, and could be profitably used at least metaphorically (or mimetically) to trace out that substitution and its usefulness.[25] Despite what I consider their more successful progressive engagement with politics, don't Tomlin and Hoch also use their characters for their own ends? Is the difference here (as with Smith's work) because the "characters" of *The Laramie Project* are real? Perhaps the care, respect, and love with which a real character or a fictional type becomes a means to an end makes the difference.

In the original production of *The Laramie Project*, the Tectonic Theatre Project performers captured the townspeople's dialogue and the iconicity of their clothing and mannerisms, but I felt they remained aloof from these people's souls, because the production told the ethnographers' story more fully than it did Laramie's. The company's intentionally Brechtian self-consciousness about their positions as outsiders to the town and its tragedy didn't seem to provide a politically inflected critical frame. The Tectonic performers, oscillating between playing themselves and playing others, conveyed most clearly their own mystification with the culture of Laramie, rather than a considered deconstruction of their own powerful perspectives as the ones shaping the telling of this story in this forum. Critics hailed the production for its topicality, for trying to create an empathetic picture of how ordinary people managed a tragedy and its aftermath. But I wonder if finally (and ironically), the Tectonic performers failed to "affiliate," which Nussbaum defines in part as "being able to live for and in relation to others, to recognize and show concern for other human beings, to engage in various forms of social interaction . . . [and] being able to imagine the situation of another and to have compassion for that situation."[26] While her definition sounds eerily like conventional method acting, something about the Tectonic performers' more distanced style, which I found salient in the New York production, made their own ethnography the end in itself, rather than the means to greater social affiliation. The Zachary Scott Theatre production in Austin, on the other hand, was more conventionally "method," rather than completely Brechtian, since the local actors performed two layers of characters who remained characters, and reverted less frequently to the bedrock of self.[27]

Saying It Correctly: Laramie Meets Austin

The Austin production took the occasion of the play to create a new public of attentive listeners, and built social capital by drawing spectators into the place and its people and asking us to measure our own relationships to these Laramie citizens' responses to Shepard's death. The Austin production seemed to perform *with* the people of Laramie, rather than *at* them (or the audience). Perhaps the more conventional acting style did allow a more direct expression of empathy, of inhabiting the "as is" of a painful past, and establishing the "what if" of a more compassionate future.[28] The production turned shame to hope, and constituted among the audience a utopian performative that let us experience how we might learn from this wound in our common humanity and move toward a more loving, just, harmonious future.

The Zach Scott Theatre production used aesthetics, tone, and mood to evoke and particularize the geography in which Shepard's murder occurred, projecting slides and video of the dusty, vast Wyoming prairie settling into itself under the light of an infinitely blue, expansive sky. Sergeant Hing, describing Laramie early in the play, says, "It's a good place to live. Good people, lots of space. . . . [A]nd uh, well, it was a beautiful day, absolutely gorgeous day, real clear and crisp and the sky was that blue that, uh . . . you know, you'll never be able to paint, it's just sky blue—it's just gorgeous" (8). The Zach Scott production, designed by Michael Raiford, somehow captured this indescribable color and the infinity of feeling and landscape it evokes. The crisp and illuminating Austin production values used mostly light to create a textured sense of the barren prairie, its cozy domesticity standing against the rigor of the Wyoming climate. In some ways, the production's beauty mitigated the ugly politics of the crime; Laramie seemed close to heaven and Matthew Shepard an angel. So close to heaven, the violence and hatred that motivated Shepard's death was already positioned as aberrational, abnormal. The town's heteronormativity gently embraced Shepard's queer body; difference, the elegant production seemed to say, can be beautiful, too. The center never changes, but can generously tolerate the margins. This production, too, acquiesced to the liberal humanism of the script.[29]

The production used the theater's height to dwarf the actors with the environmental beauty captured by the images; the actors' stature shrank to everyday size when they paced under the sign of Wyoming's enormous landscape. The original New York production of *The Laramie Project* played on a shallow stage with a wide proscenium, built quite high above the spectators, who were seated on a very low, not very well raked floor in the Union Square Theatre. This put the performers in a position of power and authority over the spectators, physically and ideologically. The Zach Scott Theatre production, on the other hand, was performed on a thrust stage floor with the audience steeply angled up from the playing space on three sides, looking down on the actors. This physical setting might have contributed to the sense of the actors' compassion I felt in the Zach Scott production.

Perhaps, too, Austin is just that much closer to Laramie, compared to New York, which kept performers and audiences respectful instead of condescending. Austin becomes somewhere between there and there, between Laramie and New York, which makes it an insistent yet elastic kind of "here." That is, Austin provides another point of contact, and creates a triangle between the urban/rural, here/there, sophisticated/naive binaries that the play otherwise institutes. Because Austin rests somewhere in the middle of all these binaries—not as naive as Laramie but not as sophisticated as New York, for instance—spectators here can see the play and its events differently. In the Zach Scott production, as theater scholar Jaclyn Pryor noted, a "third party" appeared "on stage as well as in the audience, a performative interlocutor—the actor, the ethnographer, and the Laramie subjects taken together seemed more truly intersubjective."[30]

If the Tectonic Theatre performers seemed godlike, omniscient in a community to which they didn't belong, the actors at Zach Scott performed a kind of humility, and tried to reveal quotidian humanity instead of virtuosic, redeeming allure, prompted by respect for a community and a landscape of which they were clearly not a part. The Tectonic actors seemed larger than the characters; the spare, frontally oriented New York production didn't evoke the place so much as the actors within it. The characters the Zach Scott actors played became theatrically and politically iconic rather than stereotypical and, in an odd way, more sympathetic. The Zach Scott actors played two levels of character: the people of Laramie and the Tectonic Theatre Project performers who appear as themselves in the script. As a result, the performer-ethnographers were held up for a certain level of scrutiny instead of being played for truth.

The Austin production established vigorous, attentive listening as the social gestus of the play, rather than self-conscious showing or "showingness." Director Dave Steakley positioned the actors to listen closely and visibly to each other, staging their interactions in groups or pairs of people talking together, which demonstrated the attentiveness the production sought from its audience. Like the poets in *Def Poetry Jam,* the actors watched each other perform and listened empathetically, even when they weren't directly involved in a scene; actors who weren't performing stood at the sides of the stage or sat unobtrusively nearby. Their continual presence onstage, under the signs of Matthew projected like operatic supertitles over the scene, evoked the town as a collective body, mutually sorrowful that such hatred could happen there. The lights, too, moved from one character to another, as though the set itself watched and listened carefully. Under such a gaze, the theater became a site of ethical inquiry, one in which the performance apparatus turned onto the social like a microscope probing into the DNA of the event.

Yet at the same time, the Austin production somehow stayed rooted in the quotidian life of the town, insistent that this was tragedy among common people. As theater theorist Alan Read suggests, "Theatre, when it is good, enables us to know the everyday in order better to live everyday life." "In all situations," he says, "the everyday has to be known before its theatre can be understood."[31] In simple embodied ways, with small domestic props redolent of "home," the Austin production of *The Laramie Project* re-created a respectful view of Laramie's everyday life, so that it could analyze with empathy and through affiliation the crisis it endured. Read suggests,

> [I]t is useful to think of the everyday as that which escapes everything which is specialized, the ill-defined remainder to everything in life thought worthy of writing and record. It is habitual but not unchangeable and is therefore worth taking seriously, for it is the reality which we are made aware of when theatre is good and return to when theatre is done. . . . Everyday life must be known, and intimately, for good theatre to happen.[32]

Although neither production I saw of *The Laramie Project* was full of domestic details, both opting instead for more Brechtian modes of suggestion and gestus, the more material hints of daily life provided in Zach Scott's production grounded the performance in that "ill-defined" yet all important "remainder," the emotions and affect, the wound and the struggle to heal it, that persists in everyday life after a tragedy. The acting style, too, seemed more humane and less caricatured than in the New York production; I remember the performers' warmth in Austin, and recall from my experience in New York only distance and posturing among the Tectonic actors.[33]

The Zach Scott production, as suggested in the script, used real-time video to represent the large role the media played in the events in Laramie. For example, when the town's sheriff is interviewed about Shepard's death and the trial of his murderers, several actors assumed the role of television news crews, and filmed his press conference live, with the reporters facing the audience, the sheriff with his back to the audience, his face visible only on the screen that projected and magnified his image across the width of the stage. Seeing his words mediated by technology demonstrated that speech is not transparent, that we always gather and understand information through those who frame it from particular perspectives. The video camera directs our view; the editing process manipulates our emotions, just as performance, too, frames and mediates our knowledge of any event.

But the Zach Scott production tried to acknowledge its own complicity in framing the images and words it reconstructed, to acknowledge and use its difference from the real event to attempt to extend the story into the local Austin community and to point out our collusion in both the violence and the hope for redemption the Shepard tragedy encompassed. At the play's end, the cast asked the audience to pick up and hold the candles placed discreetly under our seats. Spectators stood up while actors moved through the house to light the wicks. Once our small candles flickered, we became part of what the text calls the "sparkling lights of Laramie" (101). Laramie became Austin, and we became part of the "now," part of a moment that honored the history and importance of a tragedy that didn't seem far from us, after all.

I was moved in spite of myself by this moment, even as I understood that the performance manipulated my feelings. I found myself surprisingly willing to be part of this witnessing, part of this ritual honoring of loss, of grief, of wrenching, unexpected change that I can only hope will eventually lead to some sort of deliverance. Bloch suggests the "theatre [is a] rehearsal for the example . . . a laboratory of the right theory-praxis on a small scale, in the form of play, as though it were a case on stage that might provide the experimental experience for the serious case," although in this example, the story's truth allows the stage to rehearse other ways of feeling about the "serious case."[34] The candlelit moment represented a kind of forgiveness; it implied that we, too, metaphorically represent the citizens of Laramie. Our actions meant we were willing to take our places beside them in their pain and sorrow and to share the burden of their civic responsibility for what happened not only in Laramie, but for what continues to happen in too many towns and cities and states around the country and the world. Bloch says, "As soon as the rehearsal for the example is staged the goal is clearly visible, but the stage, being experimental, that is, being a state of anticipation, tries out the ways in which to behave in order to achieve them."[35] The final moments of the Austin production, in which the audience, transformed, held their candles aloft, rehearsed an example, offering spectators ways to behave better in the face of senseless hate.

Then again, the Austin production was not without its detractors. Although the play received glowing reviews, some students who'd been assigned to see the production as part of their Introduction to Theatre course at the University of Texas performed their alienation from the play and from the rest of the audience. Robert Newell, one of the performers in the Zach Scott production, reported over email his dismay at students who were "sitting there stone-faced and . . . not moved by the play, some of them sleeping, some of them listening to a basketball game on the radio with an earphone discreetly placed in one ear."[36] Their behavior distracted the actors working very close to them on the theater's thrust floor; Newell continued,

> You are on stage, working very hard and sharing something very personal to the audience and you look out and see a bunch of [students] sunken in their chairs asleep with their baseball caps pulled over their heads. . . . Some . . . even refused to have their candles lit in the final moment of the play, by waving us off and making a clear gesture that they did NOT want to participate. In addition, several . . . actually started down the aisle when the candle-lighting began, awkwardly and forcibly trying to make their way around [actor] Martin Burke as he was in the aisle lighting candles. It's like they were threatened by the political implication of holding a lit candle with everyone else at the end of the play.[37]

These students clearly demonstrated their choice not to believe in the utopian performativity of the moment.

Newell's email circulated in our department and prompted much discussion among the instructors and some of the students in the intro course, as well as among graduate students and faculty. Some of the course instructors shared Newell's email and talked about the practices of Brechtian theater as a way to address the issue. One said, "Many of the production responses I am grading discuss *The Laramie Project* in a reasonably sophisticated manner. Many of them were moved. Many wrote about having their eyes opened to hate crimes. Some wrote about confronting homophobia for the first time. . . . Some students will behave badly because they are boorish or feel threatened or are just bored. But others are experiencing the kind of empathy and thoughtful examination of their beliefs that socially conscious theatre aspires to engender."[38] Many of us tried to understand the message these students intended to send. Why did they refuse to "play"? Why did they perform resistance to what they presumably felt was the production's bid for communitas? Why didn't they "like" the play, if that's what their behavior signified? How is it that dislike apparently translates into disrespect, especially for productions gauged toward politically empathetic responses? Acting out against the communitas the production intended to engender quickly became tantamount to not caring about Matthew Shepard's death; the well-meant calculus of empathy slipped too easily into coercive, mandatory sympathy.[39]

Perhaps the students resisted the imposition of a *feeling*, the production's insistence on sentiment, in which "[e]mpathy is an ethical rule," as a too easy substitute for effective action.[40] Perhaps they refused the rhetoric of feeling "badly" about injustice and so refused the candles meant to signify feeling "good." Or perhaps simple boredom led them to perform their resistance. Berlant says that "while on all sides of the political spectrum political rhetoric generates a high degree of cynicism and boredom, those same sides manifest, simultaneously, a sanctifying respect for sentiment";[41] conservatives and progressives both find themselves acquiescing to a certain rhetorical manipulation of emotion, in which feelings are used to sanctify, perhaps without enough critical examination, a fervently expressed opinion.[42] On the other hand, the students' response could have stemmed from simple homophobia and their resentment at being required to see a "gay" play.

These students' performance of resistance and their disregard for the production's sentiment points to the multiple layers of community and communitas that might circulate in the same production at the same moment. As I noted in the introduction, everyone in the audience at *Menopausal Gentleman* probably didn't feel as moved as I did when Peggy Shaw entered the house to shake spectators' hands while she sang. Likewise, while I might have been moved by the Austin production of *The Laramie Project*'s invitation to participate in its utopian performative, others might have felt as uncomfortable as the student spectators, who overtly performed their separateness, their unwillingness to join what perhaps they saw as a falsely intimate performance moment. The production forces a "choice moment" from the spectator, whose action or inaction makes visible the potential for agency as well as the necessity of taking some sort of stand.[43] My partner, in fact, refused to participate; she remained seated, her candle ignored, not necessarily because she didn't want to honor Matthew Shepard, but because she preferred not to have her emotions managed. In my own theatergoing history, I too have resisted participatory performance events that insisted I join in supposedly sanctified ritual moments. In my early days of participating in and critically engaging with feminist theater, for example, I strongly resisted performances that asked me to close my eyes or to take another spectator's hand or to somehow participate bodily in what I always felt was the manipulative emotional sentiment of the moment.[44] How did I become a spectator willing to light her candle and hold it high in a theater in Austin, Texas, to commemorate the death of Matthew Shepard? Is it my desire for or relationship to community that's changed? My desire for a piece of (or the peace of) redemption? Is the utopian performative I seek in performance ultimately just chimerical?

As I said in chapter 2, writing about feminist solo performers Holly Hughes, Peggy Shaw, and Deb Margolin, I'm willing to risk sentimentality, if only to excavate it further, to deliberate its power and the potential of its affects. Trying to analyze these moments of reception and response, it's impossible to know why some spectators stand and why others remain seated.[45] I can only read the moment and my fellow spectators' reactions through my own response hoping that my description of the emotional energy I felt in the room is in some small way accurate and apt. I was moved as I stood at *The Laramie Project,* joining others who may or may not have felt the same way. A bit embarrassed by how easily my hope surged, I nonetheless appreciated this communal gesture, this chance to lend my body, my candle-holding hand and my heart, to honor Matthew Shepard's life and to embody my own sorrow at his death, my own knowledge that in other places and at other times, his fate could have been mine or one of the people I love. Call this identification; call this empathy; call this naive emotional sentiment. I'd rather call it a utopian performative. I was glad to be invited to stand in that theater with other spectators after that play to enact our hope that what happened to Matthew Shepard wouldn't happen again. In that moment, the theater opened itself to the city and the nation outside; performance became a public practice that modeled civic engagement.[46]

If utopia, as Luisa Passerini suggests, "means not struggling for something to come, but starting right now to put it into practice,"[47] then the Austin production of *The Laramie Project* did demonstrate its desire to envision a more socially just, peaceful world. Describing the events of May 1968 in Europe, Passerini says, "The movements were united by links that were neither of book nor ideology . . . but rather were of elected affinity, based on affective and cognitive choices. The community, understood in this way, was a space where the divisions between public and private were broken down, and where the utopia of direct communication with anybody suddenly became true."[48] In some ways, this describes the political, utopic work of *The Laramie Project*; the ruptured polis becomes a place where elected affinity replaces kinship structures based on family or politics, where tragedy induces the private to become public, and in the process, allows the citizenry to speak to each other and to the world from their minds and their hearts. Affinity allows Marge Murray to tell performer Greg Pierotti that she loves him; for the moments of time they share together, they strike an intimate understanding, even if it doesn't last through their lifetimes.

Engaging performance as a public practice, as a rehearsal for an example that yearns toward something better and more just than the social arrangements that divide us now, theater becomes a sort of temple of communion with a future we need to practice envisioning. Jennifer Nelson, a Washington, D.C.–based theater artist, has asked, "What would our world look like if there was a theatre on every block, if theatre was as much a part of our lives as church?"[49] I'm caught by this vision of theater as a place where we go regularly with great need and desire to practice our humanity, where we go to enact the possibilities of honorable, ethical civic engagement, where we *must* go to say what needs to be said, and to respond to what needs to be heard. I'm struck, too, by my own persistent use of metaphors of prayer or communion to describe performances that I'd rather argue engaged civic participation than religious fervor.[50]

I do believe in the spiritual aspects of utopian performatives and the way they call me to something ineffable and strangely full of solace. People who criticize my work have called it, among other things, "religious." A colleague, lesbian and feminist performance theorist Sue-Ellen Case, for example, has insisted that I "come out of the closet" about the religious aspects of the utopian performative, an insistence I find amusing as a lesbian scholar and as a Jew.[51] Surely, the practice of "coming out" is one I engage in continually, through both of these complex identity positions. I'm not sure, in this case, why my admitted longing to articulate a spiritual effect in performance should be reduced to religiosity or, worse, fundamentalism. In the same discussion at which she suggested I "come out," Case talked with admiration about the "slow food" movement, which works to bring food producers and consumers closer together, avoiding the capitalist effects of agribusiness and the health effects of overly processed food shipped long distances prior to its consumption. The utopian performative, it seems to me, might prompt a kind of "slow the-ater" movement, in which audiences and performers linger together, bask-ing in the intangible yet deeply *felt* effects of performance's production.

I don't believe that theater should be like church, although I respect Jennifer Nelson's use of the metaphor. And when I use the word *mes-sianic*—which gives my colleague Case particular pause—I don't mean it in a fundamentalist sense but in a Benjaminian way. I mean it to refer to some always deferred moment of transformation, images toward which, without knowing their real contours, without the necessity that they be fixed or real, we direct our hope. As writer Rami Shapiro says, in a fine cri-tique of messianic excess,

> The whole point of messianism is to perfect the future and rescue us from our imperfect present. To make this happen, messianists work tirelessly to free humanity from its ... capacity for evil. This is not only ridiculous, it is dangerous. ... The greatest evil is always done with mes-sianic hype, claiming to cleanse the world of that which the messianists fear most: the messiness of human life. ... Humility is the antidote to messianism. Messianism knows what is right. Humility does not.[52]

Certainly, the utopian performative, as I've argued here, is grounded in the humble, messy attempt to seek out human connectedness, rather than a grandiose, fixed vision of *one* perfect future or *one* fixed idea of a better life. This critique of messianism's inherent fascism has also been launched against utopianism in general, and I've agreed with it throughout this book.

And yet I'm touched by the way, for instance, Deb Margolin, in *O Wholly Night,* makes of the Messiah a literary trope, a poetic figure of hope and redemption, rather than a site of surety, rightness, ontology, or coer-cion toward a fixed ideal. For me, "religion" works the same way in the utopian performative; it's not organized, coherent, or coercive, but deeply spiritual, ineffable, and at the same time, profoundly *human.* Human interconnectedness is an ethical, not a religious, impulse in utopian per-formatives. As Michael Lerner, the founding editor of *Tikkun* ("a bi-monthly Jewish and Interfaith critique of politics, culture, and society"), says, "The fundamental truth of our time is the interconnectedness and mutual interdependence of all human beings on this planet. ... [w]e need a deeper understanding of what it is to be human. ... We call this approach a Politics of Meaning or an Emancipatory Spirituality—recognizing that people have a need for a meaning to their lives that transcends the narrow utilitarian logic of the competitive marketplace and its materialist assumptions about what is important in human life."[53] I agree with Lerner when he says, "I am committed to a world based on love, awe and wonder, generosity and open-heartedness, gratitude, joy and celebration at the miracle of life and consciousness itself, nonviolence, peace, and social justice, and the mutual interdependence and interconnectedness of all people on this planet, and I'm not going to get intimidated by those who claim that speaking that way, articulating a politics of meaning, is New-Agey, utopian, or unrealistic."[54] Lerner's words could easily be my own.

While I readily underline the spiritual aspects of utopian performatives, I'll emphasize, again, that I fervently wish for theater to claim its place as a vital part of the public sphere. I yearn for performance to be a practice in everyday life, not so that it will become banal and predictable, but so it will provide a place for radically democratic dissension and debate, consensus and hope, a discursive place like Greenwich Village in the late 1800s and the 1960s, or the Left Bank salons and cafés in Paris in the 1920s, where a high level of conversation and debate among artists and politicians and educators and other people was imperative. Theater can be a secular temple of social and spiritual union not with a mystified, mythologized higher power, but with the more prosaic, earthbound, yearning, ethical subjects who are citizens of the world community, who need places to connect with one another and with the fragile, necessary wish for a better future.

chapter six

Militant Optimism

Approaching Humanism

The musicking that moves us most will be that which most subtly, comprehensively and powerfully articulates the relationships of our ideal society—which may or may not have any real, or even possible, existence beyond the duration of the performance. The ambivalence of the emotions which such musicking arouses in us, posed between joy and melancholy . . . can be seen as a response to the realization of that fall from perfection which is present as an element of virtually all cultures and religions. The ambivalence reflects the simultaneous experiencing of the ideal and the impossibility of realizing it. . . . At the same time the musicking can exhilarate us with a vision of that ideal which is not just intimated to us but actually brought into existence for as long as the performance lasts. While it does we *can* believe in its realizability, and the exhilaration and the joy, outlasting the melancholy, can persist long after the performance is over. This is not surprising, for it confirms us in our *feelings,* which, as Geertz says, we must know before we know what we think, about what are right and true relationships.
—Christopher Small, *Music of the Common Tongue*

Myths are the earliest forms of science. . . . It has been said that the myth is a public dream, dreams are private myths. Unfortunately we give our mythic side scant attention these days. As a result, a great deal escapes us and we no longer understand our own actions. So it remains important and salutary to speak not only of the rational and easily understood, but also of enigmatic things: the irrational and the ambiguous. To speak both privately and publicly.
—Mary Zimmerman, *Metamorphoses*

I find myself with a keen desire to reclaim a commitment to human commonality. I know that gender, race, sexuality, ability, class, and other vectors of identity remain entrenched as discriminatory benchmarks in public discourse and in the distribution of social and political power. But more and more, I find myself feeling affinity without regard to the specifics of identity. As performance scholars Josh Abrams and Janelle Reinelt have both remarked, the ethical move in current politics and culture seems toward a responsibility to each other *as* each other, both in our radical differences and in our common capacity to embrace the fullness of our potential humanity.[1]

The climate after September 11, of distrust and racial profiling, of simplistic and chillingly effective calls to a thoughtless, knee-jerk nationalism, spurs me to claim my place as part of a progressive human community that rejects such radically conservative values and actions. The desire for social change should always strain above material circumstances, should always point us toward an ideal, a utopia imagined as a hopeful possibility that will always place us within its own process of production, a wish that needs to be made again and again. I want to feel myself part of a public that participates in a slow but sure remaking of the world. Activist-scholar Michael Warner says, "Publics, . . . lacking any institutional being, commence with the moment of attention, must continually predicate [or demand or imply] renewed attention, and cease to exist when attention is no longer predicated [or directed]."[2] Alarmed at a response to the possibility of terrorism that strips U.S. citizens of our civil liberties and that empowers the government to access personal information to an extent unprecedented in American history, I fear the imposition of a militarized state. Devastated by the Democrats' loss in the 2004 election, I take solace in the words and actions of people who continue to believe in the possibility of radical political change. Demeaned and demoralized by politicians and pundits who insist that "moral values" drove people to the polls to vote for George W. Bush against John Kerry, I'm buoyed by the determination and activism of other queer social pariahs determined to expose the hypocrisy of those who dismiss our lives as amoral while they turn their backs on U.S. poverty and genocide in the Sudan and support a war in Iraq fought for fabricated reasons. I am drawn to a progressive public that commences, as Warner suggests, with our common attention to the injustices of the moment. Warner says, "The appellative energy of publics"—that is, how they call things into being by virtue of naming them—"makes us believe our consciousness to be decisive. The direction of our glance can constitute our social world."[3]

Since theater and performance direct our glances in just such constitutive ways, they offer a public space for renewing our critical attention to the machinations of dominant ideology. Theater provides a place to practice the hope in what theologian Martin Buber calls "fantasy pictures," the wishful aspect of utopia. Likewise, philosopher Ernst Bloch believes that hope points to possibilities and that its goal is "real humanism," one that overthrows all conditions of oppression and enslavement.[4]

> For Bloch, humanity is imbued with the ability to strive for a better life. Wherever people have experienced hard times, their daydreams have offered them visions of something better. This is the manifestation of what Bloch refers to as the utopian principle. The utopian principle is constituted by "expectation, hope, intention towards possibility that has not become." Bloch seems to be arguing that it is only through the juxtaposition of immediate social relations with a sharp utopian consciousness that one can successfully navigate the darkness permeating day-to-day life.[5]

Performance can describe, through the fulsome, hopeful, radically humanist gesture of the utopian performative, how social relationships might change. I go to see performances anticipating transformative experiences, ones that will let me see a sliver of a vision, let me feel for a moment in my body and my soul what the world might be like were some form of social justice or progressive social change or some consistent act of real, human love, even partially accomplished. The performatives I'm engaging here aren't iterations of what *is,* but transformative doings of what *if.* This kind of hope represents an opening up, rather than a closing down, of consciousness of the past and the future in the present;[6] this kind of hope relies on the active doings of faith, which too often, too daily, I feel slip when I listen to the radio or read the newspaper. Hope, like faith, demands continual reaffirmation; theater gives me faith and persistently shores up my ability to hope.

I want to end *Utopia in Performance* by describing three productions in which I found utopian performatives that gave me hope and that stirred me toward the possibility of reanimating humanism as a desirable goal that can be productively modeled at the theater: one, a solo performance by artist-choreographer Ann Carlson that I saw at the University of Texas "Fresh Terrain" festival; the second, a production of Mary Zimmerman's ensemble play *Metamorphoses,* which I saw at Second Stage Theatre off-Broadway before it transferred to Circle in the Square on Broadway; and the third, Deborah Warner's production of *Medea* with Fiona Shaw, which I saw when it moved to Broadway from London's West End. In all three of these performances, I experienced what author-activist Angela Davis calls a "special form of social consciousness that can potentially awaken an urge in those affected by it to creatively transform their oppressive environments."[7] All three performances address life and death, transformations wrought publicly by history and privately by age; they evoke, in singular ways, a rather melancholic yearning for a different future, fueled by wistful but persistent hope; all three travel an axis of time in which the most powerful emotions become ephemeral, evanescent moments of feeling; all three performances trade in imagistic and semantic anachronisms to depict a Benjaminian sense of the simultaneity of time; and all three performances find a fragile beauty in the ironies of cruelty and the possibility of heroism.

Ann Carlson's *Blanket:* Diving into the Wreck of the Present

Ann Carlson's *Blanket* was part of the "Fresh Terrain" festival and critical symposium at the University of Texas in January 2003.[8] Carlson's postmodern, everyday movement-oriented choreographic work blends dance, voice, sound, and visual elements, and she often creates site-specific pieces in collaboration with local communities and nontraditional performers. She typically develops thematic series of work; her first, *Real People,* begun in 1986, is an ongoing group of performances created with and performed by people gathered together by a common profession, activity, or other relationship. These pieces represent and disassemble stereotypes and present opportunities for people to be "themselves." Carlson calls hers "experiential research," and says the heart of her process entails going into communities and learning their signs and symbols, while staying aware of the danger of appropriation and superficiality.[9] Jennifer Dunning says, "Carlson has an extraordinary gift for connecting the real and the imaginary in ways that leave their mystery vibrantly intact."[10] Carlson's work resembles Tomlin's, Hoch's, and Smith's, which I discussed in chapter 3, and even the Tectonic Theatre Project's work in Laramie, which I discussed in chapter 5. But where those performers impersonate their subjects by absorbing their characters into their own skin, Carlson stages community efforts in which people's signs and symbols are represented as art, often by the engagement of their own bodies, along with hers. Carlson's second series of work, *Animals,* incorporates live animals into performance and looks at the presence of animals in our lives as symbols, pets, and as reflections of our own animal instincts. Her third series, *White,* includes nuns, visually impaired performers, modern dancers, schoolchildren, ballet dancers, and a video installation by Carlson's artistic and life partner Mary Ellen Strom to create a performance event that examines issues of privilege and love in American culture.

Blanket is a solo performance originally commissioned by the American Dance Festival in 1990 and first performed on the eve of the Gulf War. At the University of Texas, Carlson performed the piece in the department's four-hundred-seat theater on a completely empty proscenium stage with a white cyclorama stretched taut across the back wall. (A cyclorama—or as it's commonly called, a "cyc"—is a stage-size piece of muslin that separates the stage from the backstage area, on which designers project light or images. The designer for *Blanket* lit the cyc so that it appeared to glow with a kind of subtle warmth.) Alone on stage, Carlson created a disjuncture between the presentness of her body and the visually absent but aurally recalled progress of history that brought her and an ethically and politically framed "we" to this moment. *Blanket* embraces Einstein's theory that "all time exists in the present," which Carlson regularly quotes when discussing her work.[11] Although she herself is middle-aged, Carlson performs as an elderly woman in *Blanket,* while the performance's sound environment chronicles each molting stage of an American woman's life—from birth in the 1950s to the present in 2003 to an intimation of the endings in her future—as Carlson walks an almost aimless, not quite neat circle around the stage.

The timescape in which *Blanket* evolves represents only fifty or so years of life in America, but Carlson's character appears much older, perhaps in her eighties, embodying the future that coexists with her present and her past. Because Carlson uses the putative "character" of an elderly woman—signaled by her age makeup, rather than by establishing a psychological narrative history—the audience expects to be drawn into some sort of relation to the "as if" of fiction. When character appears, the audience expects relation—that is, we expect that we'll be asked to identify with this other person, who's called into being by the performer for a clear representational purpose. We expect to mark the similarities and differences between ourselves and the character with empathy, sympathy, or doubt.[12]

Carlson plays on that probability by constantly disappointing our expectations of character and by displacing the operations of identification from story-driven "self" to history. That is, Carlson uses the device of the visual image of age to conjure our identification with a common history of the nation, rather than with an individual, psychological character. The moments she selects also represent identifiable, iconic points in American or world history. The performance doesn't invite partisan sympathies for the events it evokes; it simply sets in motion of the operation of memory and the piquing of acknowledgment. That Carlson creates an older woman (who may or may not be a reflection of her self) calls history into the present while at the same time foreshortening her (if not "the") future. Carlson's selection of certain historical moments, which resonate from *Blanket*'s soundscape (constructed by Andy Kirshner), admits to a partial, particular, progressive view of American history, one that subtly underlines American inhumanity—segregation, nuclear explosions, Vietnam, political assassinations—to create a precondition for the performance of a newly human gesture later in the piece.

In the University of Texas performance, Carlson began her journey in slow motion from the far upstage right corner of the stage, stiffly, almost shuffling her feet. She approached center stage tentatively, testing the air, securing her understanding of the tangible charge brought by the simple white lights and the audience's preparatory anticipation (or perhaps, from Bloch's perspective, "anticipatory illumination"). She took two slow steps at a time, one foot precariously going forward, the other rushing to catch up in a rhythmic staccato two-step that propelled her forward. Carlson wore a deep purple coat rubbed to a sheen by use, or perhaps glistening with some rich material like silk. She wore black tie shoes with a small heel that reminded me of the shoes my elementary school teachers wore in the early 1960s—sensible, functional, unaesthetic shoes. A straight seam ran up the back of her stockings.[13]

Her initial entrance was abrupt and brief. She stood for a moment far up stage, then hurried off again, returning with a bouquet of just-fading tulips bending slightly over her wrist, yellow and red bulbs outlined by a bit of black that appeared on their way to closing themselves again. Throughout the performance, these flowers seemed active interlocutors, poised as they were on the sharp edge before their demise. The tulips established a structure of anticipation the same way guns forewarn their own firing, as they sit waiting for their climactic moments on the domestic mantelpieces of the box set. We give flowers *to* one another, intending them as gestures of beauty and generosity. And since we know that like performance, they won't last, but that their splendor will retreat into memory, such cut flowers point to the passing of time. Since Carlson performed alone, the flowers presaged an unknown recipient, and signified mystery and generosity around her journey's goal.

Carlson and her tulips wandered the stage, while the sound environment pulled the audience into an aural kaleidoscope of the last fifty years of the American past. We heard news reports of President Kennedy's assassination, of Cambodia, Kent State, the Supreme Court upholding the death penalty, Jim Jones and the mass suicides he orchestrated in Guyana; radio news of *Brown v. the Board of Education* and the end of school segregation and of HUAC and Eisenhower. Perry Como music played; newscasters counted down to the explosion of the first atomic bomb in the Nevada desert. Popular music and snippets of public memory intertwined to pull the audience through their own nostalgic, poignant reminiscences.[14]

Over this historical soundtrack, Carlson spoke through a body mic that magnified each of her breaths and her every murmur. She spoke first in a gurgling baby voice, forming the prelinguistic utterings of a happy, curious infant, filling with sounds that can't, at first, be translated into meaning. Carlson created a productive, even shocking, friction between sound and image, asking us to interpret the pristine, innocent noise of babyish delight against the visual background of a performatively elderly body stumbling through space, while we listened to the recorded sounds of history that charted the baby's (or more metaphorically, the "subject's") growth. We could see the baby's destiny at the moment of her birth; we looked through present history at the past through the incongruence of Carlson's posture and her babble. When the atomic bomb's burst punctuated the soundtrack, the baby who was Carlson began to cry, a primal, nerve-wracking wail that sounded like the pain inflicted on all of humanity in that moment of technological "achievement." The soundtrack of news, noise, and music described the mushrooming nuclear cloud. The baby's cry expressed in a moment how much we lost by what we gained.

Fragments of history bumped against each other in the loop of found sound that anchored the performance, which served as an aural palimpsest of history. Even though she never changed her elderly posture or gestures, Carlson's vocalizing represented her development from a preverbal baby to a child as she starts coming into language. She formed small words ("bomb," "cookie," "blanket"), the juxtaposition of which wove the child's story into the world's story. As her voice grew from child to adult, she demonstrated how social sounds, echoes from the public sphere, trickle down into consciousness, teaching us words whose meaning we won't grasp until it's too late to forestall the events they predict.

The woman/child's voice grew inevitably, inexorably, moving from innocence and light to something more ominous, signaled by the distortion of the *Andy of Mayberry* theme song that played over the next generation of her life. Carlson's soundscape here evoked the trappings of small-town domesticity, yet underneath this section of the performance ran a current of lost innocence, trickling away with the dissipating smoke of the nuclear cloud. "I hate you," she said to someone who lived in her imagination, the outline of a friend's body we could all flesh out with our own imaginings. "Not it"; "Yes you are," she said, playing her own game of memory tag, as Carlson's body maintained its deliberate pace, "slowly travers[ing] the stage from left to right, like words on a page,"[15] never speeding up or slowing down to reflect the activity chronicled by her voice.

"This is a test of the emergency broadcasting system," she said, mocking the ubiquitous, ominous, inevitably ineffective warning recalled from minutes of monotones on the radios that once centered social life. Those words instructed people to listen closely; they signaled some vague, future emergency and urgency, and the always lurking possibility of the need to mobilize against danger. Reference to the emergency broadcasting system calls up a specific moment in history, one that perhaps organizes spectators' experiences differently, as not everyone will remember the imperious monotone on the radio, accompanied on television by a single, stark image of warning. *Blanket* invites spectators into its memorial stream at their own pace, while it encourages us to note the time that extends through our personal remembrances. The piece historicizes time and requires that we constantly remember what comes before us and anticipate what might come after.

Ambiguity and ambivalence haunted the piece, punctuated by Carlson halting her looping arcs around the stage several times to face out to the audience and ask, "What time is it now?" as if to secure the moment in the present, while acknowledging that time is slipping away, that there's only so much time, that it's running out even as we watch. When she first asked, about twelve minutes into the forty-odd-minute performance, the audience took a collective breath and surreptitiously glanced about, wondering if she was really talking to us. She repeated the question, directly out to the audience, looking for a spectator who would answer her. Finally, someone braved this invitation to break theatrical convention, and responded from the house, "It's 7:12," and later, "It's 7:24," and finally, "It's 7:39," announcing real time in all its digital precision. Carlson repeated these times carefully, as if to acknowledge the importance of the timekeepers' participation in marking these moments. Carlson asked us to mark the passing of time with her, even though from the audience, time is quotidian, theater time, while on stage, it's monumental, performer's time.[16] We were drawn into the porous border between performer and audience that made *Blanket* about *our* American history, which created an "our," an "us," a "we," that made the performance about our own presence in the past, and made us aware of our shared responsibility for the present and perhaps the future. Her gesture underlined the "now" that her performance conjured so eloquently.

Carlson's movement vocabulary communicated precisely yet elliptically through the whole piece, reined in to the careful two-step, the slightly bent stoop, the hand holding the flowers, and the other hand moving constantly, fingers rubbing against each other in an almost subconscious, automatic, unstoppable gesture of feeling the texture of the air, of measuring the thickness of her wordless description of life. The gesture seemed a little like palsy and a little like obsession, but it also represented rubbing against memories of experience, a certain feeling for what she's taken into her hands, between her fingers, over the many years we heard going by. As she walked in her deliberate circle, her laces bounced against her shoes, highlighting her prosaic perambulations. History sped up as she walked; the rhythms of language on the soundtrack raced to catch up to her in the present. They moved inexorably toward a now in which the words on the tape began to sound incomprehensible, as though when history arrives at the present, it confronts its own inability to mean anything. In some ways, the performance exemplifies Bloch's notion of the three dimensions of temporality, in which he

offers us a dialectical analysis of the *past* which illuminates the *present* and can direct us to a better *future*. . . . [F]or Bloch, history is a repository of possibilities that are living options for future action. . . . This three-dimensional temporality must be grasped and activated by an

anticipatory consciousness that at once perceives the unrealized emancipatory potential in the past, the latencies and tendencies of the present,
and the realizable hopes of the future.[17]

Carlson's anticipatory consciousness animates *Blanket.*

Carlson's intention gathered as she arrived, finally, at a destination
downstage left as far as possible from the point at which she started, evoking onstage, beautifully, the arcing line of life. As she began to lower the
tulips to the floor, the space instantly evoked a cemetery, as if she'd been
walking deliberately all along toward a grave, bringing her flowers to
honor, nonspecifically, "the dead." The light brightened; she bent carefully
to put the flowers down; then she lost her balance and fell in a crumpled
heap on the stage floor. Eventually, she began painfully to rise, first getting
to her knees with excruciating effort. Once halfway up, she held out her
hand to the audience, entreating. Was she asking us to help her, just as
she'd asked us for the time? Or was her entreaty to a larger "us," to perhaps
a "we," or to a "United States," or to an "America" that she wants not to let
her down? The tension built as we watched Carlson struggle to stand. Her
hand stayed suspended, shaking in the air over the stage; she looked out at
us. Regardless of the public she saw metaphorically, *we were there,* physically, the recipients of her gesture of asking—for help? for hope? for
acknowledgment?

One night during *Blanket*'s "Fresh Terrain" run, Tamara Smith, a graduate student in the University of Texas Theatre and Dance Department,
stood up as soon as Carlson fell, immediately convinced that Carlson
needed help. Smith made her way to the aisle of the theater and then
toward the stage. She stood near the proscenium, as the audience watched
her and watched Carlson, wondering, as the tension grew, if Smith
intended to mount the stage to help Carlson stand up. Some of us knew
that at the top of the short set of risers that led to the apron, the stage
dropped away, into the orchestra pit, which the lights and the otherwise
dark stage floor hid from view. Some of us worried that propelled to her
feet by her impulse to help, Smith would climb the stairs and fall into the
pit, leaving Carlson on the ground, stuck in her gesture of entreaty while
Smith would hurt herself. But Smith instead stood close to the wall at the
front of the house, willing Carlson to rise without her physical assistance.
Later, Smith said she was waiting for Carlson to make eye contact, to tell
her, through a glance, that she really did need help. Carlson later said she

purposely didn't make eye contact, so that the moment would remain suspended and she would remain alone.

What impulse moves one spectator out of her seat to help, while others remain immobilized, even if riveted by the actions unfolding before us?[18] Only a performance as powerful as Carlson's could propel a person into action, could signal as if through the flames a rather Artaudian sense of need, urgency, and desire and yet defer, disallow, the very assistance her gesture seemed to seek. Smith's impulse to help, though, confirmed the presence of a utopian performative. Carlson's earlier entreaties, her requests for time, made possible Smith's later gesture of assistance. Something had happened between Carlson and the audience, represented by our time-telling and Smith's leap to her feet, a utopian performative that allowed us to rehearse the possibilities of a humane, humanist "what if." Yet because she wouldn't make eye contact, Carlson stayed in control, in command of a moment that never became trite or facile.

Silence engulfed the stage as Carlson slowly stood to full height, gazing with recovered dignity out into the house. Her image brightened, and then the lights began the slowest fade I've ever seen in the theater. The picture of her body, once the light finally went out, had seared itself on my retina, so that I saw her figure outlined in the afterimage that remained on my eye. Seeing Carlson's absence there comforted and awed me, as though this powerful presence hadn't disappeared, but would linger, always.[19] The intimacy of the performance made something as private as someone's death a part of the public, pointing to the intermingling of the personal and the political and to the ways public discourse penetrates our bodies and our minds, whether we know it or not.

The performance exacted a particular affect—we weren't explicitly asked to identify *with* the elderly woman who carried our contemporary history, but we were implicated in the necessity to *identify* this history, to claim our part in it, not for nostalgia or sentimentality, but so that we could chart our own course into the future. As Dunning says, Carlson has a "gift for dryly suggestive evocation. Hers is an unsentimental eloquence."[20] Carlson's utopian performative gesture wasn't toward some perfected end-state of hegemonic idealism; rather, she participates in "possible futures-in-process," which, once recognized, enact the "first step to understanding the responsibility each of us has to the future in deciding how to live our lives in the present."[21] Carlson's intensely intersubjective performance presented our responsibility to the future by making tangible the present choices we make toward each other as human beings. People "require a heroic image of their own future in order to stimulate and sustain the energy capable of bringing out the best of their being."[22] By channeling so specifically American history to put in context our present, Carlson's old woman became a hero for the future into which she looked, out over our heads, as she asked, "What time is it now?" Wrenching the audience from the quotidian time of the theater to the constellated time of the stage, Carlson's utopian performative draws us toward a profitable conflation of past, present, and future: "The present is understood at each point as a transition to something new; it lives with an awareness that historical events are accelerating and an expectation that the future will be different."[23]

Dunning says, "Carlson has an extraordinary gift for connecting the real and the imaginary in ways that leave their mystery vibrantly intact."[24] Another reviewer notes, "Carlson's meticulous technique—her remarkable ability to segue from senility to cradle, for example, and her multiple voice ranges and timbres—is next to invisible. She never seems to be pulling tricks; each of her characterizations has an unimpeachable integrity and truth. But there's also nothing in the least artificial about her impersonations—it's as though she's naturally able to get under the skin of a plethora of human stereotypes, without reducing any of her subjects to caricature."[25] By working the intimate line between public and private, *Blanket* poised on a limen in which life becomes the threshold to a place imagined but not necessarily articulated elsewhere. In this respect, Carlson takes up the challenge to make theater what artist-critic Thulani Davis calls

> a public space where many private worlds can be seen and heard . . . a public space where the fictional boundaries of the past can be our metaphors, rather than our prisons. American theatre is the natural public space for a society no longer able to keep its fictional fences standing. It is a space of creative energy that is a shelter where people try to understand a world in which we are all materially, spiritually, elbow-to-elbow interdependent.[26]

Walking on Water:
Mary Zimmerman's *Metamorphoses*

The surest, and the quickest, way for us to arouse the sense of wonder is to stare, unafraid, at a single object. Suddenly—

miraculously—it will look like something we have never seen before.

—CESARE PAVESE, *Dialogue with Leuco*

Metamorphoses, director Mary Zimmerman's theatrical adaptation of Ovid's mythological tales, also employs a Benjaminian sense of all time as "now," as happening in the present. By creating a set of rich theatrical metaphors rife with witty anachronisms, Zimmerman uses mythic Greek stories to reassure the people gathered in the theater of our common humanity, of our understandable need to reassure ourselves that we're here, that we survive, by telling each other and ourselves the stories of our pasts, our presents, and our futures. Zimmerman, a company member of the Lookingglass Theatre in Chicago, where the play premiered, also teaches performance studies at Northwestern University in Evanston. The MacArthur Foundation awarded her with a "genius grant" in 1998 and she won a 2002 Tony Award for her direction of *Metamophoses.*[27] Zimmerman's work "attempts to find the magical intersection of the beautiful and the spiritual."[28] Her story-theater style of devising performance has produced *The Notebooks of Leonardo da Vinci* (2003), *Arabian Nights* (2004), and *Journey to the West* (1995), among others, all compiled of various narrative source materials in other genres. Zimmerman collaborates with ensemble casts to create the written and visual script for each performance, refreshing and surprising collisions of word and image, often formed as anachronisms that observe no unity of time or action.

When *Metamorphoses* opened off-Broadway in October 2001, critic Michael Kuchwara wrote that "Zimmerman's beautiful story-theatre production . . . serves as a consoling antidote to the tragedies of Sept.11, especially in the ways it deals with grief."[29] Ben Brantley, in the *New York Times,* said that the play "could surely never have had the resonance it has acquired in the aftermath of Sept. 11," admitting that "[i]n another context, it might have registered as too precious."[30] Other critics noted that "September 11 made Ovid seem more relevant than ever. . . . [A]udiences were deeply moved by its depiction of love, death and human resilience"; audiences "responded to the play as if gripped by the cathartic effect of an ancient Greek drama."[31] Another said that "audiences responded with open emotion to the way it confronted the ineluctable."[32] Critics rarely remark on audience response to productions, yet the coincidence of the play's opening with the September 11 attack in New York produced a wealth of direct observation of spectators' reactions. These reviews evoke with exceptional clarity the feelings that permeated audiences at the play when it opened.

Zimmerman uses the stories of loss and yearning abounding in Greek mythology to explore the contours of grief and longing, but transforms them into compassionate and somehow sustaining human lessons and parables. In fact, the play's utter humanity drives its utopian performatives. Zimmerman uses myth as an organizing structure to demonstrate how narrative orders our experience. Just as Holly Hughes, Peggy Shaw, and Deb Margolin use autobiographical stories to analyze the social and its potential for change, Zimmerman uses the familiar stories of Western myth to reassure us that transformation happens all around us all the time. We've heard many of these stories before, if not in exactly this way, and their repetitions in *Metamorphoses* remind us that life, like narrative, has a structure, that life can be told, that we can derive hope from our lives and insights that might teach us something joyful or painful about who we are and who we might become. The play foregrounds storytelling: each vignette has a narrator, a position that rotates among members of the ensemble of ten actors, who calls attention to how our lives are ordered by how we describe, tell, predict, and learn from them. One critic noted that "the low-tech simplicity of [the play] is a reminder that since ancient times, nothing has been more basic to theatre than live spoken word and well-done make-believe."[33] Because the play deftly theatricalizes these stories, metaphor brings them clarity, often breathtaking understandings that come from what we see on stage as well as what we hear.

If storytelling orders our experience, transformation keeps it fluid and unpredictable and always gives it potential for change and growth. The first speech of the play sets this tone: A woman performer says, "Bodies, I have in mind, and how they can change to assume / new shapes—I ask the help of the gods, who know the trick: / change me, and let me glimpse the secret and speak, / better than I know how, of the world's birthing, / and the creation of all things, from the first to the very latest" (5). The play "depicts constant change as a creative and inevitable life force";[34] *Times* critic Margo Jefferson said that "gods, mortals, and animals keep changing places, and the boundaries between what we feel and what we should feel keep getting erased, then redrawn."[35] The injunction to change encapsulates all of time; although the play narrates myths, the performers enact them in the present, with an affectionate, hopeful eye toward the past and the future.[36] The play's content and form—both intent on the possibilities for transformation—line up neatly and pleasurably. The stories connect the present and the past and point toward a future through the utopian performatives they use to illuminate their meanings. For example, in the story of Erysichthon, as a woman transforms in and out of various characters, including an old woman and a little girl, the narrator tells the audience, "To this day, at every hour, somewhere in the world, you can still catch a glimpse of that child playing by the shore" (39). Somewhere in the world, somewhere in time, moments repeat themselves eternally.

Metatheatricality and metaphysics align as well in *Metamorphoses*. The gods appear above the scenery, looking over the stage as they did in classical theater conventions, but here, they bear themselves with the studied casualness of the Western monied elite rather than the imperious guise of the kind or vengeful omnipotent miracle workers of myth. When Zeus first appears, he lights a cigarette, cleverly employing the idiom of anachronism in which the play delights.[37] The narrator announces that "[o]nce these distinctions were made and matter began to behave, / the sky displayed its array of stars in their constellations—*(The lights of the chandelier begin to glow)*" (6). Electric lights stand in for the firmament and, in the play's most fruitful metaphor, a shimmering twenty-seven-foot-wide pool stands in for the ocean and the earth and all the ground beneath our feet. Into this paradise walks "man," as Zeus and the woman narrator note, "A paradise, it would seem, except one thing was lacking: words. . . . And so man was born. He was born that he might talk" (6). "One way or another, people came—erect, standing tall, / with our faces set not to gaze down at the dirt beneath our feet, / but upward toward the sky in pride or, perhaps, nostalgia" (7). People, then, are born not just to talk, but already, at the moment of our genesis, to remember, to long for the "before" the now that haunts us always.

The actors transform from character to character—or from one narrative function to another—quickly, in full view of the audience, by changing their posture or a prop, or simply by moving out of one story's frame and into another. As in the performances of Tomlin, Hoch, and Smith, the play and its production free the actors from the fixity of identity, encouraging them to try on other ways of being human that might let them mean differently and continually. The story and its workings write on the performers; through their actions, the play tells its tale. Rather than being sutured to character, the performers become figures in a panoply of humanity, in which the function they serve supports the telling of the tale and its progress toward something humane and whole. Simple actions represent huge feelings—Midas makes his devastating wish, and his daughter turns to gold in his arms, demonstrating in an iconic moment how much he loses with the little wealth he gains.[38] The production's physicality writes the body simply and evocatively.

I saw *Metamorphoses* during its off-Broadway run in December 2001.[39] The production, directed by Zimmerman and cast with performers who'd participated in the play's workshop and development in Chicago, stripped down the stage to highlight images made by bodies that, like Carlson's old woman in *Blanket*, served as carriers of historical and utopian meanings. Storytelling ushered the audience into a world of imaginative play that took pleasure in its own theatricality. The performers became objects, places, other people—they aged, they became young again, they lost each other, they traveled great distances, they found each other, they died, and they were resurrected as already ancient, beneficent gods, always watching those still mired on earth.

The mythological stories took various shapes and forms, performed around the large rectangular pool of water far downstage that brought metaphors of transformation to life. Images shimmered in reflections on the water's surface, presenting to the audience a translucent, literally fluid surface on which to see animated tales of yearning, longing, loss, and redemption enacted and recalled. The light reflected in the water felt elemental, as if it were caused by sunlight or moonlight, rather than theatrical light; our eyes were tricked into seeing nature where the artifice of theater only imagined it. Art critic and activist Carol Becker says that a kind of Marcusian notion of "the beautiful"—which certainly describes *Metamorphoses*—lets people confronting art "consider what no longer exists, what resides in dreams, memories of a time (whether real or imagined) when life was fulfilling and people's relationship to it seemed less estranged. . . . [I]t is important to note that, in the context of many social movements, the seemingly retroactive emotion of *longing* has propelled people forward."[40] By reanimating mythic history, *Metamorphoses* captured this longing toward a better future, offering an aesthetic experience of the beautiful in performance that also let the audience feel utopia, calling attention to the sad, inherent loveliness of an always changing world.

Zimmerman worked the magic of water on stage to craft irreducible performances, and gave the actors' virtuosic bodies the space and depth required to shine, to glisten with desire or grief. In one story, the water became a roiling ocean, on which miniature ships waged a battle; in another, the water became a grave, into which an actor submerged himself and disappeared. Sometimes, the actors stood in the water as if it wasn't there, telling stories of people changing into other things found so often in myth. The mood changed quickly from pleasure to mourning, to demonstrate how close these emotions reside and how often they accompany each other in our lives and our stories.

The myths narrate tests. For example, in the Orpheus and Eurydice story, when Orpheus pleads for Eurydice to be sent back from Hades with him, the gods say, "Your song has moved us, Orpheus, and you may have her on one condition. . . . If you look at her before you reach the sunlight, she is ours. Forever" (42). We can only watch, as Eurydice follows her beloved out of hell toward the sun, and feel helpless when Orpheus turns back to make sure she follows and loses her once again to the gods. The gods challenge faith and belief, patience and trust, and demonstrate how human people are, and how difficult it is to meet the challenges that strain our devotion. The legendary story of Midas frames the play: When he asks the gods that everything he touches should turn to gold, his daughter transforms from precious flesh into solid metal before his eyes. When Midas appeals to the gods, Bacchus says, "Walk as far as the ends of the earth. Look for a pool of water that reflects the stars at night. Wash your hands in it and there is a chance that everything will be restored" (19). The gods' moral emphasizes that our fundamental humanity, what courses in our hearts and our souls, matters more than material goods.

If the old stories resonate with familiarity, the production's anachronisms and colloquialisms startle us into recognizing, as Carlson insists after Einstein, that all time exists in the present. The story of Phaeton perhaps most cleverly illustrates such simultaneity; Zimmerman stages the myth with Phaeton in a bathing suit wearing sunglasses, floating in the pool on a brilliant yellow raft while his therapist sits beside the pool on a lounge asking questions. Phaeton adopts the vernacular to tell the story of his father, Apollo, and the boy's fateful ride in his father's chariot, translating the tale into one of a disgruntled teenager who wants the keys to his father's car and proceeds to crash, driving, despite Apollo's instructions, too close to the sun. The amusing parody of Freudian psychoanalysis also works to illustrate man's arrogance and greed, but because the play and production handle contemporary analogies with a light touch, these tales avoid moralizing and revel instead in humanizing their characters, along with all of us. *Metamorphoses* speaks into the public of the private, inviting audiences to be present in the simultaneity of time; "Zimmerman envisions the world of playmaking as a place where public life and private fantasy overlap for an ephemeral hour or so. Throughout the play, the physical expression of emotion and exquisite stagecraft exert a powerful bond of imagination between the players."[41] "Remember how apples smell?" a narrator asks toward the end of the play. The stage directions indicate, "A pause. Everyone inhales and remembers. They continue" (80). We're invited to breathe deeply of the common, prosaic bouquet of living, to remember the everyday, to see the art in life.

Like *The Laramie Project,* Zimmerman's text and direction of *Metamorphoses* uses Brechtian devices to frame its stories. Tales are punctuated by "she said" (21), calling attention to the telling of the story so that the audience doesn't forget that we're witnessing a reenactment. That is, the production resisted a kind of monumentalism that might have left it a museum piece, the fate so many remountings of classic plays suffer, and instead undercut its own authority with references to contemporaneity and history, at once. The production underlined the play's metaphors; for example, in the story of Alcyone and Ceyx, "ALCYONE falls asleep in the shallow waters of the pool. A SECOND NARRATOR appears. As he speaks, SLEEP enters, wrapped in a black velvet blanket, with eyeshades. APHRODITE slowly drops white letter Z's from the sky" (26). These metaphorical anachronisms and theatrical representations remind us of the contemporary with sweet, gentle humor, while the words describe, luxuriously, the way the bodies on stage should amplify, rather than just "act out," the words. As Zimmerman says, in her introduction to the published play, "The staging should rarely be a literal embodiment of the text; rather, it should provide images that amplify the text, lend it poetic resonance, or even sometimes contradict it" (3).

The words help the audience imagine what exceeds the capacities of the stage, but the combination of word, image, and feeling provides a lush experience of visual, aural, and sensual engagement with our minds and imaginations, as well as with the stuff of theater. Margo Jefferson says, "An illusion can flaunt the fact that it's an illusion and thus heighten your belief in it. Imagination rules."[42] Many critics of the production commented on the "collusion" of performer and audience in the faith *Metamorphoses* exacts to make its meanings. One said,

> [Zimmerman's] work is spare and simple, frequently playful, but at the end of each tale, when a transformation takes place, it is not just the brilliant stagecraft or the actors' technique that makes the audience respond. What elicits consent, what makes the work "click," is the felt

rightness of the outcome, which is another way of saying that the weight of the culture is behind it.[43]

The utopian performative appears in this moment, when the work "clicks" with the audience because something true, something recognizable, something felt and mutually believed, even though only imagined, passes among those present. Zimmerman has said, "What attracts me to theatre is the collusion between the audience and what is happening onstage, believing what they know not to be true."[44] By suspending disbelief, we affirm a "communal self with deeply humanist values" and give ourselves over to the potential of not just personal but political transformation.[45]

Marcuse "struggled to articulate the ineffable," Becker says.[46] "Fundamental to Marcuse's understanding of the possibility of human liberation was his belief in the imagination—its regenerative abilities to remain uncolonized by prevailing ideology, to continue to generate new ideas, and to reconfigure the familiar. It was within the imagination that the desire to envision the idealized state of utopia and to push the world to its realization resided."[47] Elegantly executed performance work like *Metamorphoses*, generated from the bodies and minds and hearts of the ensemble, offers a series of utopian performatives, since in their doing, the audience's imagination is stretched to see new things in the quotidian materials of daily life.

Neo-utopian Heroism: Warner and Shaw's *Medea*

Metamorphoses created fantastical images supported by a contemporary rewriting of ancient mythology. Deborah Warner and Fiona Shaw's production of *Medea*, too, held transformational potential and, despite its tragic outcome, a measure of utopian hope.[48] Theirs also illustrates a different use of Greek narratives; they intended not to see myth as nostalgic or transcendent, but to see the repetition of a familiar narrative as an opportunity for critical thinking, if not for changing its outcome. Warner and Shaw frequently collaborate on productions, as they share a belief in the transformative power of theater alongside a healthy skepticism about its challenges. Shaw tells a reporter that she "calls the art of acting a 'heightening of all human dimensions.'" The reporter says:

She tells me that "I prefer, if I have health, the self-definition of doing a play" but in the same breath says that she loathes theatre. It's not a contradiction, she says. It's part of the reason that she works so much with Deborah Warner, who she says has "an integrity and patience beyond anyone on the planet." Warner shares her ambitions, to turn what is "a dull art form" into an experience in which the audience is changed, emotionally, when they leave the theatre.[49]

Warner and Shaw made Euripides' tragedy colloquial and personal; the play, Shaw says, "is a healing experience. 'The stage is where tragedy should be. All cultures need tragedy even when they don't think they do.'"[50]

Like *Metamorphoses,* Warner and Shaw's production of *Medea,* too, used a pool of water to stress the body's materiality, its mutability and the changeable nature of the present within history. The pool sat centered in the town square in which Warner sets the production. Medea's sons used it to float their toy boats; it offered a gathering place for the action, a place for community highlighted by the blocking. Yet the pool also waited, ominously, still water running deep, and was in fact used most effectively at the play's wrenching finale. Behind the pool, the stage of the Broadway theater seemed emptied out, its back wall bare cinder blocks, fronted by large, opaque glass doors that slid open to reveal an outdoor pathway, presumptively into an attached house placed somewhere in the stage left wings. Blocks of concrete, as if either recently taken apart or in a suspended state of waiting for reconstruction, lay stacked around the stage.

Soccer balls rolled across the floor, along with other remnants of interrupted child's play, toys that seem strangely (and purposefully) anachronistic beside each other: an abacus, a wooden sailboat, little action figures, stuffed animals, and a plastic dinosaur combined to signify a mixture of the contemporary and the ancient. Because the stage extended into the lap of the orchestra, people in the front row placed their *Playbills* carelessly along its edge, and put their feet up on the concrete steps that led from the house to the apron. These *Playbills* enacted the same sort of anachronism as those in *Metamorphoses*—the breaking of time from the present of the play to the "now" of the theater, into the "then" of the classic story. The obviousness of the watching represented by those programs on the stage seemed to emphasize how the production wanted to highlight that distraction, that critical interpretation of the real. This and other decisions—including Shaw's frequent choice to play out to the audience, nearly in direct address—subtly undercut the production's mimesis. The production signaled a desire to break the fourth wall, to remind us that the separation of public and private breaks down in any theater, but particularly in this one. Shaw emphasizes this insistent avoidance of fourth-wall pretense when she says that "from her perspective, acting is more about imagination than psychology."[51] Warner's choice of theatrical equivalences, of metaphors that illustrate her conception of the meaning of the tragedy, used imaginative means to solder phases of time—the past to the present to the future. Likewise, Shaw says, "Styles of acting keep changing. . . . The eye and the ear use things up. You carry your time with you. There has to be something new." A performance is "only valid in that moment."[52]

The doors upstage center looked like the doors that open onto the lobbies of prestigious corporate firms. Center stage, the square pool sat surrounded by blue tile; the pool at the center of a city square signified a public place, while the upstage glass doors implied something more private, even if it was corporate instead of domestic. Through the play, the doors came to divide the peculiarly public realm of Medea and the women and the children from the interior place of private commerce where people's actions have public resonance (like the corrupt actions of the executives at Enron). By putting Jason's machinations inside a semiotically corporate space while Medea pondered her fate in the public square, Warner reversed the assumption of interiority as female and private and exteriority as male and public, lending the production some of its feminist verve. The set's cool blue and gray color palette belied the heat of the emotions that would shortly fill it. The steely set mirrored Medea's resolve, her determination, despite her offhand opening gambit, in which Shaw set the audience up for a startling contrast between Medea's joking, shrugging, self-deprecating beginning and the furious bloodlust inevitably waiting for her at the end.

The set was already pregnant with a certain kind of ominous life, even before the first actor walked onto it. Sounds, too, conveyed foreboding; we heard rumblings, doleful bells, eerie noise, all of which filled the stark, abstract, postmodern scene with the pull of ancient, malignant emotions. Shaw and Warner made Medea's rage personal and urgent and colloquial. Critic Robert Brustein writes,

> Angular, gaunt, intense . . . [Shaw] makes her first entrance in a flowered skirt and cardigan sweater, wearing sunglasses over her tear-puffed eyes. Speaking the colloquial translation of Kenneth McLeish and Frederic Raphael, she excavates the mordant comedy that comes from a pit of festering hatred, surgically slicing everything away from

her character except the sinews, bones, and nerves. . . . [S]he is volcanic in the extreme . . . [displaying] the anger of the abandoned wife and the displaced immigrant.[53]

Medea became both iconic and somehow more real, as Shaw began with the specificities of character, then propelled herself into a more universal demonstration of rage at the long history of female betrayal. In some ways, this movement from iconic to real (and back) also describes the actors in *The Laramie Project,* who represent real—and through the media circus, familiar—characters, but who become icons of a traumatic national moment through the constant retelling of Shepard's (like Medea's) story. In that movement between icon and real circulates a reconfigured possibility for "the universal," one that uses despair at human degradation to decry its operation. Universality adheres not to Medea's or Shepard's actual situations, but to the ways, as Gitlin says, we only need to be human beings to understand their tragedies.[54]

Although her Medea was palpably human, pushing up her sleeves, picking up the children's toys, asking things of the servants and interacting with the chorus of worried townswomen, Shaw moved her from humiliated and incredulous over Jason's betrayal to fury that transcended the moment and entered historical time. One critic called Shaw's Medea "a woman who is being slowly tortured on the rack of her own feelings."[55] She began as an ordinary woman whose emotions catapult her into wailing laments, operatic outbursts, breathless physical flailings through the water in the pool, deeply symbolic poses in which her drenched overshirt drips with water and finally, with her children's blood.

Against the cool, static set, Shaw burned with anger, requiring intense attention from the audience in the house, insisting on capturing our glance and thereby creating a public anew with each performance. She captivated and disturbed those on the stage who represented the citizens who urge her away from revenge, who try to calm her passion, and who, finally, bear the consequences of her rage with her. Resisting all admonishments, Medea finally ran into the interior through those glass doors, which remained open, framing the blood that streaked in a single brilliant swathe against the back wall as she slashed her children's throats. The splash of blood horrified the audience, shocked us with its materiality, even though we knew it wasn't real. The red splatter seemed something you could touch, a sticky remnant of the life of the bodies in which it had just coursed. When Medea entered after the murder, her children's blood ran from her in rivulets; she splashed through the pool to confront Jason, flicking him with water to irritate him, as though those pink droplets might make him angrier than the death of his sons. Shaw's wet shirt clung to her body, outlining the palpable, vulnerable urgency of her presence.

As in *Metamorphoses*, the water on stage brought performers and spectators together into a "now," highlighting the continual rearrangement of molecules that living entails. Water on stage outlines the body's materiality, its vulnerability, its porousness, as water is something to move clumsily through and to drink in, to take into the body, for healing. Water lets us look deeply into infinity; it mirrors a past and a future that dissolves as we touch it. Water changes unpredictably, like performance, never appearing the same way again (wasn't it Brecht who said we can never step into the same stream twice?). Medea's rage roiled the waters, but she (and perhaps we) found some measure of relief when the pool settled down, a tragic relief colored with her sons' diluted blood.

The *New York Times* reviewer wrote, "The anxious perfume that saturates this production is a compound of the passion, terror, and existential ambivalence that have plagued humans for as long as they have been able to think."[56] The sheer size of the role and the performance provided audiences with an encounter with human extremes, taking us to the edges of human experience and back, in a way that stretched what we could each imagine as our own potential for suffering (and implicitly, for joy). Shaw says about Medea, "These great characters stay just this side of rationality, but they carry with them enormous irrational feelings, which is what we all carry. And so they carry the potential of human behavior with them."[57] The tragedy, played by a woman as strong and as expert as Fiona Shaw, offered a shimmering, painful, luminescent hope. "Shaw thinks there's a particular reason why American audiences are responding so passionately to *Medea*, which is that in the stressful aftermath of the Sept. 11 terror attacks, classical tragedies resonate differently. 'America is probably more open to tragedy than it's ever been, because America's wearing its nerves on its skin,' she says. . . . 'And the purpose of tragedy now, I suppose, is the same as the purpose of tragedy then, which is that its compassionate possibilities are enormous.'"[58] Shaw's Medea, like Carlson's old woman, "describe[d] [a] new mood—the yearning for a heroic image of the human future":

> Secular humanism . . . has been one of the foundation blocks of Modernist ideology. But its growing spiritual inadequacies, such as its lack

of certainty about the future, have led to the radical moral relativism of New Age Postmodernism on the one hand and return to the bedrock certainties of religious fundamentalism on the other hand. . . . Only a Neo-Utopianism can offset this double trend and reinvigorate the secular humanism that is the necessary meta-ideological underpinning of constitutional democracy.[59]

A neo-utopianism "would want to change the focus of Romanticism. It would want us to be romantic about the future—not about the past."[60] Shaw's performance hinted at this romantic, heroic hope—the enormity of her emotion put the past to rest, and looked voraciously to the future. Her spectacular anger, after she murdered her sons, forced her to dwell no longer in the past, but to look forward, beyond even the contemporary era of this production of the ancient play, to a future in which her fury might be answered.

In very different ways, *Medea, Metamorphoses,* and *Blanket* use performance to stage a reanimated, more radical humanism. They begin with the particular—with classic stories, with ancient mythologies, with an extended moment of American history—then insistently extend it to a more complex universal, one that doesn't require transhistorical agreement on the importance of a tragedy or a character or an event, but that can recognize and feel and acknowledge the consequences of an action in its moment and the various, complicated ways it resonates in some of our own. A complex universal doesn't insist on transcendent value but, like a utopian performative, sees itself as a moment in time, as progressive, partial, unfinished, and open.[61] These performances allow audiences to deepen their connection to their political and social lives by rehearsing a depth of feeling that can demonstrate effective and *affective* civic engagement. Thomas de Zengotita, arguing for a return to humanism in *Harper's,* says radical politics requires seeing quotidian, prosaic life—like those referenced in *Blanket, Metamorphoses,* and *Medea*—as part of a larger web of culture and requires empathy and connection over space and time. De Zengotita says that "deep political engagement . . . takes something extra to influence people in this way, to cause them to extend their sense of self to encompass multitudes of strangers, to [identify] with all humanity and each human being." The principles of humanism, he says, "depend on the fundamental identification of each of us with all of us, with the sheer human being abstracted in the ideal from concrete contexts of history and tradition."[62] The utopian performative acknowledges the impossibility of an ideal but finds "good enough for now" in a moment.

De Zengotita acknowledges the important work of identity politics, arguing that it, too, is based on an idealist abstraction of what any particular identity means. Identifying with a gay community, in his example, is as abstract as identifying with "humanity." He argues that progressives should reinhabit the language of humanism. He says, "We have . . . allowed the right to abscond with the very categories of political philosophy that have nourished progressive movements since the seventeenth century."[63] He urges us to take our sense of outrage at inequity and reapply it to all of humanity, knowing what we now know about differences in identity contexts and cultures, but admitting that finally, it's our understanding of broadly applied injustice that motivates our pressing activism.

The Unfinished Symphony: Finding Hope and Humanity at the Theater

In addition to reanimating humanism (after we've deconstructed the blind, transcendent universalisms it once espoused), progressives need to reclaim other languages that theater and performance can help us articulate. Searching for ways to define the utopian performative in performance, or to see the ongoing hope for utopia in daily life, I'm most moved by words that our work in theory once cast into doubt, words like *love, truth,* and *beauty,* as well as the capacious holding place called "humanity." I'm moved by the potential that performance offers for polishing away the tarnish of cliché that clings to these words. Historian Robin Kelley asks, "How do we transcend bitterness and cynicism and embrace love, hope, and an all-encompassing dream of freedom, especially in these rough times?"[64] Despair could break us; theater might renew us, by inviting us to imagine—along with the material, fleshy, so vulnerable and mortal performers' bodies that create fantasy-pictures for us, embellished with light and color and sound and depth—ways to be fully human together. Kelley describes what his mother called "the Marvelous," as "aesthetic moments of appreciation that are free, that are about being in the world and noticing its treasures." Kelley says, "I inherited my mother's belief that the map to a new world is in the imagination, in what we see in our third eyes rather than in the desolation that surrounds us."[65] The imagination can connect us to a renewed understanding of our separate corporealities, can let us appreciate commonality alongside our new and deep understanding of difference.

In theater and performance, we can harness what Rabbi Abraham Joshua Heschel calls "radical amazement." Heschel says that "no work of art [has] ever brought to expression the depth of the unutterable, in the sight of which the souls of saints, poets, and philosophers live. The attempt to convey what we see and cannot say is the everlasting theme of mankind's unfinished symphony."[66] Marcuse describes this as "the ineffable"; Raymond Williams calls it "structures of feeling"; I call this a utopian performative. In the theater, we can encounter our inarticulate longings toward a future that, through utopian performatives, might still remain *mute*, but can on some deeper level be *felt*. We can join theater and performance to social movements that, as Kelley says, "transport us to another place, compel us to relive horrors and, more importantly, enable us to imagine a new society."[67]

The emptiest stage in a theater can be filled with utopic visions. The body of an actor treading those boards can always make a gesture of utopian performativity. Breathlessly, yearning to be able to see her outline still, I watched with others as Ann Carlson stood astride a grave, but looked out in hope, to humankind, to an imagined, better, much better future that builds on the history that brought her feet to this edge. Horrified, I and my fellow spectators witnessed Medea shaking an old world order, splashing through its detritus to begin to imagine the new, metaphorically harnessing the collective desires of a nation to forge on, to recreate the state. With pleasure and admiration, the audience and I saw performers in *Metamorphoses* play in a pool, rearranging the elements into ever more aesthetic forms with their presence. I drank in the stories that splashed from the stage, reassured that old myths imagined in new ways continue to live, but that we can also create new mythologies.

These performances also trade in what feminist theater-maker and activist Joan Lipkin has called "a politics of tenderness."[68] In some ways, they also create "the proliferation of new political spaces,"[69] which point to

the diffusion of political sites across the surface of the social itself, to the elaboration of "the political" beyond its modernist enclosure within the territorially-bounded juridical institutions of the state into the far more fluid and shifting domain of cultural representation and social practices. . . . [T]his postmodern pluralism opens the possibility of a quotidian politics—a politics which extends the terrain of political contestation to the everyday enactment of social practices and the routine reiteration of cultural representations.[70]

Performance brings these quotidian politics and social practices home, as it were, literally and metaphorically. They become both more real—in that we grasp them more fully through their embodiment and ours at the theater—and less real, in that theatricality makes glorious, hopeful spectacles of the possibilities of everyday social life. These performances offered daydreams, which Bloch calls "signs of the not-yet-conscious," "where individuals have presentiments of what they lack, what they need, what they want, and what they hope to find."[71] As Ernst Fischer, one of Bloch's contemporaries said, "Art is necessary in order that [people] should be able to recognize and change the world. But art is also necessary by virtue of the magic inherent in it."[72] The magic of performance, the privilege of relief from banality and the pleasure of working at creating the ever shifting, always partial understandings and empathy that the stage allows, models a way to be together, as human beings, in a culture and a historical moment that's working much harder to tear us apart.

Epilogue

Finding Hope at the Theater

[T]he courage to care, to feel deep agony and anguish, to deal
with the tears generated by the suffering that people experience . . . this is not only a matter of following some objective
and rational moral law, but is also rooted in the blood-
drenched tear-soaked traditions of resistance, critique, and
contestation—and in the agency of the wretched of the earth.
The courage to hope, like laughter and dance, is an attempt
to endure, to persevere, to fight, and to struggle come what
may. Nothing can extinguish or crush radical hope—no matter what we continue to think critically about, care deeply for,
or hope substantively to achieve—and this is the blues shining through the darkness.
—Cornel West, "Celebrating Tikkun and Tragicomic Hope"

We need to reject the reactionary contention that, unless
properly mediated by irony, matter related to emotion and
content are out of place in "real" art. Against the exploitative
circularity of this mode of thinking only a rejection of cynicism for its own sake can return art to its true social function—which is to give imaginative shape to humanity's hope
for a better and more inclusive future. There is nothing facile
about an art that denounces the conditions of present-day
social and economic exploitation in order to seek change.
—Bram Dijkstra, "The Dialectic of Hope"

Crafting . . . a new political language will require what I call
"educated hope." Hope is the precondition for individual
and social struggle. Rather than seeing it as an individual pro-
clivity, we must see hope as part of a broader politics that
acknowledges those social, economic, spiritual, and cultural

conditions in the present that make certain kinds of agency
and democratic politics possible.
—HENRY A. GIROUX, "When Hope Is Subversive"

Throughout *Utopia in Performance*, I've suggested that moments of liminal clarity and communion, fleeting, briefly transcendent bits of profound
human feeling and connection, spring from alchemy between performers
and spectators and their mutual confrontation with a historical present
that lets them imagine a different, putatively better future. In my attempt
to recapture those moments of communitas, of spectacular yet subtle
beauty and grace in the performances I chronicle here, I've been challenged to write in a way that in itself mirrors the alchemical combustions
of those utopian performatives. In critical reflection and writerly specula-
tion, I've been inspired by reimagining and however briefly resurrecting
those performative acts as (via Bloch) rehearsals for examples of a social
utopian goal. Writing, like performance, is always only an experiment, an
audition, always only another place to practice what might be an unreach-
able goal that's imperative to imagine nonetheless. Writing, like performance, lets me try on, try out, experiment with another site of anticipation, which is the moment of intersubjective relation between word and
eye, between writer and reader, all based on the exchange of empathy,
respect, and desire. Writing *Utopia in Performance*, I've made my own
wish for the future and I've conjured, through memory, my experience of
the past. Trying to capture something of performance itself—even if it's
those inarticulate, ineffable, affective exchanges that are felt and gone even
as we reach out to save them—is also a "doing," a kind of performative
that attempts to fill the "aporia between logos and the body," the gap in
which performance inevitably, spectrally swirls.[1] Perhaps that gap congenially ushers in both theory and practice, providing a home for however
temporary a meeting between mind and body, thought and deed, feeling
and affect.

Utopian performatives capture the contradictory status of performance
as absence, as performance theorist Peggy Phelan has elegantly argued, and
the apparently separate doings of writing and gesture, which dance scholar
(and my colleague) Ann Daly has evocatively attempted to conjoin.[2] How
might utopian performatives harness those contradictory separations and
offer the possibility to experience both sides of the binary at once in a crystalline moment of past-present-future "now" time? Utopian performa-

tives gather power through their attachment to particulars—particular moments in time, spaces in geography, constellations of spectators joined as audiences to witness specific configurations of performers. Perhaps utopian performatives move and stir us because they're inevitably specific and local products of a here and now that passes into there and then even as we experience them.

How can we take the space opened in performance and imagination and actively encourage utopian performatives? Isn't this what any group of actors and directors tries to do each time they set out to create a performance? Not to "mount a production" like a museum piece, but to create the present/absent, fluid, breathtaking "goneness" of performance?[3] What strategies of artistic and critical production might enable the proliferation of utopian performatives, without commodifying them and emptying them of their necessarily spiritual, idiosyncratic is-ness? Will other spectators know utopian performatives when they feel them? Or can they only be discerned after the fact, in the removed space of contemplation and remembrance when spectators—alone or in reconstituted groups—recall what they felt and resummon the magnitude of what it might have meant? The artist-scholar-citizen challenged to apprehend utopian performatives requires a readiness, a willingness to be transported out of the banal, emotionally moved elsewhere. The materials of such transport can be modest; that is, impressive scenery and helicopters hovering in the flies of a stage aren't required to provoke such feeling.

In *Utopian in Performance*, I've also asked how might we document affect. How can we chronicle an audience's response, in the moment of performance? Utopian performatives challenge reception studies because they focus resolutely on the present, while that very present encourages us to see an immaterial, desirable future. Because that gesture—the doing of the utopian performative—is inarticulate, a structure of feeling prior to its enunciation, securing its end point in language is both improbable and undesirable. As queer theorist (and my colleague) Ann Cvetkovich says, there's a "difficulty [to] gathering even a history of the present and [a] challenge, even for experimental ethnography, of documenting emotional life."[4] Yet without such "evidence," such certainty, how do we know when communitas happens? Can we assume it's the same for everyone?

What, finally, do communitas and the utopian performative *do?* What is their action in the world? Or do we burden them by even posing this question? Perhaps utopian performatives create the *condition* for action;

they pave a certain kind of way, prepare people for the choices they might make in other aspects of their lives.[5] Perhaps our goal shouldn't be to formulate or implement how utopian performatives can have social effect outside the theater, but should be to focus our activism on getting more and different kinds of people into the theater in the first place, so that they, too, might experience their affective power. We too often flounder on the shoals of "what does this *do*," when how something *feels* in the moment might be powerful enough.[6]

At the end of a book in which I've tried to evoke the power of utopian performatives, I'm left with these potent questions. In my attempt to answer them, they keep circulating and affirming the importance and possibilities inherent in a performance-based performative. I admire and believe in a utopia-in-process as a social goal, even if it remains a beautiful, intangible product of the ineffable (via Marcuse) or the marvelous (via Kelley). I've argued here that showing up begins the chain of reactions that creates a fertile environment for utopian performatives; going to see performance at all is an act of social faith, of belief in art as a rehearsal for an example of freedom and justice. If audiences are always temporary publics, as Michael Warner theorizes them, then they become crucibles of thought, feeling, and the potential for action in which a whiff of utopia might be fermented. Perhaps because our love for theater propels us to see performance, a precondition is already met for the necessary faith, belief, and desire, out of which utopian experiments and imaginings can be forged, however ephemerally. In the always dialogic space of performance, in the endless potential of utopian performatives, thinking and creating propels movement through something.

Utopia is always a metaphor, always a wish, a desire, a no-place that performance can sometimes help us map if not find. But a performative is not a metaphor; it's a doing, and it's in the performative's gesture that hope adheres, that communitas happens, that the not-yet-conscious is glimpsed and felt and strained toward. Humanism, too, can be a performative, one that (after feminism and critical race theory and queer theory and postmodernism) needs to be continually recreated, so that we never presume its transparency.[7] Emotion and affect, too, are performative, stagings done in a moment of feeling that need to be shown to have effect. Like emotion and affect, utopian performatives can't be predicted; they exist as wishes, as desire, crystallizing from our labor to construct a temporary public that constitutes a multiplicity of presence, hoping to be recognized, extended, and shared. A utopian performative gives us a mode of thinking and seeing; it can't be confined in a set of stable, immobile criteria, because it relies on the magic of performance practice, on our belief in social justice and a better future, on the impact and import of a wish, and on love for human commonality despite the vagaries of difference.

Notes

CHAPTER ONE

1. Russell Jacoby, *The End of Utopia: Politics and Culture in an Age of Apathy* (New York: Basic Books, 1999), 10. See also, among the many commentators on this theme, Sam Gindin and Leo Pantich, "Rekindling Socialist Imagination: Utopian Vision and Working-Class Capacities," *Monthly Review*, March 2000, 36–52. On the deep pessimism within the Left, they say, "Overcoming this debilitating political pessimism and keeping some sense of transformative possibilities alive is the most important issue anyone seriously interested in social change must confront" (36).

2. See Michael Moore, *Fahrenheit 9/11*, Lions Gate Films, 2004.

3. Marvin Carlson, "The Theatre Journal Auto/Archive," *Theatre Journal* 55, no. 1 (2003): 211.

4. David Román, in his book *Acts of Intervention: Performance, Gay Culture, and AIDS* (Bloomington: Indiana University Press, 1998), explicates the refrain "return to performance" (223).

5. I've seen several other interesting uses of *performative* modified in the way I mean to use it here. Queer theorist Lauren Berlant actually uses the phrase "utopian performative" to refer to Michael Jackson's "Black or White" video, which, she says, by referring to the dominant intertext of the black panther, "signals the amnesiac optimism or the absolute falseness of the utopian performative 'It don't matter if you're black or white'" (*The Queen of America Goes to Washington City: Essays on Sex and Citizenship* [Durham, N.C.: Duke University Press, 1997], 213). The way I understand her to use this phrase, however, is to modify Jackson's performative "It don't matter if you're black or white" with "utopian" to describe it as impossible or unrealizable. I'm using the phrase to indicate a performative that "does" utopia in its utterance. Theater scholar Vivian M. Patraka, in *Spectacular Suffering: Theatre, Fascism, and the Holocaust* (Bloomington: Indiana University Press, 1999) refers to what she calls "the Holocaust performative": "Theater reiterates the Holocaust, then, by announcing itself as performative" (6); "The Holocaust performative acknowledges that there is nothing to say to goneness and yet we continue to try and mark it, say it, identify it, memorialize the loss over and over" (7).

6. J. L. Austin, *How to Do Things with Words* (Cambridge: Harvard University Press, 1975). The wedding ceremony is Austin's example. For foundational work on "performativity," see also Eve Kosofsky Sedgwick, *The Epistemology of the Closet* (Berkeley and Los Angeles: University of California Press, 1990) and *Performance and Performativity*, ed. Andrew Parker and Eve Kosofsky Sedgwick (New York: Routledge, 1995). Parker and Sedgwick critique Austin's marriage example in their introduction

(9–13). Also see José Estaban Muñoz, *Disidentifications: Queers of Color and the Performance of Politics* (Minneapolis: University of Minnesota Press, 1999), in which he argues for what he calls "disidentification" as a practice of performativity for queer people of color that happens within the social. He says, "Rather than pit performativity against performance or stack them next to each other in a less than interactive fashion, I have chosen to employ a methodology that stresses the performativity of *or* in performance. It is my contention that *the doing* matters most and the performance that seems most crucial are [*sic*] nothing short of the actual making of worlds" (200). Muñoz's impulse toward seeing performance as building worlds in both the future and the present, "which is to say that disidentificatory performance offers a utopian blueprint for a possible future while, at the same time, staging a new political formation in the present" (200), is sympathetic to my intent with what I'm calling "utopian performatives."

7. Elin Diamond, *Performance and Cultural Politics* (New York: Routledge, 1996), 5.

8. Quoted in Virginie Magnat, "Theatricality from the Performative Perspective," *SubStance* 31, nos. 2–3 and 98–99 (2003): 154.

9. Magnat, "Theatricality," 154.

10. Angelika Bammer, *Partial Visions: Feminism and Utopia in the 1970s* (New York: Routledge, 1991), 2.

11. Bammer, *Partial Visions*, 4.

12. Bammer, *Partial Visions*, 7.

13. Chris Ferns, *Narrating Utopia: Ideology, Gender, Form in Utopian Literature* (Liverpool: Liverpool University Press, 1999), x.

14. See, for excellent critical work on Brecht, gestus, and utopian performatives, Shannon Baley, "Death and Desire, Apocalypse and Utopia: Feminist *Gestus* and the Utopian Performative in the Plays of Naomi Wallace," *Modern Drama*, special issue on utopian performatives, 47, no. 2 (2004): 237–49. See also Jost Hermand, "Brecht on Utopia," in "Marxism and Utopia," special supplement of *Minnesota Review*, spring 1976, who writes that Brecht "clearly sees how necessary it is to put some utopian images in the hands of the people, but immediately emphasizes that these should be employed only as long as they are practical and useful" (103).

15. See Augusto Boal, *Theatre of the Oppressed* (New York: Theatre Communications Group, 1975), in which he coined the term "rehearsal for revolution"; and also Bertolt Brecht, *Brecht on Theatre: The Development of an Aesthetic,* trans. and ed. John Willett (New York: Hill and Wang, 1964). For my own engagement with performance as revolution, see Jill Dolan, "Rehearsing Democracy: Advocacy, Public Intellectuals, and Civic Engagement in Theatre and Performance Studies," *Theatre Topics* 11, no. 1 (2001): 1–17.

16. Ruth Levitas, *The Concept of Utopia* (Syracuse: Syracuse University Press, 1990), 148.

17. For a study of utopian contents in drama, see Dragan Klaic, *The Plot of the Future: Utopia and Dystopia in Modern Drama* (Ann Arbor: University of Michigan Press, 1991).

18. For instance, Sarah Kane's play, *Blasted* (in Sarah Kane, *Complete Plays* [London: Methuen, 2001]), while violent, dystopic, and nearly unwatchable on stage, might

still promote an experience of the utopian performative in certain moments of production.

19. John Rockwell, "Reverberations: Living for the Moments When Contemplation Turns to Ecstasy," *New York Times,* October 24, 2003, B4.

20. Phillip E. Wegner, "Horizons, Figures, and Machines: The Dialectic of Utopia in the Work of Frederic Jameson," *Utopian Studies* 9, no. 2 (1988): 61.

21. Performance theorist Peggy Phelan perhaps best captures the dialectic of appearance and disappearance in which our attempts to engage performance get caught. See *Unmarked: The Politics of Performance* (New York: Routledge, 1993).

22. Ann Daly, *Critical Gestures: Writing on Dance and Culture* (Middleton, Conn.: Wesleyan University Press, 2002), xiv.

23. For a useful explication of this problematic in historical research on musical theater, see Stacy Wolf, *A Problem Like Maria: Gender, Sexuality, and the American Musical* (Ann Arbor: University of Michigan Press, 2002).

24. Daly, *Critical Gestures,* xv.

25. Another Frankfurt school German philosopher, Walter Benjamin, has been very useful regarding the simultaneity of time and on the potential of utopian, messianic thought. See his "Theses on the Philosophy of History," in *Illuminations: Essays and Reflections,* ed. Hannah Arendt, trans. Harry Zohn (New York: Schocken, 1968), 253–64.

26. Janelle Reinelt's "The *Theatre Journal* Auto/Archive," *Theatre Journal* 55, no. 1 (2003): 385–92 was the first auto/archive Román published.

27. Jill Dolan, *The Feminist Spectator as Critic* (Ann Arbor: University of Michigan Press, 1991) and *Presence and Desire: Essays on Gender, Sexuality, Performance* (Ann Arbor: University of Michigan Press, 1993). For excellent studies of theater reception practices, see Susan Bennett, *Theatre Audiences: A Theory of Production and Reception,* 2nd ed. (New York: Routledge, 1997); Herbert Blau, *The Audience* (Baltimore: Johns Hopkins University Press, 1990); and Wolf, *A Problem Like Maria.*

28. Nancy Fraser, "Rethinking the Public Sphere: A Contribution to the Critique of Actually Existing Democracy," in *Habermas and the Public Sphere,* ed. Craig Calhoun (Cambridge: MIT Press, 1992), 112.

29. Fraser, "Rethinking the Public Sphere," 122.

30. Fraser, "Rethinking the Public Sphere," 124.

31. On communitas, see Victor Turner, *Drama, Fields, and Metaphors: Symbolic Action in Human Society* (Ithaca, N.Y.: Cornell University Press, 1974), 274. See also Victor Turner, *From Ritual to Theatre: The Human Seriousness of Play* (New York: Performing Arts Journal, 1982), 45–51.

32. Fraser, "Rethinking the Public Sphere," 125.

33. Rob Zellers and Gene Collier, *The Chief,* dir. Ted Pappas, O'Reilly Theater, Pittsburgh Public Theater, November 7, 2003.

34. See Joe Tucker, *Steelers' Victory after Forty* (New York: Exposition, 1973).

35. As Julia Kristeva says, "[W]e are confronted with two temporal dimensions: the time of linear, *cursive* history, and the time of another history, that is, a *monumental* time . . . that incorporates these supranational sociocultural groupings within even larger entities" ("Women's Time," in *New Maladies of the Soul,* trans. Ross Guberman [New York: Columbia University Press, 1995], 203).

36. Frederic Jameson, "Of Islands and Trenches: Neutralization and the Production of Utopian Discourse," *Diacritics* 7, no. 2 (1977): 2–21.

37. Wegner, "Horizons, Figures, and Machines," 61.

38. Bammer, *Partial Visions,* 48.

39. Elizabeth Grosz, "The Time of Architecture," in *Embodied Utopias: Gender, Social Change, and the Modern Metropolis,* ed. Amy Bingaman, Lise Sanders, and Rebecca Zorach (London: Routledge, 2002), 268.

40. Grosz, "The Time of Architecture," 271.

41. Turner, *Drama, Fields, and Metaphors,* 24.

42. Turner, *Drama, Fields, and Metaphors,* 47.

43. Turner, *Drama, Fields, and Metaphors,* 202.

44. Turner, *Drama, Fields, and Metaphors,* 208.

45. Reinelt, "Auto/Archive," 392.

46. Reinelt, "Auto/Archive," 388.

47. Reinelt, "Auto/Archive," 391.

48. For an interesting study of a community theater and its operations, see Leah Hager Cohen, *The Stuff of Dreams: Behind the Scenes of an American Community Theater* (New York: Viking, 2001). See also Stacy Wolf, "Theatre as Social Practice: Local Ethnographies of Audience Reception," Ph.D. diss., Department of Theatre and Drama, University of Wisconsin, Madison, 1994, and her "'Being' a Lesbian: Apple Island and the Performance of Community," in *The Queerest Art: Essays on Lesbian and Gay Theatre,* ed. Alisa Solomon and Framji Minwalla (New York: New York University Press, 2002), 183–202.

49. Quoted in Lynn M. Thomson, "Teaching and Rehearsing Collaboration," *Theatre Topics* 13, no. 1 (2003): 118.

50. Bert O. States, "Phenomenology of the Curtain Call," *Hudson Review* 34, no. 3 (1981): 374.

51. Quoted in Alice Echols, *Scars of Sweet Paradise: The Life and Times of Janis Joplin* (New York: Henry Holt, 1999), 260. Echols goes on to say, of her main subject, Janis Joplin, "For Janis, using heroin became a way of prolonging the onstage high by fending off the inevitable postperformance depression" (260).

52. See Richard Schechner, *Performance Theory,* rev. ed. (New York: Routledge, 1988). For a critical engagement with lesbian bars, see Kelly Hankin, *The Girls in the Back Room: Looking at the Lesbian Bar* (Minneapolis: University of Minnesota Press, 2002).

53. David Román evokes such moments in lovely, poignant ways in his introduction to *Theatre Journal*'s special issue on dance, *Theatre Journal* 55, no. 3 (2003).

54. See Ramón Rivera-Servera, "Choreographies of Resistance: Latina/o Queer Dance and the Utopian Performative," *Modern Drama,* special issue on utopian performatives, 47, no. 2 (2004): 269–89.

55. Herbert Marcuse, *The Aesthetic Dimension: Toward a Critique of Marxist Aesthetics* (Boston: Beacon Press, 1978), 33.

56. Marcuse, *The Aesthetic Dimension,* 46.

57. See Jacoby, *The End of Utopia.*

58. Mary Dietz, "Context Is All: Feminism and Theories of Citizenship," in *Dimensions of Radical Democracy: Pluralism, Citizenship, Community,* ed. Chantal Mouffe (London: Verso, 1992), 75.

59. Chantal Mouffe rightly cautions against the exclusions that democracy, too, can

enact. She says, "Political life concerns collective, public action; it aims at the construction of a 'we' in a context of diversity and conflict. But to construct a 'we' it must be distinguished from the 'them' and that means establishing a frontier, defining an 'enemy.' Therefore, while politics aims at constructing a political community and creating a unity, a fully inclusive political community and a final unity can never be realized since there will permanently be a 'constitutive outside,' an exterior to the community that makes its existence possible. Antagonistic forces will never disappear and politics is characterized by conflict and division. Forms of agreement can be reached but they are always partial and provisional since consensus is by necessity based on acts of exclusion" ("Democratic Citizenship and the Political Community," in *Dimensions of Radical Democracy*, 235).

60. Turner, *Drama, Fields, and Metaphors*, 243.

61. For more scholarship on hope, see Mary Zournazi, *Hope: New Philosophies for Change* (Annandale, NSW, Australia: Pluto Press, 2002), in which she stages a series of conversations with academics and intellectuals from around the world.

62. Gitlin, *Letters to a Young Activist* (New York: Basic Books, 2003), 158.

63. Gitlin, *Letters*, 168. After the exposure of American soldiers' brutality toward Iraqi prisoners at Abu Ghraib prison in Baghdad, we need more than ever such an international commitment to common ethical standards.

64. Gitlin, in *The Twilight of Common Dreams: Why America Is Wracked by Culture Wars* (New York: Metropolitan Books, 1995), says, "Today it is the Right that speaks a language of commonalities. . . . To be on the Left, meanwhile, is to doubt that one can speak of humanity at all" (84). Unfortunately, I agree with Gitlin; *Utopia in Performance* participates in an argument about changing just that equation. I should note that Gitlin's often-derogatory dismissal of identity politics elsewhere in his work can be destructive, and that he fails to account for their importance to particular moments in political history. But his best ideas can be borrowed without endorsing his entire platform of opposition to identity politics.

65. Martha C. Nussbaum, *Sex and Social Justice* (New York: Oxford University Press, 1999), 71. Speaking specifically of feminism, she says, "Feminism needs to operate with a general notion of the human core, without forgetting that this core has been differently situated and also shaped in different times and places. We should not overlook the questions raised by these differences, and we cannot formulate a just social policy if we do. But insofar as feminism denies the value of the whole idea of a human core, it gives up something vital to the most powerful feminist arguments." I'd like to thank Maurya Wickstrom for calling Nussbaum's book to my attention.

66. Nussbaum, *Sex and Social Justice*, 39.

67. Nussbaum, *Sex and Social Justice*, 49.

68. Robin D. G. Kelley's work to reinvigorate the word "humanism" by combining it with "radical" provides an excellent model for my attempts here. I first read the expression "radical humanism" in a paper Kelley presented at a faculty colloquium at the CUNY Graduate School in the late 1990s. Kelley's books, *Freedom Dreams: The Black Radical Imagination* (Boston: Beacon Press, 2002); *Race Rebels: Culture, Politics, and the Black Working Class* (New York: Free Press, 1994); and *Yo' Mama's Disfunktional! Fighting the Culture Wars in Urban America* (Boston: Beacon Press, 1997), as well as his other work around these themes, has been influential in my own thinking.

69. Josephine Lee raised this question when I presented portions of this work at the University of Minnesota in April 2003.

70. Peggy Phelan's essay on Operation Rescue in *Unmarked* offers an excellent explication of the Right's antiabortion strategies. See also on the Right's tactics of building communities of belonging, Linda Kintz's study *Between Jesus and the Market: The Emotions That Matter in Right-Wing America* (Durham, N.C.: Duke University Press, 1997).

71. See Gitlin, *Letters*, 111–17, who describes persuasively the differences in strategy between activists on the Right and the Left. He does a particularly good job describing the Left's suspicion of power, and its determination to theorize and engage intellectually with the new politics and society it espoused, especially in the 1960s. Gitlin's argument, of course, is about instrumentality; that is, he points to the Right's single-minded desire to get things done, to make social change happen their way, as its greatest asset, and ruefully blames the Left for its "anarchist" tendencies and less effective organizational strategies. I want to note, again, that I disagree with Jacoby's anti-identity politics stance and that I personally see nothing wrong with a healthy dose of anarchy. But I do think he's articulate about the ways the Right has been able to marshall power, compared to the inefficiency of the Left.

72. Pierre Bourdieu, *Distinction: A Social Critique of the Judgment of Taste*, trans. Richard Nice (Cambridge: Harvard University Press), 1984.

73. Gitlin, *Letters*, 129.

74. The second iteration of the "Throws Like a Girl" series was in 2002, for which we produced Marty Pottenger's *City Water Tunnel #3*, Peggy Shaw's *To My Chagrin*, and Terry Galloway's *Lardo Weeping*. The 2005 series hosted Marga Gomez and Carmelita Tropicana in their collaboration *Single Wet Female*; Deb Margolin in her writerly solo show *Index to Idioms*; and Peggy Shaw and Lois Weaver in a revival of their late 1980s two-hander, written by Holly Hughes, *Dress Suits to Hire*.

75. See Jessica Hester's review of the festival in *Theatre Journal* 55, no. 3 (2003): 519–22.

76. Michael Walzer, "The Civil Society Argument," in Mouffe, *Dimensions of Radical Democracy*, 107.

77. Martin Esslin, *An Anatomy of Drama* (New York: Hill and Wang, 1976), 26, quoted in Magnat, "Theatricality," 157.

78. Daniel MacIvor, "Entrepreneurial Strategies" panel, "Fresh Terrain" symposium, January 25, 2003, Department of Theatre and Dance, University of Texas at Austin.

79. Ben Cameron, "New Directions in Contemporary Theatre" panel, "Fresh Terrain" symposium, January 25, 2003; Mark Russell, "Developing Performance Art/Performance Theatre" panel, "Fresh Terrain" symposium, January 26, 2003, Department of Theatre and Dance, University of Texas at Austin.

80. Madge Darlington, "Entrepreneurial Strategies" panel, "Fresh Terrain" symposium, January 26, 2003, Department of Theatre and Dance, University of Texas at Austin.

81. Eric Bentley, "The Theatrical Occasion," in *The Life of the Drama* (New York: Atheneum, 1967), 179.

82. Bentley, "The Theatrical Occasion," 181.

83. See Joni Jones, "Performance Ethnography: The Role of Embodiment in Cultural Authenticity," *Theatre Topics* 12, no. 1 (2002): 1–15.

84. Iris Marion Young, "The Ideal of Community and the Politics of Difference,"

in *Feminism/Postmodernism,* ed. Linda J. Nicholson (New York: Routledge, 1990), 300–323.

85. For an introduction to some of the ideas in this section, see Rabbi Abraham Joshua Heschel, *Man Is Not Alone: A Philosophy of Religion* (New York: Jewish Publication Society of America, 1951). See also Margo Jefferson, "Suddenly Onscreen, It's All about Wonder," *New York Times,* February 8, 2003, B9.

86. Ann Wilson, "Bored to Distraction: Auto-performance and the Perniciousness of Presence," *Canadian Theatre Review* 79–80 (summer–fall 1994): 37.

87. Wilson, "Bored to Distraction," 33.

88. Tim Miller, introduction to *My Queer Body,* in *Body Blows: Six Performances* (Madison: University of Wisconsin Press, 2002), 83.

89. David Savran, "Choices Made and Unmade," *Theater* 3, no. 2 (2001): 89–95.

90. Román, *Acts of Intervention,* xxvi. Jaclyn Pryor, Paul Bonin-Rodriguez, and I have developed an extension of Román's notion of critical generosity that we call "colleague criticism." First proposed by Bonin-Rodriguez, then extended with Pryor, and then later with myself, colleague criticism is a practice reminiscent of participant observation in ethnography and exemplifies a standing *beside* rather than above the work in question. Through it, we express our concern for what the work does and how it lives in the world. As Bonin-Rodriguez says, "We define colleague criticism as public criticism openly informed by private, collegial knowledge. As colleague-critics, we write about performance as artists, as colleagues, as friends, and as scholars in the field; we speak to our knowledge of both the work at hand and the experience and context of making work; we keep our theory and practice in a state of present dialogue; and we work to expand the role of the artist in local, public arts discourse. Colleague-critics foreground their relationship with one another and offer an informed undertanding of process, context, subjectivity, and the critical object or event, raising questions about meaning and expanding understandings of the artist's material practice and the process of reception." See Pryor, Bonin-Rodriguez, and Dolan, "Colleague-Critic: Performance, Activism, and Public Practice," presented at "Abriendo Brecha/Haciendo Camino: Activist Scholarship on Race, Identity and Mestizaje in the Americas," jointly sponsored by the Center for Mexican American Studies, the Lozano Long Institute for Latin American Studies, and the Rockefeller Foundation Humanities Fellowship program, University of Texas, Austin, February 25, 2005.

91. Stanton B. Garner, *Bodied Spaces: Phenomenology and Performance in Contemporary Drama* (Ithaca, N.Y.: Cornell University Press, 1994), 3. Phenomenology is the study of subjective perceptual experience. Garner says, "[P]henomenological reading seeks to reembody, materialize the text, draw out this latency . . . as an intrinsic component of dramatic textuality itself" (7). Phenomenology is a "particular mode of attention" (5), which makes it a useful methodology for teasing out utopian performatives in performance. In many ways, *Utopia in Performance* uses phenomenological methods to, as Garner suggests, adopt "its own version of Clifford Geertz's 'thick description'—a description, in this case, designed to reembody the field that we inhabit and perceive, to reclaim such experiential 'stuff,' forgotten and disowned, as even theory is made on" (14).

92. Garner, *Bodied Spaces,* 4.

93. Garner, *Bodied Spaces,* 14.

CHAPTER TWO

1. As Holly Hughes says ironically, "Theater tends to happen in theaters, whereas performance art tends to happen in spaces. A theater will be defined . . . as somewhere with a stage, some lights, a box office, a dressing room, head shots, and people who know how to run these things. A theater is a place that has been designed for theater, whereas a space has been designed for some other purpose: it's a gas station, an art gallery, somebody's living room, a church basement, and it's always better suited for pancake suppers and giving oil changes than for performing" (*Clit Notes: A Sapphic Sampler* [New York: Grove Press, 1996], 15).

2. For an in-depth discussion of these pedagogical principles, and for an argument about theater's necessary relationship to civic life, see my *Geographies of Learning: Theory and Practice, Activism and Performance* (Middleton, Conn.: Wesleyan University Press, 2001).

3. Klaic, *Plot of the Future*, 2.

4. Frederic Jameson says that the utopian principle might be seen as "a hermeneutic or technique of decipherment, in opposition to the examination of the content of individual utopian visions" ("Introduction/Prospectus: To Reconsider the Relationship of Marxism to Utopian Thought," "Marxism and Utopia," special supplement to *Minnesota Review* [spring 1976]: 56).

5. Gregory Claeys and Lyman Tower Sargent, eds., *The Utopia Reader* (New York: New York University Press, 1999), 1.

6. Victor Turner, speaking of "communitas"—a moment of liminality and cohesion in performance and ritual that inspires my notion of the utopian performative—says, "When communitas becomes force rather than 'grace,' it becomes totalism, the subordination of the part to the whole instead of the free creation of the whole by the mutual recognition of its parts. Yet when communitas operates within relatively wide structural limits it becomes, for the groups and individuals within structured systems, a means of binding diversities together and overcoming cleavages" (*Drama, Fields, and Metaphors*, 206).

7. Roland Schaer, Gregory Claeys, and Lyman Tower Sargent, eds., *Utopia: The Search for the Ideal Society in the Western World* (New York: Oxford University Press, 2000), 7.

8. Schaer, Claeys, and Sargent, *Utopia*, 8.

9. Rustom Bharucha, "Contextualizing Utopias: Reflections on Remapping the Present," *Theater* 26, nos. 1–2 (1995): 37.

10. For an exhaustive history of utopias and their ideologies, see Frank E. Manuel and Fritzie P. Manuel, *Utopian Thought in the Western World* (Cambridge: Belknap Press of Harvard University Press, 1979).

11. Dragan Klaic, "Utopia Sustained," *Theater* 26, nos. 1–2 (1995): 61.

12. See, for example, theater critic Erika Munk, who, in a special issue of *Theater*, the journal that she then edited, marks the absence of theater from writings on utopia. See her "Exiled from Nowhere," *Theater* 26, nos. 1–2 (1995): 101–11. Ann Pellegrini has pointed out to me that it would be interesting to think about utopia in relation to Aristotelian catharsis, which ultimately promotes a kind of static, conservative resolution (to which I'm not aspiring here), and to Freud's death drive, given that utopia is a kind of stasis. See also Lynda Hart and Peggy Phelan, "Queerer Than Thou: Being and Deb

Margolin," *Theatre Journal* 47, no. 2 (1995): 269–82, in which they demonstrate their own desire through Margolin's work, and wrestle, through performance, against the death drive: "I want something as flimsy and precarious as performance. Because, despite all the yelling about mimesis and realism and the tyranny of the couple, I want something to match the tentativeness of the lives and love I, and I hope we, make on the other side of the death drive" (280).

13. Richard Dyer, *Only Entertainment* (New York: Routledge, 1992), 18. See also Fredric Jameson, "Reification and Utopia in Mass Culture," *Social Text* 1 (1979), in which he suggests that "the hypothesis is that the works of mass culture cannot be ideological without at one and the same time being implicitly or explicitly Utopian as well: they cannot manipulate unless they offer some genuine shred of content as a fantasy bribe to the public about to be so manipulated" (146).

14. Schechner, *Performance Theory*, 169.

15. Anne Bogart, "Utopia Forum," *Theater* 26, nos. 1–2 (1995): 182.

16. Philip Auslander, *Liveness: Performance in a Mediatized Culture* (New York: Routledge, 1999), 2. See also Wilson, "Bored to Distraction," 33–37, for a critique of what she sees as nostalgia for premodern, authentic presence.

17. Playwright Sarah Schulman quotes performance artist Jeff Weiss, who said to her in reference to the AIDS crisis, "We have a moral and ethical obligation to persist in the living of real (as opposed to 'reel') time. That is the power of theater. We're all in this together, at the *same* time. We're totally engaged in being human together, sharing the identical instants as our time advances, parallel, in unison" (*Stagestruck: Theater, AIDS, and the Marketing of Gay America* [Durham, N.C.: Duke University Press, 1998], 61).

18. Auslander, *Liveness*, 55.

19. Blau's comment is actually, "When we speak of what Stanislavski called Presence in acting, we must also speak of its Absence, the dimensionality of time through the actor, the fact that he who is performing can die there in front of your eyes; is in fact doing so. Of all the performing arts, the theater stinks most of mortality" (*Take Up the Bodies: Theater at the Vanishing Point* [Urbana: University of Illinois Press, 1982], 83). I'd like to thank Amy Steiger, who reminded me of the exact quotation by citing it in her M.A. thesis in the Department of Theatre and Dance at the University of Texas at Austin, spring 2001.

20. See Ed Cohen, "Who Are 'We'? Gay 'Identity' as Political (E)motion (a Theoretical Rumination)," in *Inside/Out: Lesbian Theories, Gay Theories,* ed. Diana Fuss (New York: Routledge, 1991), especially 84–85.

21. Anna Deavere Smith, "Systems of Lights," *Theater* 26, nos. 1–2 (1995): 50–51.

22. I'd like to thank Rude Mechs company members Madge Darlington, Lana Lesley, Kirk Lynn, Sarah Richardson, and Shawn Sides for their help in managing and producing this series.

23. See Richard Schechner, *Performance Studies: An Introduction* (New York: Routledge, 2002); and Marvin Carlson, *Performance: A Critical Introduction* (New York: Routledge, 1996).

24. The texts for the class included, among others, Schechner's *Performance Theory;* Carlson's *Performance;* selections from Jo Bonney, ed., *Extreme Exposure: An Anthology of Solo Performance Texts from the 20th Century* (New York: Theatre Communications Group, 2000); Mark Russell, ed., *Out of Character: Rants, Raves, and*

Monologues from Today's Top Performance Artists (New York: Bantam, 1997); C. Carr, *On Edge: Performance Art at the End of the 20th Century* (Middleton, Conn.: Wesleyan University Press, 1993); and Holly Hughes and David Román, eds., *O Solo Homo: The New Queer Performance* (New York: Grove, 1998).

25. The story has it that the head of the University of Texas Board of Regents was an opera fan and wanted the Bass Concert Hall stage built to accommodate the Met's productions, which still toured at the time. Various professional scene designers and colleagues have told me that while the dimensions might be similar, the backstage and fly space is not as sophisticated as the Met's.

26. See Stacy Wolf, "Civilizing and Selling Spectators: Audiences at the Madison Civic Center," *Theatre Survey* 39, no. 2 (1998): 7–23, for an analysis of how cultural capital works within city arts centers. Despite my rather critical description of the hall here, I must say that I quite enjoyed myself seeing *Mamma Mia* and *Jesus Christ Superstar* at Bass, even though I didn't exactly experience utopian performatives at either performance.

27. Despite the marginalized geography of the theater, the audiences it attracts tend to be predominantly white. The Rude Mechs, however, as the space's producers, try to position themselves as a company running a space available for the local the Latino/a community. Their summer series, "Grrrl Action," is a community-based theater project in which local teenagers from around Austin spend several weeks exploring autobiography through performance, and present their monologues for public audiences. The Rude Mech's second stage, a late-night series of performance slots offered at low rent, attracts performers with fewer resources and less access to conventional production. The space is not a large, prestigious production site, and the Rudes aren't considered part of Austin's cultural elite. On the other hand, other East Austin theaters do attract a more racially diverse clientele. The Tillery Street Theatre at ALLGO (Austin Latina/o Lesbian/Gay Organization, which now calls itself a "queer people of color organization"), for instance, regularly produces solo performance, spoken word evenings, and other performative work by local and national people of color. ALLGO's theater is farther east than the Off Center but within the same general neighborhood, and it serves as a community center as well as a performance space.

28. Dyer, *Only Entertainment*, 20–21.

29. For historical and critical work on the Wow Café, see Dolan, *The Feminist Spectator as Critic;* and Alisa Solomon, "The WOW Café," in *The Drama Review: Thirty Years of Commentary on the Avant-Garde*, ed. Brooks McNamara and Jill Dolan (Ann Arbor: UMI Research Press, 1986), 305–14.

30. There is, by now, a vast and expanding archive of critical and theoretical work on feminist performance. See, for only several key examples, my own *Feminist Spectator as Critic* and *Presence and Desire;* Sue-Ellen Case, *Feminism and Theatre* (New York: Methuen, 1988), and her edited collection, *Performing Feminisms* (Baltimore: Johns Hopkins University Press, 1990); Elin Diamond, *Unmaking Mimesis* (New York: Routledge, 1997); Phelan, *Unmarked;* Lynda Hart, ed., *Making a Spectacle: Feminist Essays on Contemporary Women's Theatre* (Ann Arbor: University of Michigan Press, 1989); Lynda Hart and Peggy Phelan, eds., *Acting Out: Feminist Performances* (Ann Arbor: University of Michigan Press, 1993); and Carol Martin, ed., *On and Beyond the Stage: A Sourcebook of Feminist Theatre and Performance* (New York: Routledge, 1996).

31. Schulman, *Stagestruck*, 149–50.

32. See Kate Davy, "The Storefront: Creating Feminist Space and a 'System of Anarchy,'" unpublished, 2000.

33. See Tim Miller and David Román, "Preaching to the Converted," *Theatre Journal* 47, no. 2 (1995): 169–88. See also Vicki Patraka's interview with performance artist Robbie McCauley, in Martin, *On and Beyond,* 205–38, in which McCauley says about preaching to the converted, "I think that criticism is a cop-out. First of all, how much do the converted know? And things resonate, ripple out. This is not to say that you do not work constantly for audience development; we need to grapple with finding ways to expand audiences. But we don't need to put that problem in the way of doing the work, making our work clear and beautiful for our audiences. The whole issue is just a block" (234).

34. I was struck, listening to Hughes talk, about how vital it is that progressives recuperate the term *faith-based* from the ways it's pressed into service by the George W. Bush administration. The notion of faith, it seems to me, detached from religion, is undertheorized in its effect on political commitments. And certainly after the 2004 election, with its undefined and conservatively effective emphasis on "moral values" that seem to exclude anyone but the most fundamentalist Christian, such theorizing is more necessary than ever. For excellent work on the political use of religion, see Janet Jakobsen and Ann Pellegrini, *Love the Sin: Sexual Regulation and the Limits of Religious Tolerance* (New York: New York University Press, 2003).

35. For selected commentary on the NEA debacle, see, for example, Dolan, *Geographies of Learning;* Richard Meyer, "'Have you Heard the One about the Lesbian Who Goes to the Supreme Court?' Holly Hughes and the Case against Censorship," *Theatre Journal* 52, no. 4 (2000): 543–52; Peggy Phelan, "Serrano, Mapplethorpe, the NEA and You: 'Money Talks,'" *Drama Review* 34, no. 1 (1990): 4–15; and Wendy Steiner, *The Scandal of Pleasure* (Chicago: University of Chicago Press, 1995).

36. Holly Hughes, *Preaching to the Perverted,* unpublished script, 2000. Subsequent references will be included in the text. I'm very grateful to Hughes for giving me a copy of this script. If *Preaching* clearly describes the opposite of utopia, presenting our current culture as intensely dystopic, Hughes's short clip, *The Mystery Spot,* which I've seen her perform on numerous occasions, might be addressed as one of her more utopian performance moments. In this piece, she leaves the confines of her parents' car to travel alone to "the Amazing Mystery Spot, where billboards promised we could witness phenomena that defied the laws of nature" (*Clit Notes,* 11). As she follows the allure of this tantalizing place, her road takes her, eventually, to the WOW Café in New York, where her career as a performance artist begins, making of WOW the utopia it in some ways was.

37. Meyer, "Have You Heard," 552.

38. Meyer, "Have You Heard," 552.

39. Dennis Harvey, *Variety,* October 18, 1999, 54.

40. Robert Nesti, Arts and Life, *Boston Herald,* October 2, 1999, 25.

41. See Richard Schechner on the performance sequence in *Between Theater and Anthropology* (Philadelphia: University of Pennsylvania Press, 1985), 16–21.

42. See Román, *Acts of Intervention:* "Critical generosity is a practice that sets out to intervene in the limited perspectives we currently employ to understand and discuss AIDS theater and performance by looking beyond conventional forms of analysis. Critical generosity therefore forces us not only to rethink traditional criteria by

which evaluations are made but also to acknowledge the ideological systems that promote canonical prejudice. . . . Critical generosity understands that criticism can be much more than simply a procedure of critique or means for qualitative analysis. Criticism can also be a cooperative endeavor and collaborative engagement with a larger social mission" (xxvi–xxvii).

43. For the collected plays of Split Britches and a historical introduction to their work, see *Split Britches: Lesbian Practice/Feminist Performance,* ed. Sue-Ellen Case (New York: Routledge, 1996).

44. As Phillip Zarrilli writes, "A reified subjectivist notion of 'presence' is as complicit in a dualist metaphysics as is the Cartesian 'mind.' Neither provides an adequate account of the 'body' in the mind, the 'mind' in the body, or of the process by which the signs read as 'presence' are a discursive construct" ("Introduction to Part I," in *Acting (Re)Considered,* ed. Zarrilli [New York: Routledge, 1995], 15). I'd once again like to thank Amy Steiger, whose M.A. thesis recalled my attention to this quotation.

45. Peggy Shaw, *Menopausal Gentleman,* unpaginated, unpublished script, 1997. I'm very grateful to Shaw for giving me a copy of this script.

46. This is also partly what allows Shaw to undercut the image of the "White Man" that she might otherwise project. Hilary Harris writes that white women are complicit in white supremacist heteropatriarchy by the way in which they reflect the "white man" back to himself at twice his natural size. Shaw participates in an antiracist project by, among other things, cutting the white man down to a more prosaic scale. See Hilary Harris, "Failing 'White Womanhood': Interrogating the Performance of Respectability," *Theatre Journal* 52, no. 2 (2000): 183–209.

47. See Virginia R. Domínguez, "For a Politics of Love and Rescue," *Cultural Anthropology* 15, no. 3 (2000): 361–93. Domínguez argues that love and affection have a place in cultural (even in scholarly) discourse. Domínguez is writing specifically to scholars in anthropology, but her comments on the necessity for love and affection in our discourse resonate usefully here. See also David Román, "Comment—Theatre Journals," *Theatre Journal* 54, no. 3 (2002), n.p., for a persuasive argument about love and performance research.

48. Richard Dyer, "In Defense of Disco," in *Out in Culture: Gay, Lesbian, and Queer Essays on Popular Culture,* ed. Corey K. Creekmur and Alexander Doty (Durham, N.C.: Duke University Press, 1995), 413.

49. Francine Russo, *Village Voice,* June 16, 1998, 172; Christopher Rawson, Arts and Entertainment, *Pittsburgh Post-Gazette,* January 20, 2003, D6; and Ed Siegel, Arts and Film, *Boston Globe,* March 25, 1998, C6.

50. Russo, 172.

51. Siegel, C6.

52. Turner, *From Ritual to Theatre,* 47–48.

53. Lynda Hart, introduction to *Of All the Nerve: Deb Margolin Solo,* ed. Lynda Hart (London: Cassell, 1999), 5.

54. Hart, *Of All the Nerve,* 8.

55. Deb Margolin, *O Wholly Night and Other Jewish Solecisms,* in Hart, *Of All the Nerve,* 140. Subsequent references will appear in the text.

56. Michael Loewy, "Jewish Messianism and Libertarian Utopia in Central Europe," *New German Critique* 20 (1980): 107.

57. Dyer, "In Defense of Disco," 413.

58. Hart, *Of All the Nerve*, 8.
59. Harris, "Failing 'White Womanhood,'" 184, 204.
60. Harris, "Failing 'White Womanhood'," 202.
61. See Hart, *Of All the Nerve*, 7.
62. Benjamin, "Theses," 253–67.
63. Patraka, *Spectacular Suffering*, 103.
64. J. Hillis Miller, "Narrative," in *Critical Terms for Literary Study*, ed. Frank Lentricchia and Thomas McLaughlin (Chicago: University of Chicago Press, 1990), 69.
65. Miller, "Narrative," 69. Miller also says, "By 'performative' I mean the power of a narrative to make something happen, as opposed to its power to give, or to appear to give, knowledge" (78).
66. Hughes, *Clit Notes*, 2–3.
67. Hughes, *Clit Notes*, 9.
68. Schulman, *Stagestruck*, 91.
69. Schulman, *Stagestruck*, 69.
70. Dyer, "In Defense of Disco," 413.
71. Turner, *From Ritual to Theatre*, 58.
72. Turner, *From Ritual to Theatre*, 51.

CHAPTER THREE

I've borrowed the evocative phrase "finding our feet" from Clifford Geertz, "Thick Description," in *The Interpretation of Cultures* (New York: Basic Books, 1973), 3–30.

1. Kelley, *Freedom Dreams*, 9.
2. For feminist work on the limitations of realism and on the possibilities of postmodern forms, see, for example, Elinor Fuchs, *The Death of Character: Perspectives on Theater after Modernism* (Bloomington: Indiana University Press, 1996); Jill Dolan, "'Lesbian' Subjectivity in Realism: Dragging at the Margins of Structure and Ideology," in Case, *Performing Feminisms*, 40–53; Diamond, *Unmaking Mimesis*.
3. For the literature on feminist reception theory in performance, see Bennett, *Theater Audiences*; Wolf, *A Problem Like Maria*; and Wolf, "Theatre as Social Practice."
4. Román, "Comment—Theatre Journals."
5. MacIvor, "Entrepreneurial Strategies" panel.
6. Eva Illouz, *Consuming the Romantic Utopia: Love and the Cultural Contradictions of Capitalism* (Berkeley and Los Angeles: University of California Press, 1997), 7–8.
7. Raymond Williams, *Marxism and Literature* (London: Oxford University Press, 1977), 132.
8. Williams, *Marxism and Literature*, 129.
9. Williams, *Marxism and Literature*, 131.
10. Williams, *Marxism and Literature*, 132.
11. Michael Peterson, *Straight White Male: Performance Art Monologues* (Jackson: University of Mississippi Press, 1997), 14.

12. Bruce McConachie, "Approaching the 'Structure of Feeling' in Grassroots Theatre," *Theatre Topics* 8, no. 1 (March 1998): 40.

13. For an excellent overview of the form's history, see Peterson, *Straight White Male.*

14. Harry Elam, "Towards a New Territory in 'Multicultural' Theatre," in *The Color of Theatre: Race, Culture, and Contemporary Performance,* ed. Roberta Uno with Lucy Mae San Pablo Burns (New York: Continuum, 2002), 98.

15. Elam, "Towards a New Territory," 98.

16. Peterson, *Straight White Male,* 5.

17. Jones, "Performance Ethnography," 7.

18. Jones, "Performance Ethnography," 14.

19. Jane Wagner, *Search for Signs of Intelligent Life in the Universe* (New York: Harper and Row, 1985). Subsequent references will appear in the text.

20. See Monique Wittig, "The Point of View: Universal or Particular," in *The Straight Mind and Other Essays* (Boston: Beacon Press, 1992), 59–67, for an insightful argument about the universal and the particular, from which I borrow here.

21. I'd like to thank Janelle Reinelt, who suggested that Trudy is a "cock-eyed optimist" when I presented an earlier version of this chapter on a "Fresh Print" panel at the Association for Theatre in Higher Education conference in San Diego in 2002.

22. Gestus, as I discuss in chapter 1, is a concept developed by Marxist playwright-theorist Bertolt Brecht to describe a simple gesture that illuminates a complex set of social relations.

23. Jen Graves, "The 'Search' Resumes: The Incomparable Lily Tomlin, Older but Wise as Ever, Returns to Where it All Started with Her Most Celebrated One-Woman Show," *News Tribune* [Tacoma, Wash.], September 5, 2002, www.lilytomlin .com/reviews/TacTribune/tt01.html.

24. Jen Graves, "Lily Tomlin Terrific in One-Woman 'Search': Actress Brings Great Characters to Life in Funny, Profound Show," *News Tribune* [Tacoma, Wash.], September 13, 2002, www.lilytomlin.com/reviews/TacTribune/tt02/html.

25. Graves, "Lily Tomlin Terrific."

26. Graves, "Lily Tomlin Terrific."

27. Lily Tomlin, "Ms. Universe," interview by Sarah Goodyear, *Time Out New York,* November 2000, 220.

28. The original production of *Search for Signs* ran 398 performances at the Plymouth Theatre in New York, winning the 1986 Tony Award for best actress in a play. The show also won a Drama Desk Award and a New York Drama Critics Award. *Search for Signs* reopened at the Booth Theatre in New York November 16, 2000; it ran for 184 performances, closing on May 20, 2001.

29. Quoted in Bonney, *Extreme Exposure,* 56.

30. Kristi Turnquist, "Signs of Intelligent Life? Tomlin's Got 'Em," *Oregonian,* February 23, 2002, B1.

31. Jamie Painter Young, "Why Lily Tomlin Remains a Pioneer of Performance," *Backstage, BPI Entertainment News Wire,* April 3, 2002, available from LexisNexis.

32. Anthony D'Alessandro, "'Intelligent Signs' Point to Tomlin Tribute," *Daily Variety,* February 26, 2002, A4.

33. Sonja Kuftinec, "A Cornerstone for Rethinking Community Theatre," *Theatre*

Topics 6, no. 1 (1996): 67. See also Kuftinec's full-length study, *Staging America: Cornerstone and Community-Based Theatre* (Carbondale: Southern Illinois University Press, 2003).

34. José Esteban Muñoz, "Feeling Brown: Ethnicity and Affect in Ricardo Bracho's *The Sweetest Hangover (and Other STDs),*" *Theatre Journal* 52, no. 1 (2000): 67.

35. David Harvey, *Spaces of Hope* (Berkeley and Los Angeles: University of California Press, 2000), 225.

36. Danny Hoch, *Jails, Hospitals, and Hip-Hop* and *Some People* (New York: Villard, 1998). Subsequent references will appear in the text. For other work by and about Hoch, see www.dannyhoch.com and www.hiphoptheaterfest.com.

37. Eisa Ulen, "Danny Hoch's 'Hyper-conscious' Hip-Hop: This White Boy Tells It Like It Is," *Horizon*, October 2000 (cited March 28, 2003), www.horizon mag.com/1/danny-hoch.asp.

38. Quoted in Bonney, *Extreme Exposure*, 354.

39. "Danny Hoch: Jails, Hospitals & Hip-Hop," *Revolutionary Worker*, October 28, 2001, http://rwor.org/a/v23/1120–29/1124/danny_hoch.htm. As performance theorist Dwight Conquergood notes, "Often I have been gratified to see the way the performance of a story can pull an audience into a sense of the other in a rhetorically compelling way" ("Performing as a Moral Act: Ethical Dimensions of the Ethnography of Performance," *Literature and Performance* 5, no. 2 [1985]: 3).

40. Bruce Weber, "Hip-Hop's Distinct Voice Is Reshaping Theatre," *New York Times*, June 25, 2002, late ed., final, E5.

41. Peterson, *Straight White Male*, 27. Critic Jonathan Kalb agrees: "Every sketch in Hoch's shows is as preoccupied with the business of looking shrewdly at the process of looking as it is with the enacted pictures and behaviors themselves" ("Documentary Solo Performance: The Politics of the Mirrored Self," *Theater* 31, no. 3 [2001]: 27).

42. Peterson, *Straight White Male*, 28.

43. Peterson, *Straight White Male*, 165.

44. Peterson, *Straight White Male*, 166.

45. Cameron made these remarks on the "New Directions in Contemporary Theatre" panel.

46. Quoted in Young, "Lily Tomlin." Performer-writer Lisa Kron's latest "solo performance with some other people in it," *Well,* addresses the issue of authenticity by asking actors of color to embody her memories of her African American grade school friends and neighbors. Although the play is autobiographical, and purposefully tells Kron's memory of a significant moment in her life, the actors continually break out of "character" as Kron has constructed them to comment on the action of the play. The play empowers the actors to doubt publicly Kron's authenticity, as part of its general address. As a result, the whole question of authenticity—of memory, as well as of the performance of race and ethnicity—becomes overt. I saw *Well* on March 27, 2004, at the Public Theater in New York City.

47. For theoretical work that complicates notions of community, see Miranda Joseph, *Against the Romance of Community* (Minneapolis: University of Minnesota Press, 2002); one of her examples is Theatre Rhinoceros, a gay/lesbian theater in San Francisco.

48. Ulen, "Hyper-Conscious."

49. Aida Mashaka Croal, "Danny Hoch Wants to Change the Word," *Africana.com*, October 12, 2001, http://www.africana.com/articles/daily/index_ 20011012.asp.

50. "Danny Hoch: Jails, Hospitals & Hip-Hop."

51. David Román, in his lecture "Contemporary American Culture: The Question of the Performing Arts," Third Annual Distinguished Lecture Series in Performance as Public Practice, University of Texas, Austin, February 25, 2005, astutely critiqued the notion that building theater audiences requires luring young people to the theater. He described this as a heteronormative investment in reproduction, which denies the impact and import of middle-aged and older people who continue to frequent the theater.

52. Weber, "Hip-Hop's Distinct Voice."

53. Peterson, *Straight White Male*, 170.

54. Peterson, *Straight White Male*, 171.

55. Dorinne Kondo, "[Re]Visions of Race: Contemporary Race Theory and the Cultural Politics of Racial Crossover in Documentary Theatre," *Theatre Journal* 52, no. 1 (2000): 102.

56. Harvey, *Spaces of Hope*, 245.

57. Young, "Lily Tomlin."

58. Conquergood, "Performing as Moral Act," 9.

59. As Kondo notes, when she hears "academic dismissals of race, gender, and sexuality as mere 'identity politics,'" she wonders, "'Hello, from which site of privilege do you speak?'" ("[Re]Visions of Race," 103).

60. Harvey, *Spaces of Hope*, 238.

61. See Maria Lugones, "Playfulness, 'World'-Traveling, and Loving Perception," in *Making Face, Making Soul, Haciendo Caras: Creative and Critical Perspectives by Women of Color*, ed. Gloria Anzaldúa (San Francisco: Aunt Lute, 1990), 390–402.

62. Anna Deavere Smith, *Fires in the Mirror* (New York: Random House, 1993), xxxiii.

63. Smith, *Fires in the Mirror*, xxxii.

64. Kondo, "[Re]Visions of Race," 83.

65. Kondo, "[Re]Visions of Race," 85.

66. Smith, *Fires in the Mirror*, xxiii.

67. Quoted in Bonney, *Extreme Exposure*, 178.

68. Theodore Shank, *Beyond the Boundaries: American Alternative Theatre*, 2nd ed. (Ann Arbor: University of Michigan Press, 2002), 245.

69. Quoted in Bonney, *Extreme Exposure*, 178.

70. Ann Pellegrini, "Citing Identity, Sighting Identification: The Mirror Stages of Anna Deavere Smith," in *Performance Anxieties: Staging Psychoanalysis, Staging Race* (New York: Routledge, 1997), 71.

71. Bernice Johnson Reagon, "Coalition Politics: Turning the Century," in *Home Girls: A Black Feminist Anthology*, ed. Barbara Smith (New York: Kitchen Table Women of Color Press, 1983), 359.

72. Quoted in Bonney, *Extreme Exposure*, 177.

73. Adam Zachary Newton in *Facing Black and Jew: Literature as Public Space in Twentieth-Century America* (London: Cambridge University Press, 1999) in fact cri-

tiques Smith's insistence on the "realness" of her characters and her disappearance of herself, suggesting, "Presenting oneself as 'an empty vessel' for respectively different Black and Jewish personae (as Smith describes her role), serving as 'a repeater' of their not randomly juxtaposed utterances, can *obscure* and *dissolve* salient differences in ethnic self-understanding which, only from such a privileged, third person vantage, conveniently 'melt' into the combinatory pot of *e pluribus unum*. I cavil not because the characters in Smith's pieces are 'real people' . . . but rather because they are real people who have been wrenched free of context, at the mercy of framing juxtaposition on the one hand, and 'performance' on the other" (163). What's missing from her impersonations, he says, "is rootedness of *context,* of lifeworld—the blood and sinew of habit, practice, and belief" (164).

74. Smith, *Fires in the Mirror,* xxxviii.

75. On mimesis and mimicry, see Diamond, *Unmaking Mimesis.* On balancing on bridges and inhabiting the gaps of identity, see Phelan, *Unmarked,* especially the last chapter.

76. Smith, *Fires in the Mirror,* xxvi.

77. Tania Modleski, "Doing Justice to the Subjects: The Work of Anna Deavere Smith," in *Old Wives Tales and Other Women's Stories* (New York: New York University Press, 1998), 101–25.

78. Quoted in Smith, *Fires in the Mirror,* xix.

79. Quoted in Smith, *Fires in the Mirror,* xxii. Kondo says that the critically important task at hand is "working in alliance for social change, mounting theoretical critique that sharpens our understandings of the historical and political landscape and creating new kinds of formations to combat hegemonic forces. The theatre is a key site in contemporary culture where we can find visions of possibility for those new formations" ("[Re]Visions of Race," 105).

80. Anna Deavere Smith, *Talk to Me: Listening Between the Lines* (New York: Random House, 2000), 147. For a trenchant review of Smith's book, which points up some of the contradictions in Smith's thinking and her politics, see David Brooks, "Ms. Smith Goes to Washington," *New Republic,* December 11, 2000.

81. Linda Kintz, email to the author, September 2002.

82. Kondo, "[Re]Visions of Race," 107.

83. McConachie, "Structure of Feeling," 38.

CHAPTER FOUR

1. Fraser, "Rethinking the Public Sphere," 110.

2. Fraser, "Rethinking the Public Sphere," 111.

3. Bourdieu, *Distinction.* See also Robert Putnam, *Bowling Alone: The Collapse and Revival of American Community* (New York: Simon and Schuster, 2000), for his notion of "social capital," which he derives from Bourdieu's notion of cultural capital. Putnam defines "social capital" as the way in which social networks and connections among individuals have value, embedded as they are in dense networks of reciprocal relations (19). "Civic engagement and social capital," he says, "entail mutual obliga-

tion and responsibility for action" (23). Using Putnam's terms, then, theater and performance set up a system of "generalized reciprocity" (21), in which we can think of the spectator's attention as part of a social network that will eventually reciprocate the artist's generosity and insight with some other act of social faith. Putnam argues that we need to "make Americans more aware of the collective significance of the myriad minute decisions that we make daily to invest—or disinvest—in social capital and . . . to spark the civic imaginations of our fellow citizens to discover and invent new ways of connecting socially that fit our changed lives" (404). Choosing to create and to see theater and performance can demonstrate such a desire for social connection, in ways that can also spark our civic imaginations.

4. Christopher Small, *Music of the Common Tongue: Survival and Celebration in Afro-American Music* (New York: Riverrun Press, 1987), 50. Small explicitly sees performance as a practice, rather than a commodified object of exchange. I'd like to thank Gayle Wald for sharing this very useful source.

5. Alan Read, *Theatre in Everyday Life: An Ethics of Performance* (New York: Routledge, 1993), 16.

6. See also Maria Irene Fornes's play *Conduct of Life*, in *Plays* (New York: PAJ, 1986), 65–88, which describes through theatrical metaphors the kind of participation necessary to overthrow states governed by fascism and tyranny.

7. As Habermas says, "By 'public sphere' we mean first of all a domain of our social life in which such a thing as public opinion can be formed. Access to the public sphere is open in principle to all citizens. A portion of the public sphere is constituted in every conversation in which private persons come together to form a public" ("The Public Sphere," in *Jürgen Habermas on Society and Politics: A Reader,* ed. Steven Seidman [Boston: Beacon Press, 1989], 231).

8. Nat Hentoff's "Ashcroft Watch" columns in the *Progressive* magazine provided particularly good sources for tracking this imposition of religious morality through federal law.

9. Such a story was reported in the *Austin American-Statesman* when a University of Texas chapter of the Young Conservatives of Texas began sitting in on the classes of professors they considered liberal in order to blacklist them. See Sharon Jayson, "Group's Ideology Watch List Singles Out 10 UT Professors," *Austin American-Statesman,* October 31, 2003, B1.

10. Erin McKenna, *The Task of Utopia: A Pragmatist and Feminist Perspective* (Lanham, Md.: Rowman and Littlefield, 2001), 8.

11. McKenna, *The Task of Utopia,* 1.

12. Paul Ricoeur, *From Text to Action: Essays in Hermeneutics,* trans. Kathleen Blamey and John B. Thompson (Evanston, Ill.: Northwestern University Press, 1991), 319.

13. Ricoeur, *From Text to Action,* 320.

14. Michael Warner, *Publics and Counterpublics* (New York: Zone Books, 2002).

15. Schechner, *Performance Theory,* 157–58.

16. Patricia K. Szuhaj, "Must the Show Go On?" *Trust* 4 (fall 2001): 13.

17. Putnam, *Bowling Alone,* 60.

18. Theater theorist David Savran cites film theorists Christian Metz and André Bazin in his extended discussion of the differences between film and theater spectators, which is pertinent to my point here: "Moreover, as Metz and Bazin imply, since

the theatergoer is always more or less conscious of playing the role of spectator together with the rest of the audience, he or she always retains more of his or her social being sitting in the darkened theatre than the filmgoer does. As a result, the theatre is the site, as Metz notes, in which 'a true' audience is constituted, 'a temporary collectivity' made all the more efficacious both by the physical presence of actors' bodies as well as by the actors' awareness that they are being overseen, that they are participating willingly in the formation of 'an authentic perverse couple'" ("The Queerest Art," in *A Queer Sort of Materialism: Recontextualizing American Theater* [Ann Arbor: University of Michigan Press, 2003], 75).

19. Quoted in Kate Davy, *Richard Foreman and the Ontological-Hysteric Theatre* (Ann Arbor: UMI Research Press, 1981), 25.

20. Davy, *Richard Foreman,* 25–26.

21. Quoted in Matthew Gurewitsch, "Theater's Quicksilver Truth: All Is Change," *New York Times,* December 2, 2001, late ed., final, sec. 2, p. 1.

22. Ernst Bloch, *The Utopian Function of Art and Literature: Selected Essays,* trans. Jack Zipes and Frank Mecklenburg (Cambridge: MIT Press, 1988), 107. Ricoeur, too, puts ideology and utopia together in a conceptual framework he designates as a "theory of cultural imagination" (*From Text to Action,* 308).

23. Warner, *Publics and Counterpublics,* 8, 12.

24. Warner, *Publics and Counterpublics,* 74.

25. Warner, *Publics and Counterpublics,* 88.

26. John Fletcher, "Identity and Agonism: Tim Miller, Cornerstone, and the Politics of Community-Based Theatre," *Theatre Topics* 13, no. 2 (2003): 194. For a discussion of the politics of "preaching to the converted," see Miller and Román, "Preaching to the Converted." I discuss this issue at greater length in chapter 2.

27. For an explication of the repetitions of reception and production foundational to performance, see Marvin Carlson, *The Haunted Stage: The Theatre as Memory Machine* (Ann Arbor: University of Michigan Press, 2001).

28. Warner, *Publics and Counterpublics,* 91.

29. Román, *Acts of Intervention,* 206.

30. Román, *Acts of Intervention,* 223.

31. Lauren Berlant, "The Subject of True Feeling: Pain, Privacy, and Politics," in *Feminist Consequences: Theory for a New Century,* ed. Elisabeth Bronfen and Misha Kavlea (New York: Columbia University Press, 2001), 133.

32. See Katherine Turman's interview, "Russell Simmons: Heeding Hip Hop's Higher Calling," *Mother Jones,* September–October 2003, 92–93.

33. Simmons, interview by Turman, 93.

34. See Tracie Rozhon, "Can Urban Fashion Be Def in Des Moines?" *New York Times,* August 24, 2003, late ed., final, sec. 3, p. 1. Rozhon reports that while Simmons's public-spirited businesses seem progressive, they're still capitalist; for example, the prepaid Visa card he developed for "individuals without access to traditional banking services" requires a $19.95 fee to enroll and a monthly fee of "never more than $10," according to the chief operating official of Rush Communications, the umbrella company for Simmons's businesses.

35. See, for example, Deepti Hajela, "Young Artists Bring Performance Poetry to Broadway," *Associated Press Wire,* online, February 10, 2003, November 11, 2003, available from LexisNexis. Jon Pareles, in the *New York Times,* writes that poetry slams

"began in Chicago in the 1980s as mock-Olympics for poetry, and soon turned serious, with local teams and national championships. As each poet delivered one poem per round, slams worked like radio or MTV; if the current act wasn't entertaining, the next would be on in minutes. New York's magnet for poetry performance was the Nuyorican Poets Café [which was founded in the East Village circa 1973; see www.nuyorican.org]. Most of the *Def Poetry Jam* poets have appeared on its small stage" ("A New Platform for the New Poets," *New York Times,* November 10, 2002, late ed., final, sec. 2, p. 1).

36. I saw the Broadway production of *Def Poetry Jam* on December 29, 2002, at the Longacre Theatre in New York.

37. Mouffe, "Democratic Citizenship," 213.

38. Shannon Baley, "Simulating Slam: Representations of Gender and Reproductions of Reality in HBO's *Def Poetry Jam,*" seminar paper, RTF386C, University of Texas at Austin, December 2002. I want to thank Baley, whose insights have been very useful to my thinking here. Some of the striving for this somewhat essentialized authenticity no doubt comes from Simmons himself. The *Advocate* reported, "The hiring of gay white man Jonathan Van Meter as editor of the *Vibe* rap magazine triggered the resignation of its founder, Russell Simmons. Simmons believed the magazine should be edited by a straight black editor who is an authority on rap music" (Eric K. Washington, "The Big Dis," *Advocate,* November 3, 1992, 72).

39. Quoted in Pareles, "New Platform," 1.

40. Danny Simmons, ed., *Russell Simmons Def Poetry Jam on Broadway . . . and More: The Choice Collection,* assisted by M. Raven Rowe, conceived by Stan Lathan and Russell Simmons (New York: Atria Books, 2003), 120. Subsequent references will appear in the text.

41. Jack Zipes, "Introduction: Toward a Realization of Anticipatory Illumination," in Bloch, *Utopian Function,* xx.

42. In her review of Dael Orlandersmith's slam-influenced play *Yellowman,* Nicole Fleetwood writes, "In recent years, the delivery techniques and narrative structure of performance poetry, or spoken word, have infiltrated contemporary theatre, particularly in the works of black and Latino playwrights. This fruitful merging of performance poetry with theatre has its roots in the Harlem Renaissance and the Black Arts Movement" (*Theatre Journal* 55, no. 2 [2003]: 331).

43. After all, plenty of plays and musicals by and about people of color (although of course, never enough) have by now been presented on Broadway. See, among other examples, *For Colored Girls Who Have Considered Suicide When the Rainbow Is Enuf* (1976), to which many commentators compare *Def Poetry Jam,* no doubt because they share a poetic aesthetic; *Bring in Da Noise, Bring in Da Funk* (1996), a history of African American music and performance that George C. Wolfe brought to Broadway from the Public Theater; Suzan-Lori Parks's Pulitzer-Prize–winning *Top Dog/Underdog* (2002), also a transfer from the Public Theater; the successful 2004 revival of Lorraine Hansberry's classic, *A Raisin in the Sun* (1961), starring Sean "Puffy" Combs; and of course the many Broadway productions of August Wilson's plays. Nilo Cruz's Pulitzer-Prize–winning play *Anna in the Tropics* (2003) was the first play by and about Latino/as to be produced on Broadway. David Henry Wang's plays have long been staged in this forum (although not gay Asian-American playwright Chay Yew's). These examples, however, don't ameliorate the continued imbalance in the demographics of Broadway productions, which continue to present plays by and about mostly white middle-class men. My point is simply that *Def Poetry Jam*'s appeal to a

young audience was as innovative as its presentation of a multi-ethnic, multi-racial ensemble cast.

44. Tony Vellela, "Hip-Hop Takes Center Stage on Broadway," *Christian Science Monitor,* November 22, 2002, Arts, 19.

45. Ed Siegel, "A Promising Blend of Pop Art and High Art on Broadway," *Boston Globe,* January 19, 2003, 3rd ed., N5.

46. Elysa Gardner, "*Def Poetry Jam* Is All Relative," *USA Today,* November 15, 2002, final ed., 7E.

47. Charles Isherwood, "Russell Simmons *Def Poetry Jam,*" *Variety,* November 15, 2002, 7.

48. Pareles, "New Platform," 1. Interestingly, Pareles is the *Times*'s music critic, not its regular theater writer.

49. Gardner, "All Relative."

50. Isherwood, "Russell Simmons."

51. Siegel, "Promising Blend."

52. Arlene Croce, "Discussing the Undiscussable," *New Yorker,* December 26, 1994–January 2, 1995, 54–59.

53. This, in fact, is the audience Simmons intended for this production. For Simmons, "Broadway means 'long-standing shows that the whole world will see.' Otherwise, he is not exactly in awe of the territory. 'I try to watch what they think is hot on Broadway,' he grouses, 'and my ass starts to hurt.' Needless to say, Simmons isn't counting on the average theatergoer, so he's already putting to work a number of marketing techniques that have always worked to bring out his traditional audience of music, comedy, and clothes buyers. For example, prior to opening night, a mighty 50% of the ad budget is devoted to radio, with only 5% going to print. Most Broadway producers would reverse those figures. . . . But radio is the obvious choice for African-American-themed stage shows that successfully play the Beacon Theatre" (Robert Hofler, "Broadway Spreads 'Jam' to New Auds," *Variety,* October 21, 2002, 81). At the same time, Suheir Hammad, one of the poets in the production, told Jon Pareles, " 'We want to open this up to the traditional theatre audience.' . . . 'They may be worried that they don't relate to the hip-hop generation, but they're raising the hip-hop generation.' (Ticket prices after the opening will range from $25 to $65)" (Pareles, "New Platform," 1).

54. The singing also embodied the spectators, helping them to resist the erstwhile passivity of the Broadway house. For work on how musical theater embodies spectators, by causing them to tap their feet and move to the beat in a way that provokes positive affect, see Stacy Wolf, " 'Something Better than This': *Sweet Charity* and the Feminist Utopia of Broadway Musicals," *Modern Drama,* special issue on utopian performatives, 47, no. 2 (2004): 309–32.

55. The production of *The Chief,* at the Pittsburgh Public Theater, which I discuss in chapter 1, hails its audience in the same way.

56. The DJ, Tendaji Lathan (the son of the director, Stan Lathan), created a soundscape underneath the poets' words throughout the evening. "[H]e moved the performances . . . from one scene to another on beats that effortlessly hinge the transitions" (Simmons, *Def Poetry Jam,* 203).

57. Ann Ciccolella, the managing director of the Zachary Scott Theatre in Austin, Texas, has referred to the burgeoning local performance scene as "garage band theatre," meaning that the seventy to eighty small companies established in Austin have used the production mode of upstart music groups to form and promote themselves. In some ways, slam poetry, too, is garage band theater, in that participants and audiences can

assemble at informal neighborhood locations to "pick up" a performance. These artistic "garage" incubators foster the growth of talent that often moves on into wider cultural circulation, much like the trajectory of *Def Poetry Jam*. In addition to evoking garage doors, the set's simplicity was intentional; Robert Hofler, in *Variety,* wrote that the "capitalization of the Broadway production in the range of $1 million–$1.5 million . . . is average to low-end for a play. 'If you made it expensive and overproduced, you'd kill it,' Simmons says" ("Simmons Hopes to 'Slam' Broadway," *Variety,* June 10, 2002, 54).

58. Dyer, *Only Entertainment.*

59. Kelley, *Freedom Dreams,* 11.

60. Kelley, *Freedom Dreams,* 12.

61. The Associated Press drama critic, Michael Kuchwara, wrote, "In fact, the whole evening has a churchlike feeling, although definitely without the piety. Exhortation is the name of the game at the Longacre, and judging by theatregoers' responses at a recent performance, they were more than ready to be converted" ("A Defiant Celebration of Rap, Ranting, and Rhythm Finds its Way to Broadway," *Associated Press Wire,* online, November 14, 2002, Entertainment News, LexisNexis, November 11 2003.

62. McKenna, *The Task of Utopia,* 3.

63. Robert C. Schehr, *Dynamic Utopia: Establishing Intentional Communities as a New Social Movement* (Westport, Conn.: Bergin and Garvey, 1997), 55.

64. See, for example, Michael Giltz, "Getting Raves for Her Rants: Chinese-Jamaican Poet Staceyann Chin Brings Her Outraged Eloquence from Broadway to HBO's Def Poetry," *Advocate,* April 29, 2003, 60–62, who interviews Chin about her lesbian, multiracial identity and its relationship to her work and to American-ness. The reference to the master's tools comes from Audre Lorde, "The Master's Tools Will Never Dismantle the Master's House," in *Sister Outsider: Essays and Speeches* (Trumansburg, N.Y.: Crossing Press, 1984), 110–13.

65. As geographer David Harvey says, "[W]ithout hope alternative politics becomes impossible. Could it be, then, that a revitalization of the utopian tradition will give us ways to think the possibility of real alternatives?" (*Spaces of Hope,* 156).

66. Arundhati Roy, *Power Politics* (Cambridge, Mass.: South End Press, 2001), 32.

67. Lemon is half Puerto Rican; he grew up in Brooklyn as an "outlaw." His parents were drug addicts who died of AIDS; he went to prison on Rikers Island for armed robbery, where he taught himself to read and write, and on his release became a member of the Universes, a slam poetry performance troupe. His biography in the script reports, "'My stuff is profound,' he brags a little. 'I'm speaking for the poor peoples'" (Simmons, *Def Poetry Jam,* 134). Lemon's performance was virtuosic, although his technique, as witnessed by his tendency to mouth the other performers' words, was rudimentary. This combination of power and untrained method marked many of the performances, and also lent the production its patina of authenticity, a value stressed repeatedly by the editors of the published script. The pointed references to Lemon's prison stint also secures his authenticity and positions *Def Poetry Jam* as redemptive for the artists as well as the audience.

68. Martin Buber, *Paths in Utopia,* trans. R. F. C. Hull (Boston: Beacon Press, 1958), 7–8.

69. Ferns, *Narrating Utopia,* 23.

70. Isherwood says that the poets "are offering their own, rather more skeptical analyses of the state of the union, even as they illustrate the entrancing power of the individual human voice" ("Russell Simmons," 7).

CHAPTER FIVE

1. Moisés Kaufman and the Members of the Tectonic Theatre Project, *The Laramie Project* (New York: Vintage, 2001), vi.

2. See Michael Joseph Gross, "Pain and Prominence," *Advocate*, September 30, 2003, 26–28, 31, for an overview of the events of Shepard's murder and a report on his mother, Judy Shepard's, activism against hate crimes.

3. Kaufman, *The Laramie Project*, v. Subsequent references will appear in the text. The play was first performed at the Denver Center Theatre, opening on February 26, 2000.

4. Shelly Salamensky, reviewing Kaufman's direction of *I Am My Own Wife*, notes that "Kaufman's pursuit of objective documentary truth-making shortchanges his subjects and counters his expressed multi-perspective poststructural aims. Kaufman [reduces] richly textured experience to facile ethical debates" (*Theatre Journal* 55, no. 4 [2003]: 702).

5. Debby Thompson writes in *Theatre Journal* of seeing the Tectonic Theatre Project perform the play at the University of Wyoming in Laramie itself in 2000: "Among the many participants present were individuals portrayed in the piece itself or directly involved in the incident and its aftermath: Father Roger Schmitt, who received enthusiastic applause, and jury members of the McKinney and Henderson trials (including one jury member who commented that the performance and talkback provided the first chance the community had to de-brief and heal)" ("Performance Review," *Theatre Journal* 53, no. 4 [2001]: 644–45).

6. Judith Halberstam notes that rural life in discourses about queer culture has always been constituted as backward and "pre-modern," as geographies necessary to leave in order to flee the closet and assume an adult sexual identity. She says that "the rural is made to function as a closet for urban sexualities in most accounts of rural queer migration" (*In a Queer Time and Place: Transgender Bodies, Subcultural Lives* [New York: New York University Press, 2005], 37), yet goes on to demonstrate that many queer people report longing to return to their small-town roots after their experiences in larger cities. Halberstam focuses on the transgender murder victim Brandon Teena, who lived in Nebraska but whose story also illuminates Shepard's murder in Wyoming; both stories, Halberstam says, begin to "map the immensely complex relations that make rural America a site of horror and degradation in the urban imagination" (27). Teena, like Shepard, "represents other rural lives undone by fear and loathing, and his story also symbolizes an urban fantasy of homophobic violence as essentially Midwestern" (25). The Tectonic Theatre Company, many of whom are gay men and lesbians, fall into the trap of this logic with *The Laramie Project*.

7. Quoted in Michael Kuchwara, "On Stage: Coming to Terms with the Death of Matthew Shepard," Associated Press wire, online, February 15, 2000, LexisNexis, November 11, 2003.

8. While in the text, the narrator is simply a device, a production could conceivably use these introductions intersubjectively as a demonstration of meeting someone and getting to know them, throwing emphasis on the possibilities of human interaction. A production could point up the civic action behind such introductions and use them to truly create a community, a public of actors, characters, and spectators. A critically creative production could mine the text's potential for just these kinds of profitable interventions.

9. Quoted in Michael Kuchwara, "Out of the Matthew Shepard Tragedy Grew a Play on 'Laramie,'" *Austin American-Statesman*, February 21, 2000, E3. As Anna Deavere Smith says, "What's good about turning a historic event or current event into a work of theatre is that it allows the audience to reflect on it . . . to respond to the play in a way they didn't when the event happened, because they were too overwhelmed by it" (quoted in Jonathan Mandell, "In Depicting History, How Far Can the Facts Be Bent?" *New York Times*, March 2, 2002, late ed., final, sec. 2, p. 7).

10. That this information about the Laramie residents' response to the Tectonic Theatre Project members' presence is included in the play creates still another level of self-reflexive knowingness that treads close to self-congratulatory.

11. Quoted in Albor Ruiz, "A Private Wyoming," *New York Daily News*, sports final ed., May 4, 2000, 52.

12. As Jamie Smith Cantara says in her review of the Austin production, "Matthew Shepard is nowhere and everywhere in this play" ("Strong Performances Give *Laramie Project* Its Power and Beauty," www.Austin360.com, online, February 27, 2002. Cantara goes on to say, "Although never a physical presence onstage, his absence makes us more acutely aware of his loss."

13. Critics regularly compare *The Laramie Project* to *Our Town*. See, for one example, Robert Faires, "Our Town, Our Time," *Austin Chronicle*, March 15, 2002, 38, and Steven Oxman, *Daily Variety*, August 16, 2001, who says, "The La Jolla Playhouse is making much of how *The Laramie Project* is following a production of *Our Town*, and the comparison is not just apt but dead-on. There's no question that in his direction, Kaufman has incorporated some of Thornton Wilder's spare dramatic strokes" (16).

14. Thompson reports that Kaufman and Fondakowski said in the Laramie talkback that "the very form of theatre, and in particular their choice to focus on how individuals *changed* as a result of the incident, meant that some stories were more relevant than others, although not necessarily more authentic" ("Performance Review," 645). This by definition means that Shepard's story—since obviously he was dead and couldn't change—was not considered dramatically effective enough to be central to the play's narrative.

15. Tessa Carr, "Achieving a Radical Democratic Theatre? Notes on *The Laramie Project*," paper presented on the "Crafting Identities: The Construction of the Personal in Performance" panel, Performance as Public Practice Conference, Department of Theatre and Dance, University of Texas at Austin, February 22, 2003, 10.

16. Reviewer Elizabeth Pochoda says, "I wandered from the performance occasionally to consider, unfairly perhaps, what [the members of the Tectonic Theater Project] didn't find, and afterward I wondered whether the secret shame of Laramie might be that in this upright community there's an element of routine and absent-minded moral indifference" ("The Talk in Laramie," *Nation*, June 19, 2000, 34).

17. Krandall Krauss, writing about the published play for the gay journal *Lambda Book Report*, says, "Without exploring how we are involved and what we have in common with this incident, the play can have no universal appeal, indeed no truth. Because in the end we are all guilty of Matthew Shepard's death. Every last one of us, as part of the collective we call the United States, contributes on some conscious or

unconscious level to the atmosphere of hatred and violence that has come to define this country. *The Laramie Project* never forces (never even invites) us to explore the ways in which this is true. . . . You will have to look elsewhere and look much deeper than *The Laramie Project* in order to find the spiritual, emotional and cultural truth behind the murder of Matthew Shepard" ("Reality TV Comes to the Stage," *Lambda Book Report,* January 2002, 23).

18. *Angels in America* has now become the predictable choice for the "gay" play in university (or even regional) theaters. While I think Kushner's play has much to recommend it, and while I was fascinated by the number of 2004 Emmy Awards the HBO production received to punctuate its glowing reviews, the play, as theater scholar David Savran points out in an excellent critical essay, skimps on real attention to the politics of gender and race and promotes a standard, liberal humanist ideal of citizenship and nationalism. Choosing this production, then, to ameliorate hostility toward gays turns this complex social problem into a single issue (sexuality) instead of one that touches all aspects of identity and democracy. See David Savran, "Ambivalence, Utopia, and a Queer Sort of Materialism: How *Angels in America* Reconstructs the Nation," in *A Queer Sort of Materialism: Recontextualizing American Theater* (Ann Arbor: University of Michigan Press, 2003), 107–33.

19. Quoted in Kuchwara, "Matthew Shepard Tragedy."

20. In fact, nationalism becomes the implicit focus of the play, especially toward the end of the third act, in Dennis Shepard's speech of forgiveness for Aaron McKinney. In the course of this speech, delivered to the court, Shepard calls his son a hero, and rewrites his life under the banner of American experience from which those who hate him and gay people like him would banish him. Matt's father's speech uses the cadences of patriotism to make his son visible as a citizen, one who was denied the due process from which his murderer now profits. Kaufman insists that the events of Laramie say "something about where we are as a nation," and warns that "[w]e all need to be conscious of the perils of our democracy" (quoted in Terry Byrne, "Playwright Explores the Fluid Intersection of Life and Drama," *Boston Herald,* October 4, 2001, 64).

21. The production ran off-Broadway at the Union Square Theatre from April to September 2000, immediately following its Denver Center Theatre premiere in February 2000.

22. Nussbaum, *Sex and Social Justice,* 10.

23. Nussbaum, *Sex and Social Justice,* 11.

24. Conquergood, "Performing as Moral Act," quoted in Carr, "Radical Democratic Theatre," 12. On the other hand, critic Don Shewey, writing about the opening night performance of *The Laramie Project* at the Denver Center Theatre Company, said that "it was impossible not to be aware of the enormous responsibility that the actors felt to do justice to the people who had entrusted them with their stories and their innermost feelings" ("Town in a Mirror: *The Laramie Project* Revisits an American Tragedy," *American Theatre* [May–June 2000], 68). He sat next to a woman who was represented in the play, reporting that "she told *USA Today* that what didn't come through for her was 'the depth of grief that was a communal grief. I don't know if it's possible in any way for anybody to capture that. I think they did the best they could'" (68).

25. On performance as substitution and what he calls "surrogation," see Joseph Roach, *Cities of the Dead: Circum-Atlantic Performance* (New York: Columbia University Press, 1996).

26. Nussbaum, *Sex and Social Justice,* 41.

27. I saw the Zach Scott production on March 3, 2002. Differences in acting style and method of representation, and the kinds of empathy or affiliation those differences evoke, are also evident in the two television productions of Shepard's story. *The Matthew Shepard Story,* an NBC television movie-of-the-week first broadcast March 16, 2002, starring Stockard Channing as Judy Shepard and Sam Waterston as Matthew's father, used conventional acting styles, narrative conventions, and representational modes to bid for empathy, tolerance, and understanding. HBO's *The Laramie Project* (first presented March 9, 2002, released on VHS and DVD June 25, 2002) represents Kaufman's confused attempt to translate his project to the screen. The film version of the play drastically reedits, rearranges, and shortens the dialogue and the narrative; revises to whom the story is told and how; and inserts fictionalized details in which the citizens of Laramie, all performed by noted independent film actors, interact with each other and with the events in characterological, psychologized ways. Kaufman chose a peculiar pseudodocumentary style for the film, intercutting segments of real news stories (Tom Brokaw, for instance, reporting on Shepard's beating on the NBC *Nightly News,* and Sen. Ted Kennedy, Ellen Degeneres, and then president Bill Clinton, among other real public figures, all expressing their outrage and sorrow at Shepard's death) with self-righteous reaction shots from the actors playing the residents of Laramie. The Tectonic Theatre Company members are themselves represented by other actors, although several of the original cast have secondary roles in the film. This overly complicated, frenetically edited, and graceless layering of "truth" with pretentious, indie-style cinematography and acting completely displaces the real townspeople from the film. No Brechtian devices are employed to introduce us to these people or to represent the complex layers of representing the real that the play at least attempts.

While the play casts the Tectonic company members both as themselves and as various members of the town, the film assigns each role to only one actor, which disallows the illustration of human interconnectedness toward which the play at least gestures. In the film, each character is stabilized and fixed, an individual alone with the interviewer in an often contrived context: in a store, in a field with farm props, in a classroom, in a theater, in a hospital corridor. The New York company members are given dialogue among themselves in which they express their fear of their surroundings, and throughout, the film positions viewers to empathize with their displacement and distress. The Laramie residents wear flannel shirts and turtlenecks, their Ralph Lauren–inspired costumes contrasting stylistically but not substantively with the New Yorkers' dressed down urban chic.

The odd pretense to documentary disrupts the now conventionally structured narrative with contrived, sepia-bathed scenes of actors sitting in courtrooms watching horrified as McKinney and Henderson (actors given quite a lot of screen time with which to react—often in portentous slow motion—to the proceedings against them) sit remorselessly as the judge details their crime. The style Kaufman imposes begs the question of why he didn't simply film a documentary in the first place and clarifies his concern with the *story* rather than the actual people of the town, emphasizing his use of Laramie's citizens, as Nussbaum would suggest, as means rather than ends in themselves. His arty excesses—for example, expressionist point-of-view shots of dark streets and isolated country roads and, finally, the lonely fence where Shepard was left to die, all seen through the windshield of a moving car—sensationalize the tragedy, rather than helping viewers understand its poignant humanity.

Perhaps most egregiously, Kaufman's film moves Dr. Cantway's story about simultaneously treating McKinney and Shepard in the emergency room to the film's end, emphasizing the boys' cosmic equivalence. The narrative ends with the actors playing the company packing up their car, piling bins of audiotapes into the trunk like so much loot, while Jeremy Davies, the actor playing Jedadiah Schultz, speaks Prior's last monologue in *Angels in America* ("We will be citizens. The time has come"). It finally fades out on Doc O'Connor's reference to the sparkling lights of Laramie, represented in a blurry, rather flat long shot meant to symbolize how Shepard saw them when he was tied to the fence, dying.

28. For a compelling and precise theoretical explication of the "as if" and the "what if" in performance, see Maurya Wickstrom, "Wonder in the Heart of Empire: Deborah Warner's *Medea* and *The Angel Project*," *Modern Drama,* special issue on utopian performatives, 42, no. 2 (2004): 177–99.

29. As Janet Jakobsen and Ann Pellegrini argue in their persuasive book *Love the Sin,* the discourse of tolerance—in which *The Laramie Project* participates—is not the same as actively advocating for social equality and justice for queers and other minoritarian subjects. A more radical humanism, rather than the liberal version practiced by this play, would vociferously argue for justice and equality for all. See *Love the Sin: Sexual Regulation and the Limits of Religious Tolerance* (New York: New York University Press, 2003).

30. Jaclyn Pryor, email correspondence to the author, November 2, 2004.

31. Read, *Theatre and Everyday Life,* 1, 10.

32. Read, *Theatre and Everyday Life,* 17.

33. Of course, I live in Austin, knew many of the performers in the Zach Scott production personally, and had seen them perform in other roles many times. If anyone can characterize the acting style of a certain city, I'd hazard to say that performances in Austin seem sincere, less slick and glib than New York actors often seem, more rough-hewn and perhaps as a result more like the characters they played in *The Laramie Project.* The actors projected intelligence, commitment, and feeling in each of their roles, which also helped keep them from appearing condescending to their characters or to the citizens of Laramie.

34. Bloch, *Utopian Function,* 227.

35. Bloch, *Utopian Function,* 230.

36. Robert Newell, email to Cheryl Green, March 27, 2002. The performance in question was March 22, 2002. Newell's email was forwarded to the "Theatre-History" Listserv in the M.A./Ph.D. Program in the Department of Theatre and Dance, University of Texas at Austin, where heated exchanges about Newell's email and the incident itself were exchanged between March 28, and April 8, 2002.

37. Newell, email.

38. Maria Beach, email correspondence to the "Theatre-History" Listserv, April 1, 2002. Another instructor found the production implicitly demeaning to student spectators; she noted that all the college-age characters "seemed overblown and, frankly,

stereotyped. I couldn't help but read it as them condemning the generation who 'killed' Matthew Shepard, or who were implicated by their apathy" (Christin Yannacci, email to the "Theatre-History" Listserv, April 1, 2002).

39. Queer theorist Lauren Berlant says that what she calls the "traffic in affect" requires "subalternized [marginalized] groups . . . to forge alliances on behalf of radical social transformation through testimonial rhetorics of true pain" ("Subject of True Feeling," 132). What happens, Berlant asks, when true feeling "takes over the space of ethics and truth? . . . what happens to questions of managing alterity or difference or resources in collective life when feeling *bad* becomes evidence for a structural condition of injustice? What does it mean for the theory and practice of social transformation when feeling *good* becomes evidence of justice's triumph?" (133).

40. Berlant, "Subject of True Feeling," 145.

41. Berlant, "Subject of True Feeling," 132.

42. One of the few bad reviews I read of any production of *The Laramie Project*, published in the conservative paper the *Washington Times*, underlines Berlant's point. Jayne M. Blanchard, reviewing a production at the Olney Theatre Center in Maryland, writes that the play "fairly glows with earnestness and altruism," but says, "Whether or not that makes good theatre depends on how you feel about message plays. . . . It seems a bit indulgent to have all these theatre types from the East Coast yakking it up about their feelings, their first encounters with chicken-fried steak, and their incredulity at realizing that gays and lesbians have it much harder in Wyoming than they do in New York City. . . . To come down hard on a play about Matthew Shepard's murder is like slapping a puppy" ("'Laramie' Misses Target," *Washington Times*, 20 July 2002, final ed., D5).

43. I'd like to thank Jaclyn Pryor for the term "choice moment" (email correspondence to the author, November 2, 2004).

44. See my discussion of At the Foot of the Mountain Theatre's production of *Story of a Mother* in *Feminist Spectator as Critic*, 93–97.

45. Tessa Carr suggests that the "emotionally coercive staging" of the Zach Scott production "posits a self-congratulatory spectator or an angry spectator who must make a visible choice to leave the theater conspicuously at the performance's conclusion" ("Radical Democratic Theatre," 14).

46. On the other hand, I had not joined the crowds of people who demonstrated in the streets of New York City when news of Shepard's death traveled eastward in 1998, even though I lived there at the time. Many of my friends and colleagues did walk in the spontaneous protests that day, and several were arrested on trumped-up charges of blocking foot traffic. Some were held for long hours without appropriate food or access to medications. Perhaps my emotions at the play, about this much more safely staged protest, came from guilt over my decision not to join the demonstration in New York on the actual day of Shepard's death.

47. Luisa Passerini, "'Utopia' and Desire," *Thesis Eleven*, February 2002, 18.

48. Passerini, "'Utopia' and Desire," 23.

49. Jennifer Nelson made these remarks during the plenary session "Arts Advocacy during National Crisis: Can Arts Participation Bind a Nation?" at the Association for Theatre in Higher Education Conference in San Diego, July 26, 2002.

50. Perhaps I'm feeling some slippage toward the shoals of "civil religion." See, for

example, Robert Bellah, *The Broken Covenant: American Civil Religion in a Time of Trial*, 2nd ed. (Chicago: University of Chicago Press, 1992).

51. Sue-Ellen Case made these remarks at the "Utopian Performatives" seminar at the American Society for Theatre Research Conference, Las Vegas, November 18, 2004.

52. Rami Shapiro, "Meet the Messiah; Kill the Messiah," *Tikkun* (November–December 2004): 67–68.

53. Michael Lerner, "Tikkun at Eighteen: The Voice of Radical Hope and Practical Utopianism," *Tikkun* (November–December 2004): 34–35.

54. Lerner, "Tikkun at Eighteen," 37.

CHAPTER SIX

1. They made these remarks on the panel "Refreshing Language/Reanimating Performance 2: Politics and the Contemporary Macaronic Stage," Association for Theatre in Higher Education, New York, August 1, 2003. Abram's paper was entitled "Playing with Tongues: In Search of an Ethical Language for the Stage." Reinelt served as the respondent.

2. Warner, *Publics and Counterpublics*, 88.

3. Warner, *Publics and Counterpublics*, 89.

4. Quoted in Zipes, "Introduction," xxv.

5. Schehr, *Dynamic Utopia*, 148.

6. As Walter Benjamin says of this kind of historicism, it "grasps the constellation which [our] own era has formed with a definite earlier one. Thus [we] establish a conception of the present as the 'time of the now' which is shot through with chips of Messianic time" ("Theses," 263).

7. Angela Davis, *Women, Culture, and Politics* (New York: Random House, 1984), 199.

8. Ann Carlson, lecture, Department of Theatre and Dance, University of Texas at Austin, October 20, 2003. Carlson refers to Adrienne Rich's poem "Diving into the Wreck" (1973).

9. Ann Carlson, lecture, Department of Theatre and Dance, University of Texas at Austin, October 28, 2003.

10. Jennifer Dunning, "Enlisting Viewers' Aid While Observing Daily Life," *New York Times*, August 18, 1998, E4.

11. Carlson, lecture, October 28, 2003.

12. See Fuchs, *The Death of Character*, on the complications of character in postmodernism; see also Muñoz for critical work on the operations of what he calls "disidentification," in *Disidentifications*, which calls up doubt and ambivalence rather than sympathy and empathy.

13. Carlson told one reviewer she was dressed as if she were "ready to go to my own funeral" (Tom Strint, "Carlson Dances on the Edge of Fear; Curiosity Drives," *Milwaukee Journal*, June 24, 1990, E14).

14. Reviewer Chris Dohse remarks, "The whistled theme from 'The Andy Griffith Show' and Vietnam-era headlines place her in the USA of my own childhood" ("Flag-

Wrapping Carlson Doodles Yankee," *Dance Insider* [2002], www.danceinsider.com/
f2002/f0503_3.html, November 6, 2003).

15. Dohse, "Flag-Wrapping Carlson."

16. See Kristeva, "Women's Time," 201–36.

17. Douglas Kellner and Harry O'Hara, "Utopia and Marxism in Ernst Bloch,"
New German Critique, fall 1976, 16.

18. Interestingly, Tamara Smith is Canadian. As theater scholar Jaclyn Pryor notes,
"She took responsibility for a past/future/present that wasn't quite hers in an identi-
tarian sense but one that was perfectly hers in a humanist sense. This gesture, then,
becomes evidence of radical humanism" (email correspondence to the author,
November 13, 2004).

19. Michal Kobialka, during a reading of an earlier version of this chapter at the
University of Minnesota in April 2003, suggested that the final moment of *Blanket* was
an ontological moment rather than a representational one, in which Carlson presented her disappearance to somehow secure her presence.

20. Jennifer Dunning, "Review/Dance: Walking toward Death in Her Sensible
Shoes," *New York Times,* December 24, 1990, late ed., final, sec. 1, p. 13.

21. McKenna, *The Task of Utopia,* 2.

22. Tsvi Bisk, "Toward a Practical Utopianism," *Futurist* 36, no. 3 (2002): 24.

23. Jürgen Habermas, "The Crisis of the Welfare State and the Exhaustion of
Utopian Energies," in *Jürgen Habermas on Society and Politics,* 286.

24. Dunning, "Enlisting Viewers' Aid," E4.

25. Alan M. Kriegsman, "Ann Carlson, True to Life," *Washington Post,* April 27,
1995, D06.

26. Thulani Davis, "Theatre beyond Borders: Reconfiguring the Artist's Relationship to Community in the Twenty-first Century—Moving beyond *Bantustans,*" in
Uno, *The Color of Theatre,* 23.

27. The Lookingglass Theatre moved into the landmark Water Works building on
Michigan Avenue in summer 2003, thanks to private fund-raising and the largess of
Chicago's mayor Richard Daley, who "allotted $1.5 million of city money to the con-
struction fund and helped persuade the state legislature to appropriate another $1.5
million" (Stephen Kinzer, "Chicago Theatre Unveils Its Latest Metamorphosis," *New
York Times,* June 16, 2003, late ed., final, E3). Lookingglass founding member David
Schwimmer, who found fame in *Friends* on NBC, also contributed to the campaign.

28. Hedy Weiss, "Grant May Give Director Her 'Metamorphosis,'" *Chicago Sun-
Times,* June 3, 1998, late sports final ed., 56.

29. Michael Kuchwara, review of *Metamorphoses,* "Staging Myths of Loss and
Metamorphosis," Associated Press wire, online, October 15, 2001, LexisNexis, November 6, 2003.

30. Ben Brantley, review of *Metamorphoses,* "How Ovid Helps Deal with Loss and
Suffering," *New York Times,* October 10, 2001, late ed., final, E1.

31. Tara Pepper, "The Return of Ovid," *Newsweek,* December 2, 2002, Atlantic ed.,
58; Deborah Garwood, "Myth as Public Dream: The Metamorphosis of Mary Zimmerman's *Metamorphoses,*" *PAJ* 25, no. 1 (2003): 78.

32. William Meyers, "Cheering 'Metamorphoses,'" *Commentary,* July–August
2002, 59.

33. Garwood, "Myth as Public Dream," 70. Matthew Gurewitsch adds, "Words tell

the story, strategic bits of mime add their thunderbolt or the murmur of suggestion, and the spectator's wish to believe does the rest" ("Theatre's Quicksilver Truth," 1).

34. Pepper, "The Return of Ovid," 58.

35. Margo Jefferson, "Myth, Magic, and Us Mortals," *New York Times,* May 26, 2002, Arts and Leisure Desk, online.

36. Robert Schehr, in *Dynamic Utopia,* notes that "'the function of any myth is to facilitate action.' Myths exist in the historical memory of specific actors and may be imbued with utopian images of alternate modes of living" (144).

37. Garwood says that the "theme of mythic enchantment" allows "the playwright to theatricalize myth as a hybrid of antiquity and twentieth-century culture" ("Myth as Public Dream," 71).

38. William Meyers, writing about this moment, says, "Once again, although the story is literally fabulous, we feel unmistakably that this is how life is" ("Cheering 'Metamorphoses,'" 58).

39. The production opened at Second Stage Theatre on September 19, 2001 and ran until December 30, 2001; it transferred to Circle in the Square on Broadway in spring 2002.

40. Carol Becker, "Herbert Marcuse and the Subversive Potential of Art," in *Zones of Contention: Essays on Art, Institutions, Gender, and Anxiety* (Albany: State University of New York Press, 1996), 48. I should note here that as Dana Cloud has suggested, utopian longings for the past are sometimes conservative (see "The Rhetoric of Family Values: Scapegoating, Utopia, and the Privatization of Social Responsibility," *Western Journal of Communications* 62, no. 4 [1998]: 387–419). Writing about how the Right has co-opted the language of "family values," she suggests that they've created a utopian language of nostalgia for the past of the normative, white, middle-class, two-parent family of the 1950s. Such rhetoric, this time about "moral values," drove the polarized presidential campaign of 2004, some say handing the Right President Bush's victory. Cloud's research persuades me to clarify that what I'm calling utopian performatives enact a longing for the future, not a nostalgia for a purportedly better, simpler, more moral (all codes for white, Christian, heterosexual) past.

41. Garwood, "Myth as Public Dream," 76.

42. Margo Jefferson, "Remembering Moments of Pure Magic," *New York Times,* May 19, 2002, late ed., final, sec. 2, p. 7.

43. Meyers, "Cheering 'Metamorphoses,'" 59.

44. Quoted in Gurewitsch, "Theatre's Quicksilver Truth," 1. He also quotes actor Ian McKellen, who says, "The particularly thrilling thing in the theatre is that the audience colludes. They allow magic to happen, know it can't have happened, and are full of wonder that it did happen. . . . That's the thrill, the impertinence of a transformation in the theatre."

45. Garwood, "Myth as Public Dream," 73.

46. Becker, "Herbert Marcuse," 39.

47. Becker, "Herbert Marcuse," 37.

48. See Elin Diamond's review of the production, *Theatre Journal* 55, no. 1 (2003): 135–36, and her "Bloody Aprons: Feminism, Identity, and Globalization," paper presented to "Identities on Trial," Women and Theatre Program Conference, New York University, July 30, 2003, for critical and theoretical work on this production; as well as Maurya Wickstrom, "Wonder in the Heart of Empire: Deborah Warner's *Medea*

and *The Angel Project,*" *Modern Drama,* special issue on utopian performatives, 42, no. 2 (2004): 177–99. I saw this production on December 28, 2002, at the Brooks Atkinson Theatre in New York. See also Gordon Rogoff, "Deadly Theatre Meets Dead Horse," *Theater* 33, no. 3 (2003): 86–95 for a provocative, compelling, but much less complimentary review of the production.

49. Sarah Jones, "Profile: Fiona Shaw: An Actor Who Is Determined to Keep Shouting," *Independent* (London), Global News Wire, online, August 9, 2003, Lexis-Nexis, November 11, 2003.

50. Quoted in Mel Gussow, "A Contemporary, Human Scale for Larger-Than-Life Characters," *New York Times,* January 7, 2003, late ed., final, E1. Shaw might consider the play a healing experience, but critic Michael Kuchwara reported that "[a]t one recent performance, an audience member reportedly needed medical assistance when things got a bit intense" (Associated Press, online, December 30, 2002, Entertainment News, LexisNexis, November 11, 2003).

51. Gussow, "Contemporary, Human Scale," E1.

52. Gussow, "Contemporary, Human Scale," E1.

53. Robert Brustein, "Varieties of Histrionic Experience," *New Republic,* November 18, 2002, 28.

54. See Gitlin, *Letters,* 123–32.

55. Charles Isherwood, "Medea," *Daily Variety,* December 11, 2002, 33.

56. "Theatre Review: Fitting the Modern Age to the Classic Greek Form," *New York Times,* December 11, 2002, late ed., final, E1.

57. Quoted in Alona Wartofsky, "With *Medea,* She Didn't Just Get Mad: Fiona Shaw and the Abbey Theatre, Seeing the Humanity in an Unhinged Role," *Washington Post,* November 3, 2002, final ed., G1.

58. Wartofsky, "With *Medea,*" G1.

59. Bisk, "Toward a Practical Utopianism," 23.

60. Bisk, "Toward a Practical Utopianism," 24.

61. Martha Nussbaum, in her argument for liberal humanism as a context for feminist justice, argues that "an account of the central human capacities and functions, and of the basic human needs and rights, can be given in a fully universal manner" (*Sex and Social Justice,* 8). Her sense that the basics of human needs and rights can be usefully universalized resonates with my argument here.

62. Thomas de Zengotita, "Common Ground," *Harper's,* January 2003, 36. I'd like to thank Maurya Wickstrom for pointing me toward this article.

63. de Zengotita, "Common Ground," 42.

64. Kelley, *Freedom Dreams,* x.

65. Kelley, *Freedom Dreams,* 2.

66. Quoted in Arlene Goldbard, "The Cultural Policy Colonization of the West, or, Fattening Frogs for Snakes," in *Symposium Proceedings: Cultural Policy in the West* (Denver: Western States Arts Federation, 1999), 49.

67. Kelley, *Freedom Dreams,* 9.

68. Joan Lipkin coined this phrase on a discussion panel after Deb Margolin's performance of *Index to Idioms* at the Women and Theatre Program conference in New York, July 29, 2003. The performance was part of the "Lynda Hart Memorial" panel and was held at the Belt Theatre.

69. Ernst Laclau and Chantal Mouffe, *Hegemony and Socialist Strategy* (London: Verso, 1985), 181.

70. Kirstie McClure, "On the Subject of Rights: Pluralism, Plurality, and Political Identity," in Mouffe, *Dimensions of Radical Democracy*, 123.

71. Zipes, quoting Bloch, in his introduction to *Utopian Function of Art and Literature*, xxxii.

72. Quoted in Zipes, "Introduction," xl. See Ernst Fischer, *The Necessity of Art* (Baltimore: Penguin, 1963), 14.

EPILOGUE

1. I'd like to thank Michal Kobialka for his suggestion that the utopian performative is found in the gap between body and word, which he made during my Nolte Lectures at University of Minnesota, April 2003.

2. See Phelan, *Unmarked;* and Daly, *Critical Gestures.*

3. I'm borrowing "goneness" from Vivian M. Patraka, who uses it in *Spectacular Suffering* more specifically to describe the operations of what she calls the Holocaust performative in theater.

4. Ann Cvetkovich, *An Archive of Feelings: Trauma, Sexuality, and Lesbian Public Cultures* (Durham, N.C.: Duke University Press, 2003), 10.

5. Ji Hye, a Ph.D. student in the Department of Theatre and Dance at the University of Texas at Austin, told me that she thinks of utopian performatives as "the medicine," but not the cure, for social inequities.

6. I was inspired in this regard by Ann Cvetkovich's informal talk for the LGBTQ research cluster at the University of Texas at Austin on October 22, 2004, in which she suggested that perhaps we're asking the wrong questions to some of our political work, and that the demand that something be productive catches us in the very net of capitalism that we otherwise try to resist.

7. Part of keeping humanism radical and never assuming its transparency is the attention we continue to pay to difference, while we strive for interconnectedness. Feminist theorist Ien Ang, commenting on Rita Felski's essay "The Doxa of Difference," notes, "Incommensurability then pertains to the residue of the irreducibly particular that cannot, ultimately, be shared. It does not imply an absolute impossibility of communication, but relates to the occasional and interspersed moments of miscommunication (or breakdown of communication) that always accompany communicative interchanges between differently positioned subjects. Ironically, such moments of incommensurability, while generally not acknowledged as such, are precisely what propel us to go on communicating, forever chasing for an ultimate fullness of understanding and complete commonality that are never achieved" ("Comment on Felski's 'The Doxa of Difference': The Uses of Incommensurability," *SIGNS* [autumn 1997], 59). She concludes that "politics does not have to be premised on the construction of a solid, unified 'we'... but on the very fragility, delicacy, and uncertainty of any 'we' we forge" (61).

Bibliography

Abrams, Joshua. "Playing with Tongues: In Search of an Ethical Language for the Stage." Paper presented to the panel "Refreshing Language/Reanimating Performance 2: Politics and the Contemporary Macaronic Stage," Association for Theatre in Higher Education, New York, August 1, 2003.

Anderson, Benedict. *Imagined Communities: Reflections on the Origin and Spread of Nationalism.* London: Verso, 1983.

Ang, Ien. "Comment on Felski's 'The Doxa of Difference': The Uses of Incommensurability." *SIGNS* (autumn 1997): 57–64.

Appiah, Kwame Anthony. *In My Father's House: Africa in the Philosophy of Culture.* New York: Oxford University Press, 1992.

Artaud, Antonin. *The Theatre and Its Double.* Trans. Mary Caroline Richards. New York: Grove Press, 1958.

Auslander, Philip. *From Acting to Performance: Essays in Modernism and Postmodernism.* New York: Routledge, 1997.

———. *Liveness: Performance in a Mediatized Culture.* New York: Routledge, 1999.

Austin, J. L. *How to Do Things with Words.* Cambridge: Harvard University Press, 1975.

Baley, Shannon. "Death and Desire, Apocalypse and Utopia: Feminist *Gestus* and the Utopian Performative in the Plays of Naomi Wallace." *Modern Drama* 47, no. 2 (2004): 237–49.

———. "Simulating Slam: Representations of Gender and Reproductions of Reality in HBO's *Def Poetry Jam.*" Seminar paper RTF386C, University of Texas, Austin, December 2002.

Bammer, Angelika. *Partial Visions: Feminism and Utopia in the 1970s.* New York: Routledge, 1991.

Barnes, Clive. "New York Notebook." *Stage,* July 13, 2000, 9.

Bauman, Richard. *Verbal Acts as Performance.* Prospect Heights, Ill.: Waveland Press, 1977.

Becker, Carol. "Herbert Marcuse and the Subversive Potential of Art." In *Zones of Contention: Essays on Art, Institutions, Gender, and Anxiety.* Albany: State University of New York Press, 1996.

———. *Surpassing the Spectacle: Global Transformations and the Changing Politics of Art.* Lanham, Md.: Rowman and Littlefield, 2002.

Bell, Catherine. *Ritual Theory, Ritual Practice.* New York: Oxford University Press, 1992.

Bellah, Robert. *The Broken Covenant: American Civil Religion in a Time of Trial.* 2nd ed. Chicago: University of Chicago Press, 1992.

Benhabib, Seyla. *Critique, Norm, and Utopia: A Study of the Foundations of Critical Theory.* New York: Columbia University Press, 1986.

Benjamin, Walter. *The Arcades Project.* Trans. Howard Eiland and Kevin McLaughlin. Cambridge: Belknap Press of Harvard University Press, 1999.

———. "Theses on the Philosophy of History." In *Illuminations: Essays and Reflections.* Ed. Hannah Arendt. Trans. Harry Zohn. New York: Schocken, 1968.

Bennett, Susan. *Theatre Audiences: A Theory of Production and Reception.* 2nd ed. New York: Routledge, 1997.

Bentley, Eric. "The Theatrical Occasion." In *The Life of the Drama.* New York: Atheneum, 1967.

Berlant, Lauren. *The Queen of America Goes to Washington City.* Durham, N.C.: Duke University Press, 1997.

———. "The Subject of True Feeling: Pain, Privacy, and Politics." In *Feminist Consequences: Theory for the New Century.* Ed. Elisabeth Bronfen and Misha Kavlea. New York: Columbia University Press, 2001.

Berson, Misha. "Lily Tomlin Resumes 'The Search.'" *Seattle Times,* Arts and Entertainment, September 8, 2000, E1.

Bharucha, Rustom. "Contextualizing Utopias: Reflections on Remapping the Present." *Theater* 26, nos. 1–2 (1995): 37.

Bingaman, Amy, Lise Sanders and Rebecca Zorach, eds. *Embodied Utopias: Gender, Social Change, and the Modern Metropolis.* London: Routledge, 2002.

Bisk, Tsvi. "Toward a Practical Utopianism." *Futurist* 36, no. 3 (2002): 22–25.

Blanchard, Jayne M. "'Laramie' Misses Target: Anti-hate Message Sews Confusion." *Washington Times,* July 20, 2002, final ed., D5.

Blau, Herb. *The Audience.* Baltimore: Johns Hopkins University Press, 1990.

———. *Take Up the Bodies: Theater at the Vanishing Point.* Urbana: University of Illinois Press, 1982.

Bloch, Ernst. *The Principle of Hope.* Trans. Neville Plaice, Stephen Plaice, and Paul Knight. 3 vols. London: Basil Blackwell, 1986.

———. *The Utopian Function of Art and Literature: Selected Essays.* Trans. Jack Zipes and Frank Mecklenburg. Cambridge: MIT Press, 1988.

Boal, Augusto. *Theatre of the Oppressed.* New York: Theatre Communications Group, 1975.

Bogart, Anne. "Utopia Forum." *Theater* 26, nos. 1–2 (1995): 182.

Bonner, Stephen Eric. "Revolutionary Anticipation and Tradition: In Honor of Ernst Bloch's Ninetieth Birthday." "Marxism and Utopia," special supplement to *Minnesota Review,* spring 1976, 88–95.

Bonney, Jo, ed. *Extreme Exposure: An Anthology of Solo Performance Texts from the Twentieth Century.* New York: Theatre Communications Group, 2000.

Bourdieu, Pierre. *Distinction: A Social Critique of the Judgment of Taste.* Trans. Richard Nice. Cambridge: Harvard University Press, 1994.

Brantley, Ben. "How Ovid Helps Deal with Loss and Suffering." *New York Times,* October 10, 2001, late ed., final, E1.

Brecht, Bertolt. *Brecht on Theatre: The Development of an Aesthetic.* Ed. and trans. John Willett. New York: Hill and Wang, 1964.

Brooks, David. "Ms. Smith Goes to Washington." *New Republic,* December 11, 2000.

Brustein, Robert. "Varieties of Histrionic Experience." *New Republic,* November 18, 2002, 28–30.

Buber, Martin. *Paths in Utopia*. Trans. R. F. C. Hull. 1949; reprint, Boston: Beacon Press, 1958.

Buck-Morris, Susan. *Dreamworld and Catastrophe: The Passing of Mass Utopia in East and West*. Cambridge: MIT Press, 2000.

Byrne, Terry. "Playwright Explores the Fluid Intersec. of Life and Drama." *Boston Herald*, October 4, 2001, Arts, 64.

Calhoun, Craig, ed. *Habermas and the Public Sphere*. Cambridge: MIT Press, 1992.

Cameron, Ben. "New Directions in Contemporary Theatre" panel, "Fresh Terrain" symposium, Department of Theatre and Dance, University of Texas, Austin, January 25, 2003.

Cantara, Jamie Smith. "Strong Performances Give *Laramie Project* Its Power and Beauty." *Austin 360*, www.statesman.com, February 27, 2002, www.prfdance.org/publicity/statesman.publicity/espirit2001.htm.

Carlson, Ann, choreographer. *Blanket*. B. Iden Payne Theatre. University of Texas, Austin, January 2003.

———. Lecture. Department of Theatre and Dance, University of Texas at Austin, October 20, 2003.

———. Lecture. Department of Theatre and Dance, University of Texas at Austin, October 28, 2003.

Carlson, Marvin. *The Haunted Stage: The Theatre as Memory Machine*. Ann Arbor: University of Michigan Press, 2001.

———. *Performance: A Critical Introduction*. New York: Routledge, 1996.

———. "The Theatre Journal Auto/Archive." *Theatre Journal* 55, no. 1 (2003): 207–11.

Carr, C. *On Edge: Performance Art at the End of the Twentieth Century*. Middleton, Conn.: Wesleyan University Press, 1993.

Carr, Tessa. "Achieving a Radical Democratic Theatre? Notes on *The Laramie Project*." Presented to the conference "Performance as Public Practice," Department of Theatre and Dance, University of Texas, Austin, February 22, 2003.

Case, Sue-Ellen. *Feminism and Theatre*. New York: Methuen, 1988.

———, ed. *Performing Feminisms: Feminist Critical Theory and Theatre*. Baltimore: Johns Hopkins University Press, 1990.

———, ed. *Split Britches: Lesbian Practice/Feminist Performance*. New York: Routledge, 1996.

Chaudhuri, Una. Comment. "A Forum on Theatre and Tragedy in the Wake of September 11th, 2001." *Theatre Journal* 54, no. 1 (2002): 98.

Chin, Staceyann. ". . . And These Are Only Some of the Things I Believe." In *Russell Simmons Def Poetry Jam on Broadway . . . and More: The Choice Collection*. Ed. Danny Simmons. Assisted by M. Raven Rowe. Conceived by Stan Lathan and Russell Simmons. New York: Atria Books, 2003.

Claeys, Gregory, and Lyman Tower Sargent, eds. *The Utopia Reader*. New York: New York University Press, 1999.

Cloud, Dana L. "The Rhetoric of Family Values: Scapegoating, Utopia, and the Privatization of Social Responsibility." *Western Journal of Communication* 62, no. 4 (1998): 387–419.

Cohen, Ed. "Who Are 'We'? Gay 'Identity' as Political (E)motion (a Theoretical Rumination)." In *Inside/Out: Lesbian Theories, Gay Theories*. Ed. Diana Fuss. New York: Routledge, 1991.

Cohen, Leah Hagar. *The Stuff of Dreams: Behind the Scenes of an American Community Theater.* New York: Viking, 2001.

Cohen-Cruz, Jan. "A Hyphenated Field: Community-Based Theatre in the USA." *New Theatre Quarterly* 16, no. 4 (2000): 364–78.

Conquergood, Dwight. "Performing as a Moral Act: Ethical Dimensions of the Ethnography of Performance." *Literature and Performance* 5, no. 2 (1985): 1–13.

Cook, Dara. Review of *Russell Simmons Def Poetry Jam on Broadway*, ed. Danny Simmons. *Black Issues Book Review* 3, no. 1 (2001): 30.

Crimp, Douglas, ed. *AIDS: Cultural Analysis, Cultural Activism.* Cambridge: MIT Press, 1988.

Croal, Aida Mashaka. "Danny Hoch Wants to Change the Word." *Africana.com*, October 12, 2001, http://www.africana.com/articles/daily/index_20011012.asp.

Croce, Arlene. "Discussing the Undiscussable." *New Yorker*, December 1994, 54–59.

Curtis, Kimberley. *Our Sense of the Real: Aesthetic Experience and Arendtian Politics.* Ithaca, N.Y.: Cornell University Press, 1999.

Cvetkovich, Ann. *An Archive of Feelings: Trauma, Sexuality, and Lesbian Public Cultures.* Durham, N.C.: Duke University Press, 2003.

D'Alessandro, Anthony. "'Intelligent Signs' Point to Tomlin Tribute." *Daily Variety*, February 26, 2002, A4.

Daly, Ann. *Critical Gestures: Writings on Dance and Culture.* Middletown, Conn.: Wesleyan University Press, 2002.

Darlington, Madge. "Entrepreneurial Strategies" panel, "Fresh Terrain" symposium, Department of Theatre and Dance, University of Texas at Austin, January 26, 2003.

Davis, Angela. *Women, Culture, and Politics.* New York: Random House, 1984.

Davis, Thulani. "Theatre beyond Borders: Reconfiguring the Artist's Relationship to the Community in the 21st Century: Moving beyond *Bantustans*." In *The Color of Theatre: Race, Culture, and Contemporary Performance.* Ed. Roberta Uno with Lucy Mae San Pablo Burns. New York: Continuum, 2002.

Davy, Kate. "The Storefront: Creating Feminist Space and a 'System of Anarchy.'" Unpublished manuscript. 2000.

Dean, Jodi. *Solidarity Among Strangers: Feminism After Identity Politics.* Berkeley and Los Angeles: University of California Press, 1996.

Delbanco, Andrew. *The Real American Dream: A Meditation on Hope.* Cambridge: Harvard University Press, 1999.

D'Erasmo, Stacey. *Tea.* Chapel Hill: Algonquin Books of Chapel Hill, 2000.

Denizen, Norman K. "The Call to Performance." *Symbolic Interaction* 26, no. 1 (2003): 187–207.

de Zengotita, Thomas. "Common Ground." *Harper's*, January 2003, 35–45.

Diamond, Elin. "Bloody Aprons: Feminism, Identity, and Globalization." Unpublished paper. Presented at "Identities on Trial," Women and Theatre Program Conference. New York University, New York, July 30, 2003.

———. Review of *Medea*. Brooklyn Academy of Music. 6 Oct. 2003. *Theatre Journal* 55, no. 1 (2003): 135–36.

———. *Unmaking Mimesis: Essays on Feminism and Theatre.* New York: Routledge, 1997.

———, ed. *Performance and Cultural Politics.* New York: Routledge, 1996.

Dietz, Mary. "Context Is All: Feminism and Theories of Citizenship." In *Dimensions of*

Radical Democracy: Pluralism, Citizenship, Community. Ed. Chantal Mouffe. London: Verso, 1992.

Dijkstra, Bram. "The Dialectics of Hope versus the Politics of Stasis in Art." *Tikkun,* November–December 2004, 60–62.

Dohse, Chris. "Carlson Doodles Yankee." *Dance Insider.* 2002.www.danceinsider .com/ f2002/f0503_3.html.

Dolan, Jill. *The Feminist Spectator as Critic.* Ann Arbor: University of Michigan Press, 1991.

———. *Geographies of Learning: Theory and Practice, Activism and Performance.* Middleton, Conn.: Wesleyan University Press, 2001.

———. Introduction to special issue on utopian performatives, *Modern Drama* 47, no. 2 (2004): 165–76.

———. *Presence and Desire: Essays on Gender, Sexuality, Performance.* Ann Arbor: University of Michigan Press, 1993.

———. "'Lesbian' Subjectivity in Realism: Dragging at the Margins of Structure and Ideology." In *Performing Feminisms: Feminist Critical Theory and Theatre.* Ed. Sue-Ellen Case. Baltimore: Johns Hopkins University Press, 1990.

———. "Rehearsing Democracy: Advocacy, Public Intellectuals, and Civic Engagement in Theatre and Performance Studies." *Theatre Topics* 11, no. 1 (2001): 1–17.

Domínguez, Virginia. "For a Politics of Love and Rescue." *Cultural Anthropology* 15, no. 3 (2000): 361–93.

Dunning, Jennifer. "Enlisting the Viewers' Aid While Observing Daily Life." *New York Times,* August 18, 1998, E4.

———. "Walking toward Death in Her Sensible Shoes." Review of *Blanket. New York Times,* December 24, 1990, 13.

Dyer, Richard. "Entertainment and Utopia." In *Only Entertainment.* New York: Routledge, 1992.

———. "In Defense of Disco." In *Out in Culture: Gay, Lesbian, and Queer Essays on Popular Culture.* Ed. Corey K. Creekmur and Alexander Doty. Durham, N.C.: Duke University Press, 1995.

Echols, Alice. *Scars of Sweet Paradise: The Life and Times of Janis Joplin.* New York: Henry Holt, 1999.

Epperson, Todd. "Compassion Trumps Hatred." *QTexas,* March 1, 2002, 20–21.

Elam, Harry. "'Keeping It Real': August Wilson and Hip Hop." Unpublished manuscript.

———. *Taking It to the Streets: The Social Protest Theatre of Luis Valdez and Amiri Baraka.* Ann Arbor: University of Michigan Press, 1997.

———. "Towards a New Territory in 'Multicultural' Theatre." In *The Color of Theatre: Race, Culture, and Contemporary Performance.* Ed. Roberta Uno with Lucy Mae San Pablo Burns. New York: Continuum, 2002.

Esslin, Martin. *An Anatomy of Drama.* New York: Hill and Wang, 1976.

Evans, Everett. "'Slanguage' Speaks of Urban Experience." *Houston Chronicle,* January 18, 2003, 9.

Faires, Robert. "Our Town, Our Time." Review of *The Laramie Project. Austin Chronicle,* March 15, 2002, 38.

Fanger, Iris. Review of *Menopausal Gentleman. Boston Herald,* March 25, 1998, 43.

Feingold, Michael. "American Madness." Review of *The Laramie Project*, Union Square Theatre. *Village Voice*, May 30, 2000, 115.

Féral, Josette. "Foreword." *SubStance* 31, nos. 2–3 (2002): 3–13.

Ferns, Chris. *Narrating Utopia: Ideology, Gender, Form in Utopian Literature*. Liverpool: Liverpool University Press, 1999.

Fischer, Ernst. *The Necessity of Art*. Baltimore: Penguin, 1963.

"Fitting the Modern Age to the Classic Greek Form." Review of *Medea*. *New York Times*, December, 11 2002, E1.

Fleetwood, Nicole R. Review of *Yellowman*. *Theatre Journal* 55, no. 2 (2003): 331–32.

Fletcher, John. "Identity and Agonism: Tim Miller, Cornerstone, and the Politics of Community-Based Theatre," *Theatre Topics* 13, no. 2 (2003): 189–204.

Fornes, Maria Irene. *Conduct of Life*. In *Plays*. New York: PAJ, 1986.

Foucault, Michel. "Of Other Spaces." Trans. Jay Miskowiec. *Diacritics* 16, no. 1 (1986): 22–27.

Fraser, Nancy. "Rethinking the Public Sphere: A Contribution to the Critique of Actually Existing Democracy." In *Habermas and the Public Sphere*. Ed. Craig Calhoun. Cambridge: MIT Press, 1992.

Fuchs, Elinor. *The Death of Character: Perspectives on Theater after Modernism*. Bloomington: Indiana University Press, 1996.

Gardner, Elysa. "*Def Poetry Jam* Is All Relative." *USA Today*, November 15, 2002, 7E.

———. "Hateful Act Spurs Heartening 'Laramie.'" *USA Today*, May 19, 2000, 5E.

Garner, Stanton B. *Bodied Spaces: Phenomenology and Performance in Contemporary Drama*. Ithaca, N.Y.: Cornell University Press, 1994.

Garwood, Deborah. "Myth as Public Dream: The Metamorphosis of Mary Zimmerman's *Metamorphoses*." *PAJ* 25, no. 1 (2003): 69–78.

Geertz, Clifford. "Thick Description." In *The Interpretation of Cultures*. New York: Basic Books, 1973.

Geoghegan, Vincent. "Remembering the Future." In *Not Yet: Reconsidering Ernst Bloch*. Ed. Janine Owen Daniels and Tom Moylan. London: Verso, 1997.

Giltz, Michael. "Getting Raves for Her Rants: Chinese-Jamaican Poet Staceyann Chin Brings Her Outraged Eloquence from Broadway to HBO's Def Poetry." *Advocate*, April 29, 2003, 60–62.

Gindin, Sam, and Leo Pantich. "Rekindling Socialist Imagination: Utopian Vision and Working-Class Capacities." *Monthly Review*, March 2000, 36–52.

Giroux, Henry A. "When Hope Is Subversive." *Tikkun*, November–December 2004, 62–64.

Gitlin, Todd. *Letters to a Young Activist*. New York: Basic Books, 2003.

———. *The Twilight of Common Dreams: Why American Is Wracked by Culture Wars*. New York: Metropolitan Books, 1995.

Goldbard, Arlene. "The Crisis in Cultural Policy." Performance as Public Practice Distinguished Lecture Series, Department of Theatre and Dance, University of Texas, Austin, January 31, 2003.

———. "The Cultural Policy Colonization of the West, or, Fattening Frogs for Snakes." In *Symposium Proceedings: Cultural Policy in the West*. Ed. Maripat Murphy. Denver: Westaf (Western States Arts Federation), 1999.

Gómez-Peña, Guillermo, and Lisa Wolford. "Navigating the Minefields of Utopia: A Conversation." *TDR* 46, no. 2 (2002): 66–96.

Graves, Jen. "Lily Tomlin Terrific in One-Woman 'Search.'" *News Tribune* (Tacoma, Wash.), September 13, 2000, www.lilytomlin.com/reviews/TacTribune/tto2.html.

———. "The 'Search' Resumes." *News Tribune* (Tacoma, Wash.), September 5, 2000, www.lilytomlin.com/reviews/TacTribune/tto1.html.

Gross, Michael Joseph. "Pain and Prominence." *Advocate,* September 30, 2003, 26–28, 31.

Grosz, Elizabeth. "The Time of Architecture." In *Embodied Utopias: Gender, Social Change, and the Modern Metropolis.* Ed. Amy Bingaman, Lise Sanders, and Rebecca Zorach. London: Routledge, 2002.

Gurewitsch, Matthew. "Theatre's Quicksilver Truth: All Is Change." *New York Times,* December 2, 2001, late ed., final, sec. 2, p. 1.

Gussow, Mel. "A Contemporary, Human Scale for Larger-Than-Life Characters." *New York Times,* January 7, 2003, E1.

Habermas, Jürgen. "The Crisis of the Welfare State and the Exhaustion of Utopian Energies." In *Jürgen Habermas on Society and Politics: A Reader.* Ed. Steven Seidman. Boston: Beacon Press, 1979.

———. "The Public Sphere." In *Jürgen Habermas on Society and Politics: A Reader.* Ed. Steven Seidman. Boston: Beacon Press, 1979.

Hajela, Deepti. "Young Artists Bring Performance Poetry to Broadway." Associated Press wire, February 10, 2003, LexisNexis, November 11, 2003.

Halberstam, Judith. *In a Queer Time and Place: Transgender Bodies, Subcultural Lives.* New York: New York University Press, 2005.

Halliburton, Rachel. Review of *Menopausal Gentleman. Independent* (London), April 14, 1999, Features, 11.

Hankin, Kelly. *The Girls in the Back Room: Looking at the Lesbian Bar.* Minneapolis: University of Minnesota Press, 2002.

Harney, Emily. "Reaction and Reconsideration." Review of Ann Carlson performance. *Gay City News,* May 2002, www.gaycitynews.com/GCN2/DanceHarneyArts.html.

Harris, Hilary. "Failing 'White Womanhood': Interrogating the Performance of Respectability." *Theatre Journal* 52, no. 2 (2000): 183–209.

Hart, Lynda, ed.. *Making a Spectacle: Feminist Essays on Contemporary Women's Theatre.* Ann Arbor: University of Michigan Press, 1989.

———. *Of all the Nerve: Deb Margolin Solo.* London: Cassell, 1999.

Hart, Lynda, and Peggy Phelan, eds. *Acting Out: Feminist Performances.* Ann Arbor: University of Michigan, 1993.

———, eds. "Queerer Than Thou: Being and Deb Margolin." *Theatre Journal* 47, no. 2 (1995): 269–82.

Harvey, David. *Spaces of Hope.* Berkeley and Los Angeles: University of California Press, 2000.

Harvey, Dennis. Review of *Russell Simmons Def Poetry Jam. Variety,* July 15, 2002, 32.

———. Review of *Preaching to the Perverted. Variety,* October 18, 1999, 54.

Hermand, Jost. "Brecht on Utopia." "Marxism and Utopia," special supplement to *Minnesota Review,* spring 1976, 96–113.

Heschel, Abraham Joshua. *Man Is Not Alone: A Philosophy of Religion.* New York: Jewish Publication Society of America, 1951.

Hester, Jessica. Review of "Fresh Terrain" symposium. *Theatre Journal* 55, no. 3 (2003): 519–22.

Hoch, Danny. *Jails, Hospitals, and Hip-Hop* and *Some People.* New York: Villard, 1998.

———. *Jails, Hospitals, and Hip-Hop.* CD recorded live at P.S. 122. New York: Casero Productions, 1998.

Hofler, Robert. "Broadway Spreads 'Jam' to New Auds." *Variety,* October 21, 2002, 81.

———. "Simmons Hopes to 'Slam' Broadway." *Variety,* June 10, 2002, 54.

hooks, bell. *Salvation: Black People and Love.* New York: Perennial, 2001.

———. *All about Love.* New York: Perennial, 2000.

Hughes, Holly. *Preaching to the Perverted.* Unpublished script, 2000.

———. *Clit Notes: A Sapphic Sampler.* New York: Grove Press, 1996.

Hughes, Holly, and David Román, eds. *O Solo Homo: The New Queer Performance.* New York: Grove Press, 1998.

Illouz, Eva. *Consuming the Romantic Utopia: Love and the Cultural Contradictions of Capitalism.* Berkeley and Los Angeles: University of California Press, 1997.

Isherwood, Christopher. Review of *Medea. Variety,* December 11, 2002, 33.

———. Review of *Russell Simmons Def Poetry Jam. Variety,* November 15, 2002, 7.

Jacoby, Russell. *The End of Utopia: Politics and Culture in an Age of Apathy.* New York: Basic Books, 1999.

Jakobsen, Janet, and Ann Pellegrini. *Love the Sin: Sexual Regulation and the Limits of Religious Tolerance.* New York: New York University Press, 2003.

Jameson, Frederic. "Introduction/Prospectus: To Reconsider the Relationship of Marxism to Utopian Thought." "Marxism and Utopia," special supplement to *Minnesota Review,* spring 1976, 53–58.

———. *Marxism and Form: Twentieth Century Dialectical Theories of Literature.* Princeton: Princeton University Press, 1971.

———. "Of Islands and Trenches: Neutralization and the Production of Utopian Discourse." *Diacritics* 7, no. 2 (1977): 2–21.

———. "Progress versus Utopia; or, Can We Imagine the Future?" In *Art after Modernism: Rethinking Representation.* Ed. Brian Wallis. New York: New Museum of Contemporary Art, 1984.

———. "Reification and Utopia in Mass Culture." *Social Text* 1 (1979): 130–48.

Jayson, Sharon. "Group's Ideology Watch List Singles Out Ten UT Professors." *Austin American-Statesman,* October 31, 2003, B1.

Jefferson, Margo. "Myth, Magic and Us Mortals." *New York Times,* May 26, 2002, *New York Times Premium Archive,* November 5, 2004.

———. "Remembering Moments of Pure Magic." *New York Times,* May 19, 2002, late ed., final, sec. 2, p. 7.

———. "Suddenly Onscreen, It's All about Wonder." *New York Times,* February 8, 2003, B9.

Jones, Joni. "Performance Ethnography: The Role of Embodiment in Cultural Authenticity." *Theatre Topics* 12, no. 1 (2002): 1–15.

Jones, Sarah. "Profile: Fiona Shaw." *Independent* (London), Global News Wire, August 9, 2003, LexisNexis, November 11, 2003.

Joseph, Miranda. *Against the Romance of Community.* Minneapolis: University of Minnesota Press, 2002.

Kalb, Jonathan. "Documentary Solo Performance: The Politics of the Mirrored Self." *Theater* 31, no. 3 (2001): 13–29.

Kane, Sarah. *Complete Plays*. London: Methuen, 2001.

Kateb, George. *Utopia and Its Enemies*. London: Free Press of Glencoe, 1963.

Kaufman, Moisés, dir. *The Laramie Project*. Film. Home Box Office, 2002.

Kaufman, Moisés, and the Members of the Tectonic Theatre Project. *The Laramie Project*. New York: Vintage, 2001.

Kelley, Robin D. G. *Freedom Dreams: The Black Radical Imagination*. Boston: Beacon Press, 2002.

———. *Race Rebels: Culture, Politics, and the Black Working Class*. New York: Free Press, 1994.

———. *Yo' Mama's Disfunktional! Fighting the Culture Wars in Urban America*. Boston: Beacon Press, 1997.

Kellner, Douglas, and Harry O'Hara. "Utopia and Marxism in Ernst Bloch." *New German Critique* 9 (fall 1976): 11–36.

Kintz, Linda. *Between Jesus and the Market: The Emotions That Matter in Right-Wing America*. Durham, N.C.: Duke University Press, 1997.

Kinzer, Stephen. "Chicago Theatre Unveils Its Latest Metamorphosis." *New York Times*, June 16, 2003, late ed., final, E3.

Klaic, Dragan. *The Plot of the Future: Utopia and Dystopia in Modern Drama*. Ann Arbor: University of Michigan Press, 1991.

———. "Utopia Sustained." *Theater* 26, nos. 1–2 (1995): 60–69.

Kondo, Dorinne. "(Re)Visions of Race: Contemporary Race Theory and the Cultural Politics of Racial Crossover in Documentary Theatre." *Theatre Journal* 52, no. 1 (2000): 81–107.

Krauss, Krandall. "Reality TV Comes to the Stage." *LAMBDA Book Report* 10, no. 6 (2002): 23–24.

Kriegsman, Alan M. "Ann Carlson, True to Life." *Washington Post*, April 27, 1995, D6.

Kristeva, Julia. "Women's Time." *New Maladies of the Soul*. Trans. Ross Guberman. New York: Columbia University Press, 1995.

Kron, Lisa. *Well*. Public Theater, New York, March 27, 2004.

Kuchwara, Michael. "Coming to Terms with the Death of Matthew Shepard." Associated Press wire, February 15, 2000, LexisNexis, November 11, 2003.

———. "A Defiant Celebration of Rap, Ranting and Rhythm Finds Its Way to Broadway." Associated Press wire, November 14, 2002, LexisNexis, November 11, 2003.

———. "Delivering a Docudrama That Is a Satisfying Piece of Story Theater." Associated Press wire, May 18, 2000, LexisNexis, November 11, 2003.

———. "Finding the Tragedy, the Terror, and Even the Humor in a Modern *Medea*." Associated Press wire, December 30, 2002, LexisNexis, November 11, 2003.

———. "Out of the Matthew Shepard Tragedy Grew a Play on 'Laramie.'" Associated Press wire, February 21, 2000, LexisNexis, November 11, 2003.

———. "Staging Myths of Loss and Metamorphosis." In Associated Press wire, October 15, 2001, LexisNexis, November 6, 2003.

Kuftinec, Sonja. "A Cornerstone for Rethinking Community Theatre." *Theatre Topics* 6, no. 1 (1996): 91–104.

———. *Staging America: Cornerstone and Community-Based Theater*. Carbondale: Southern Illinois Press, 2003.

Laclau, Ernst, and Chantal Mouffe. *Hegemony and Socialist Strategy.* London: Verso, 1985.

Leonin, Mia. "Mission: Unspeakable." Review of *The Laramie Project. Miami New Times,* January 18, 2001, Art, n.p., LexisNexis.

Lerner, Michael. "Tikkun at Eighteen: The Voice of Radical Hope and Practical Utopianism." *Tikkun* (November–December 2004): 33–38.

Levitas, Ruth. *The Concept of Utopia.* Syracuse: Syracuse University Press, 1990.

Lipkin, Joan. "Lynda Hart Memorial" panel, Women and Theatre Program conference, New York, July 29, 2003.

Lisovicz, Susan. "Tragedy on Broadway." *Biz Buzz.* CNN Transcript #051904cb.109, May 19, 2000, LexisNexis.

Loewy, Michael. "Jewish Messianism and Libertarian Utopia in Central Europe." *New German Critique* 20 (1980): 105–15.

Lorde, Audre. "The Master's Tools Will Never Dismantle the Master's House." In *Sister Outsider: Essays and Speeches.* Trumansburg, N.Y.: Crossing Press, 1984.

Lugones, María. "Playfulness, 'World'-Traveling, and Loving Perception." In *Making Face, Making Soul, Haciendo Caras: Creative and Critical Perspectives by Women of Color.* Ed. Gloria Anzaldúa. San Francisco: Aunt Lute Press, 1990.

MacDonald, Ann-Marie. *Fall on Your Knees.* New York: Pocket Books, 1996.

MacIvor, Daniel. "Entrepreneurial Strategies" panel. "Fresh Terrain" symposium, Department of Theatre and Dance, University of Texas, Austin, January 25, 2003.

Magnat, Virginie. "Theatricality from the Performative Perspective." *SubStance* 31, nos. 2–3 (2003): 147–66.

Mandell, Jonathan. "In Depicting History, Just How Far Can the Facts Be Bent?" *New York Times,* March 2, 2002, late ed., final, sec. 2, p. 7.

Manuel, Frank E., and Fritzie P. Manuel. *Utopian Thought in the Western World.* Cambridge: Belknap Press of Harvard University Press, 1979.

Marcuse, Herbert. *The Aesthetic Dimension: Toward a Critique of Marxist Aesthetics.* Boston: Beacon Press, 1978.

———. *Eros and Civilization: A Philosophical Inquiry into Freud.* Boston: Beacon Press, 1955.

———. *Five Lectures: Psychoanalysis, Politics, and Utopia.* Trans. Jeremy J. Shapiro and Shierry M. Weber. Boston: Beacon Press, 1970.

Margolin, Deb. *O Wholly Night and Other Jewish Solecisms.* In *Of All the Nerve: Deb Margolin Solo.* Ed. Lynda Hart. London: Cassell, 1999.

Marin, Louis. "The Utopic Stage." In *Mimesis, Masochism, and Mime: The Politics of Theatricality in Contemporary French Thought.* Ed. Timothy Murray. Ann Arbor: University of Michigan Press, 1997.

Martin, Carol. "Bearing Witness: Anna Deavere Smith from Community to Theatre to Mass Media." In *On and Beyond the Stage.* Ed. Carol Martin. New York: Routledge, 1996.

———, ed. *On and Beyond the Stage: A Sourcebook of Feminist Theatre and Performance.* New York: Routledge, 1996.

McCauley, Robbie. "Interview with Robbie McCauley." Interview by Vivian M. Patraka. In *On and Beyond the Stage.* Ed. Carol Martin. New York: Routledge, 1996.

McClure, Kirstie. "On the Subject of Rights: Pluralism, Plurality, and Political Identity." In *Dimensions of Radical Democracy: Pluralism, Citizenship, Community*. Ed. Chantal Mouffe. London: Verso, 1992.

McConachie, Bruce. "Approaching the 'Structure of Feeling' in Grassroots Theatre." *Theatre Topics* 8, no. 1 (1998): 33–53.

McKenna, Erin. *The Task of Utopia: A Pragmatist and Feminist Perspective*. Lanham, Md:. Rowman and Littlefield, 2001.

Meyer, Richard. "'Have You Heard the One About the Lesbian Who Goes to the Supreme Court?': Holly Hughes and the Case against Censorship." *Theatre Journal* 52, no. 4 (2000): 543–52.

Meyers, William. "Cheering 'Metamorphoses.'" *Commentary*, July–August 2002, 55–59.

Miller, J. Hillis. "Narrative." In *Critical Terms for Literary Study*. Ed. Frank Lentricchia and Thomas McLaughlin. Chicago: University of Chicago Press, 1990.

Miller, Tim. *Body Blows: Six Performances*. Madison: University of Wisconsin Press, 2002.

Miller, Tim, and David Román. "Preaching to the Converted." *Theatre Journal* 47, no. 2 (1995): 169–88.

Modleski, Tania. "Doing Justice to the Subjects: The Work of Anna Deavere Smith." *Old Wives' Tales and Other Women's Stories*. New York: New York University Press, 1998.

Moore, Michael, dir. *Fahrenheit 9/11*. Lions Gate Films, 2004.

Moraga, Cherríe. "Queer Aztlán: The Re-formation of Chicano Tribe." In *The Last Generation*. Boston: South End Press, 1993.

Mouffe, Chantal. "Democratic Citizenship and the Political Community." In *Dimensions of Radical Democracy: Pluralism, Citizenship, Community*. Ed. Chantal Mouffe. London: Verso, 1992.

———. *The Return of the Political*. London: Verso, 1993.

———, ed. *Dimensions of Radical Democracy: Pluralism, Citizenship, Community*. London: Verso, 1992.

Munk, Erika. "Exiled from Nowhere." *Theater* 26, nos. 1–2 (1995): 101–11.

Muñoz, José Esteban. *Disidentifications: Queers of Color and the Performance of Politics*. Minneapolis: University of Minnesota Press, 1999.

———. "Feeling Brown: Ethnicity and Affect in Ricardo Bracho's *The Sweetest Hangover (and Other STDs)*." *Theatre Journal* 52, no. 1 (2000): 67–79.

Nelson, Jennifer. "Arts Advocacy during a National Crisis: Can Arts Participation Bind a Nation?" Plenary session presentation, Association for Theatre in Higher Education, San Diego, July 26, 2002.

Nesti, Robert. Review of *Preaching to the Perverted*. *Boston Herald*, October 2, 1999, Arts and Life, 25.

Newton, Adam Zachery. *Facing Black and Jew: Literature as Public Space in Twentieth-Century America*. London: Cambridge University Press, 1999.

Nussbaum, Martha. *Sex and Social Justice*. New York: Oxford University Press, 1999.

Oizerman, T. I. "Marxism and Utopianism." *Russian Studies in Philosophy* 39, no. 4 (2001): 54–80.

"On Danny Hoch." *Revolutionary Worker*, October 28, 2001, http://rwor.org/a/v23/1120-29/1124/danny_hoch.htm.

Oxman, Steven. Review of *The Laramie Project*. *Variety*, August 16, 2001, 16.

Pareles, Jon. "A New Platform for the New Poets." *New York Times,* November 10, 2002, B1.

Parker, Andrew, and Eve Kosofsky Sedgwick. *Performativity and Performance.* New York: Routledge, 1995.

Passerini, Luisa. "'Utopia' and Desire." *Thesis Eleven,* February 2002, 11–30.

Patraka, Vivian M. *Spectacular Suffering: Theatre, Fascism, and the Holocaust.* Bloomington: Indiana University Press, 1999.

Pavese, Cesare. *Dialogues with Leuco.* Trans. William Arrowsmith and D. S. Carne-Ross. Ann Arbor: University of Michigan Press, 1965.

Pellegrini, Ann. "Citing Identity, Sighting Identification: The Mirror Stages of Anna Deavere Smith." In *Performance Anxieties: Staging Psychoanalysis, Staging Race.* New York: Routledge, 1997.

Pepper, Tara. "The Return of Ovid." *Newsweek,* December 2, 2002, 58.

Perron, Wendy. "A Performance Piece Runs through It." *New York Times,* August 10, 2003, A26.

Peterson, Michael. *Straight White Male: Performance Art Monologues.* Jackson: University of Mississippi Press, 1997.

Pfister, Joel, and Nancy Schnog, eds. *Inventing the Psychological: Toward a Cultural History of Emotional Life in America.* New Haven: Yale University Press, 1997.

Phelan, Peggy. "Serrano, Mapplethorpe, the NEA, and You: 'Money Talks.'" *TDR* 34, no. 1 (1990): 4–15.

———. *Unmarked: The Politics of Performance.* New York: Routledge, 1993.

Piscator, Erwin. *The Political Theatre: A History, 1914–1929.* Trans. Hugh Rorrison. New York: Avon, 1978.

Pochoda, Elizabeth. "The Talk in Laramie." *Nation,* June 19, 2000, 33–34.

Porter, David. Letter to the editor. *New York Times,* June 9, 2002, late ed., final, sec. 2, p. 4.

Porter, David H. "Brief Mention: *Metamorphoses* and Metamorphosis, A Brief Response." *American Journal of Philology* 124, no. 3 (2003): 473–76.

Pressley, Nelson. "A Holly Terror: Performance Artist Holly Hughes, Weary but Unwilted by a Grueling Ten-Year Role as Culture Warrior." *Washington Post,* November 5, 2000, G1.

Pryor, Jaclyn, Paul Bonin-Rodriguez, and Jill Dolan. "Colleague-Critic: Performance, Activism, and Public Practice." Presented at "Abriendo Brecha/Haciendo Camino: Activist Scholarship on Race, Identity and Mestizaje in the Americas," the Center for Mexican American Studies, the Lozano Long Institute for Latin American Studies, and the Rockefeller Foundation Humanities Fellowship program, University of Texas, Austin, February 25, 2005.

Putnam, Robert. *Bowling Alone: The Collapse and Revival of American Community.* New York: Simon and Schuster, 2000.

Rawson, Christopher. Review of *Menopausal Gentleman.* Pittsburgh Post-Gazette, January 20, 2003, Arts and Entertainment, D6.

Read, Alan. *Theatre and Everyday Life: An Ethics of Performance.* New York: Routledge, 1993.

Reagon, Bernice Johnson. "Coalition Politics: Turning the Century." In *Home Girls: A Black Feminist Anthology.* Ed. Barbara Smith. New York: Kitchen Table Women of Color Press, 1983.

Reinelt, Janelle. "The Politics of Discourse: Performativity Meets Theatricality." *Sub-Stance* 31, nos. 2–3 (2002): 201–15.

———. "The *Theatre Journal* Auto/Archive." *Theatre Journal* 55, no. 1 (2003): 385–92.

Rivera-Servera, Ramón. "Choreographies of Resistance: Latina/o Queer Dance and the Utopian Performative." *Modern Drama* 42, no. 2 (2004): 369–89.

Ricoeur, Paul. *From Text to Action: Essays in Hermeneutics.* Trans. Kathleen Blamey and John B. Thompson. Evanston, Ill.: Northwestern University Press, 1991.

Roach, Joseph. *Cities of the Dead: Circum-Atlantic Performance.* New York: Columbia University Press, 1996.

Rockwell, John. "Reverberations: Living for the Moments When Contemplation Turns to Ecstasy." *New York Times,* October 24, 2003, B4.

Rogoff, Gordon. "Deadly Theatre Meets Dead Horse." *Theater* 33, no. 3 (2003): 86–95.

Román, David. *Acts of Intervention: Performance, Gay Culture, and AIDS.* Bloomington: Indiana University Press, 1998.

———. "Comment—Theatre Journals." *Theatre Journal* 54, no. 3 (2002): n.p.

———. "Contemporary American Culture: The Question of the Performing Arts." Third Annual Distinguished Lecture Series in Performance as Public Practice, University of Texas, Austin, February 25, 2005.

———. Introduction to special issue on dance. *Theatre Journal* 55, no. 3 (2003): n.p.

Rose, Lloyd. "Holly Hughes, Making Herself Decent." *Washington Post,* November 6, 2000, C1.

Rothstein, Edward, Herbert Muschamp, and Martin E. Marty. *Visions of Utopia.* New York: Oxford University Press, 2003.

Roy, Arundhati. *Power Politics.* Cambridge, Mass.: South End Press, 2001.

Rozhon, Tracie. "Can Urban Fashion Be Def in Des Moines?" *New York Times,* August 24, 2003, C1.

Ruiz, Albor. "A Private Wyoming." Review of *The Laramie Project. New York Daily News,* May 4, 2000, sports final ed., 52.

Ruppert, Peter. Review of *The Post-utopian Imagination: American Culture in the Long 1950s,* by M. Keith Booker. *Utopian Studies* 13, no. 2 (2002): 109–11.

Russell, Mark. "Developing Performance Art/Performance Theatre" panel. "Fresh Terrain" symposium, Department of Theatre and Dance, University of Texas, Austin, January 26, 2003.

———, ed. *Out of Character: Rants, Raves, and Monologues from Today's Top Performance Artists.* New York: Bantam, 1997.

Russo, Francine. Review of *Menopausal Gentleman. Village Voice,* June 10, 1998, 172.

Salamensky, S. I. Review of *I Am My Own Wife. Theatre Journal* 55, no. 4 (2003): 700–702.

Sargisson, Lucy. *Utopian Bodies and the Politics of Transgression.* London: Routledge, 1997.

Savran, David. "Ambivalence, Utopia, and a Queer Sort of Materialism: How *Angels in America* Reconstructs the Nation." *A Queer Sort of Materialism: Recontextualizing American Theater.* Ann Arbor: University of Michigan Press, 2003.

———. "Choices Made and Unmade." *Theater* 31, no. 2 (2001): 89–95.

———. "The Queerest Art." In *A Queer Sort of Materialism: Recontextualizing American Theater.* Ann Arbor: University of Michigan Press, 2003.

———. *Taking It Like a Man: White Masculinity, Masochism, and Contemporary American Culture.* Princeton: Princeton University Press, 1998.

Schaer, Roland, Gregory Claeys, and Lyman Tower Sargent, eds. *Utopia: The Search for the Ideal Society in the Western World.* New York: Oxford University Press, 2000.

Schechner, Richard. *Between Theater and Anthropology.* Philadelphia: University of Pennsylvania Press, 1985.

———. *Performance Studies: An Introduction.* New York: Routledge, 2002.

———. *Performance Theory.* Rev. ed. New York: Routledge, 1988.

Schehr, Robert C. *Dynamic Utopia: Establishing Intentional Communities as a New Social Movement.* Westport, Conn.: Bergin and Garvey, 1997.

Schneekloth, Lynda H. Review of *Embodied Utopias,* ed. Amy Bingaman, Lise Sanders, and Rebecca Zorach. *Utopian Studies* 13, no. 2 (2002): 107–9.

Scholem, Gershom. *The Messianic Idea in Judaism and Other Essays on Jewish Spirituality.* New York: Schocken, 1971.

Schools, Frances. "Ann Carlson Interprets Life." *Richmond Times-Dispatch,* May 13, 1996, E5.

Schulman, Sarah. *My American History: Lesbian and Gay Life During the Reagan/Bush Years.* New York: Routledge, 1994.

———. *Stagestruck: Theater, AIDS, and the Marketing of Gay America.* Durham, N.C.: Duke University Press, 1998.

Sedgwick, Eve Kosofsky. *The Epistemology of the Closet.* Berkeley and Los Angeles: University of California Press, 1990.

———. *Touching Feeling: Affect, Pedagogy, Performativity.* Durham, N.C.: Duke University Press, 2003.

Seidman, Steven, ed. *Jürgen Habermas on Society and Politics: A Reader.* Boston: Beacon Press, 1989.

Siegel, Ed. Review of *Def Poetry Jam. Boston Globe,* January 19, 2003, N5.

———. Review of *Menopausal Gentleman. Boston Globe,* March 25, 1998, Arts and Film, C6.

Shank, Theodore. *Beyond the Boundaries: American Alternative Theatre.* 2nd ed. Ann Arbor: University of Michigan Press, 2002.

Shapiro, Rami. "Meet the Messiah; Kill the Messiah." *Tikkun* (November–December 2004): 67–68.

Shaw, Peggy. *Menopausal Gentleman.* Unpublished script, 1997.

Shewey, Don. "Town in a Mirror: *The Laramie Project* Revisits an American Tragedy." *American Theatre* (May–June 2000): 14–17, 67–69.

Simmons, Danny, ed. *Russell Simmons Def Poetry Jam on Broadway . . . and More: The Choice Collection.* Assisted by M. Raven Rowe. Conceived by Stan Lathan and Russell Simmons. New York: Atria Books, 2003.

Simmons, Russell. "Russell Simmons: Heeding Hip Hop's Higher Calling." Interview by Katherine Turman. *Mother Jones,* September–October 2003, 92–93.

———, prod. *Russell Simmons Def Poetry Jam on Broadway.* Longacre Theatre, New York, December 30, 2002.

Sington, David, and Pamela Neville-Sington. *Paradise Dreamed: How Utopian Thinkers Have Changed the Modern World.* London: Bloomsbury, 1993.

Small, Christopher. *Music of the Common Tongue: Survival and Celebration in Afro-American Music.* New York: Riverrun Press, 1987.

Smith, Anna Deavere. "Anna Deavere Smith: The Word Becomes You." Interview by Carol Martin. In *On and Beyond the Stage.* Ed. Carol Martin. New York: Routledge, 1996.

———. *Fires in the Mirror.* New York: Random House, 1993.

———. "Systems of Lights." *Theater* 26, nos. 1–2 (1995): 50–51.

———. *Talk to Me: Listening Between the Lines.* New York: Random House, 2000.

———. *Twilight: Los Angeles, 1992.* New York: Dramatists Play Service, 1999.

Solomon, Alisa. "The WOW Café." In *The Drama Review: Thirty Years of Commentary on the Avant-Garde.* Ed. Brooks McNamara and Jill Dolan. Ann Arbor: UMI Research Press, 1986.

Soloski, Alexis. Review of *Preaching to the Perverted. Village Voice,* May 16, 2000, 77.

States, Bert O. "Phenomenology of the Curtain Call." *Hudson Review* 34, no. 3 (1981): 371–80.

Steakley, Dave, dir. Moisés Kaufman. *The Laramie Project.* Zach Scott Theatre, Austin, Texas, March 4, 2002.

Steiger, Amy. "Performing Beckett's Women: The Feminist Actor, Subjectivity, and the Body in Representation." M.A. thesis, Department of Theatre and Dance, University of Texas, Austin, 2001.

Steiner, Wendy. *The Scandal of Pleasure.* Chicago: University of Chicago Press, 1995.

Strint, Tom. "Carlson Dances on the Edge of Fear; Curiosity Drives." *Milwaukee Journal,* June 24, 1990, E14.

Szuhaj , Patricia K. "Must the Show Go On?" *Trust* 4 (fall 2001): 12–17.

Thompson, Debby. Review of *The Laramie Project. Theatre Journal* 53, no. 4 (2001): 644–45.

Thomson, Lynn M. "Teaching and Rehearsing Collaboration." *Theatre Topics* 13, no. 1 (2003): 118.

Tomlin, Lily. "Ms. Universe." Interview by Sarah Goodyear. *Time Out New York,* November 2000, 220.

Tucker, Joe. *Steelers' Victory after Forty.* New York: Exposition, 1973.

Turner, Victor. *Dramas, Fields, and Metaphors: Symbolic Action in Human Society.* Ithaca, N.Y.: Cornell University Press, 1974.

———. *From Ritual to Theatre: The Human Seriousness of Play.* New York: Performing Arts Journal Publications, 1982.

Turnquist, Kristi. "Signs of Intelligent Life? Tomlin's Got 'Em." *Oregonian,* February 23, 2002, B1.

Ulen, Eisa. "Danny Hoch's 'Hyper-Conscious' Hip-Hop: This White Boy Tells It Like It Is." *Horizon: People and Possibilities,* October 2000, www.horizonmag.com/1/danny-hoch.asp.

Uno, Roberta. "The 5th Element." *American Theatre,* April 2004, 26–30, 85–86.

Vellela, Tony. "Hip-hop Takes Center Stage on Broadway." *Christian Science Monitor,* November 22, 2002, Arts, 19.

Vorlicky, Robert H. "Performing Men of Color: Male Autoperformance, Highways Performance Space, the NEA, and the White Right." In *Whiteness: A Critical Reader.* Ed. Mike Hill. New York: New York University Press, 1997.

Wagner, Jane. *Search for Signs of Intelligent Life in the Universe.* New York: Harper and Row, 1985.

Walzer, Michael. "The Civil Society Argument." In *Dimensions of Radical Democracy: Pluralism, Citizenship, Community.* Ed. Chantal Mouffe. London: Verso, 1992.

Warner, Deborah, dir. *Medea.* Brooks Atkinson Theatre, New York, December 29, 2003.

Warner, Michael. *Publics and Counterpublics.* New York: Zone, 2002.

Wartofsky, Alona. "With *Medea,* She Didn't Just Get Mad: Fiona Shaw and the Abbey Theatre Seeing Humanity in an Unhinged Role." *Washington Post,* November 3, 2002, G1.

Washington, Eric K. "The Big Dis." *Advocate,* November 3, 1992, 72–73.

Weber, Bruce. "Critic's Notebook: Hip-Hop's Distinct Voice Is Reshaping Theatre." *New York Times,* June 25, 2002, late ed., final, E5.

Wegner, Phillip E. "Horizons, Figures, and Machines: The Dialectic of Utopia in the Work of Frederic Jameson." *Utopian Studies* 9, no. 2 (1998): 58–74.

Weiss, Hedy. "Grant May Give Director Her 'Metamorphosis.'" *Chicago Sun-Times,* June 3, 1998, late sports final ed., 56.

West, Cornel. "Celebrating Tikkun and Tragicomic Hope." *Tikkun,* November–December 2004, 53–54.

Wickstrom, Maurya. "Wonder in the Heart of Empire: Deborah Warner's *Medea* and *The Angel Project.*" *Modern Drama* 42, no. 2 (2004): 177–99.

Williams, Raymond. *Marxism and Literature.* London: Oxford University Press, 1977.

Wilson, Ann. "Bored to Distraction: Auto-performance and the Perniciousness of Presence." *Canadian Theatre Review* 79–80 (summer–fall 1994): 33–37.

Wilson, Elizabeth. "Against Utopia: The Romance of Indeterminate Spaces." In *Embodied Utopias: Gender, Social Change, and the Modern Metropolis.* Ed. Amy Bingaman, Lise Sanders, and Rebecca Zorach. London: Routledge, 2002.

Williams, Lee. "Hot Flash." Review of *Menopausal Gentleman. Houston Press,* May 20, 1999, LexisNexis.

Winn, Steven. "*Laramie Project* at Berkeley Rep." *San Francisco Chronicle,* January 5, 2001, C2.

Wittig, Monique. "The Point of View: Universal or Particular." In *The Straight Mind and Other Essays.* Boston: Beacon Press, 1992.

Wolf, Stacy. "'Being' a Lesbian: Apple Island and the Performance of Community." In *The Queerest Art: Essays on Lesbian and Gay Theatre.* Ed. Alisa Solomon and Framji Minwalla. New York: New York University Press, 2002.

———. "Civilizing and Selling Spectators: Audiences at the Madison Civic Center." *Theatre Survey* 39, no. 2 (1998): 7–23.

———. *A Problem Like Maria: Gender, Sexuality, and the American Musical.* Ann Arbor: University of Michigan Press, 2002.

———. "'Something Better than This': *Sweet Charity* and the Feminist Utopia of Broadway Musicals." *Modern Drama* 47, no. 2 (2004): 309–32.

———. "Theatre as Social Practice: Local Ethnographies of Audience Reception." Ph.D. diss., Department of Theatre and Dance, University of Wisconsin, Madison, 1994.

Yoran, Hanan. "The Humanist Critique of Metaphysics and the Foundation of Political Order." *Utopian Studies* 13, no. 2 (2002): 1–19.

Young, Alan. Review of *The Laramie Project,* Denver Center Theatre Company, February 26, 2000. *Variety,* March 6, 2000, 49.

Young, Iris Marion. "The Ideal of Community and the Politics of Difference." In *Feminism/Postmodernism.* Ed. Linda J. Nicholson. New York: Routledge, 1990.

Young, Jamie Painter. "Why Lily Tomlin Remains a Pioneer of Performance." *Backstage,* BPI Entertainment News Wire April 3, 2002, LexisNexis.

Zarrilli, Phillip, ed. *Acting (Re)Considered.* New York: Routledge, 1995.

Zellers, Rob, and Gene Collier. *The Chief.* Dir. Ted Pappas. O'Reilly Theater, Pittsburgh Public Theater, November 7, 2003.

Zimmerman, Mary. *Metamorphoses: A Play.* Based on David R. Slavitt's translation of *The Metamorphoses of Ovid.* Evanston, Ill.: Northwestern University Press, 2002.

———, dir. *Metamorphoses.* Second Stage Theatre, New York, December 8, 2001.

Zipes, Jack. "Introduction: Toward a Realization of Anticipatory Illumination." In *The Utopian Function of Art and Literature: Selected Essays,* by Ernst Bloch. Trans. Jack Zipes and Frank Mecklenburg. Cambridge: MIT Press, 1988.

Zournazi, Mary. *Hope: New Philosophies for Change.* Annandale, NSW, Australia: Pluto Press, 2002.

Index